The
Restaurant Lover's
Companion

Other Books by Steve Ettlinger

*The Complete Illustrated Guide to Everything
Sold in Hardware Stores*

*The Complete Illustrated Guide to Everything
Sold in Garden Centers (Except the Plants)*

The Kitchenware Book

*Don't Pick Up the Baby and Other
Old Wives' Tales About Pregnancy and Parenting*

The Restaurant Lover's Companion

A Handbook for Deciphering the Mysteries of Ethnic Menus

covering the following cuisines:

FRENCH
CHINESE
ITALIAN
JAPANESE
INDIAN
MEXICAN
THAI
GREEK
CARIBBEAN
SPANISH
MIDDLE EASTERN
GERMAN
VIETNAMESE
& AMERICAN REGIONAL

★

Steve Ettlinger
with Melanie Falick

ADDISON-WESLEY PUBLISHING COMPANY
READING, MASSACHUSETTS • MENLO PARK, CALIFORNIA
NEW YORK • DON MILLS, ONTARIO • WOKINGHAM, ENGLAND
AMSTERDAM • BONN • SYDNEY • SINGAPORE • TOKYO
MADRID • SAN JUAN • PARIS • SEOUL
MILAN • MEXICO CITY • TAIPEI

Conceived and edited by Ettlinger Editorial Projects

Many of the designations used by manufacturers and sellers to distinguish their products are claimed as trademarks. Where those designations appear in this book and Addison-Wesley was aware of a trademark claim, the designations have been printed in initial capital letters (i.e., Cheez-Whiz).

Library of Congress Cataloging-in-Publication Data
Ettlinger, Steve.
The restaurant lover's companion : a handbook for deciphering the mysteries of ethnic menus / Steve Ettlinger, with Melanie Falick.
p.   cm.
Includes index.
ISBN 0-201-40636-5
1. Cookery, International. 2. Ethnic restaurants—United States.
3. Menus. I. Falick, Melanie. II. Title.
TX725.A1E88   1995
641.59'03—dc20
94-12438

Cover design by Barbara Atkinson
Text design by Tilman Reitzle
Set in Janson and Helvetica Neue by Tilman Reitzle

1 2 3 4 5 6 7 8 9-DOC-9897969594
First printing, October, 1994

Addison-Wesley books are available at special discounts for bulk purchases by corporations, institutions, and other organizations. For more information, please contact:

Corporate, Government, and
Special Sales Department
Addison-Wesley Publishing Company
Reading, MA 01867
(800) 238-9682

*To those of us who can never
remember the difference
between an enchilada and a burrito*

CONTENTS

BARBARA ALBRIGHT (Caribbean cuisine) is a Connecticut-based food writer and cookbook author who recently had firsthand experience judging a culinary competition in St. Lucia. Among her six books are *Cooking with Regis & Kathie Lee* and a series on baked items that includes *Mostly Muffins, Simply Scones,* and *Totally Teabreads.* She also writes a food column for the Associated Press. Whenever life gets too hectic, she escapes on a mini-vacation to a Caribbean restaurant.

KATHERINE R. BOULUKOS (Greek cuisine) is a first-generation Greek-American who has researched and written extensively about Greek food. She is chairperson of the Recipe Club of Saint Paul Greek Orthodox Church, Hempstead, N.Y., and co-author of several books on Greek cooking written by this group, the latest being *The Complete Book of Greek Cooking,* published by HarperCollins. She is on the board of directors of the Greek Food and Wine Institute and has taught Greek cooking in the New York City area.

STEPHEN BREWER (Italian cuisine) is a freelance travel writer and editor based in New York City. He is the Senior Editor of the *Berlitz Travellers Guides* and is also a contributor to their guide to southern Italy, among others. He spends his summers in Tuscany and the rest of the year eating in Italian restaurants closer to home.

PENELOPE CASAS (Spanish cuisine) is the leading authority in the U.S. on Spanish cuisine. A teacher and lecturer on the subject, she has published three books: *The Foods and Wines of Spain, Tapas: The Little Dishes of Spain,* and *Discovering Spain: An Uncommon Guide,* all published by Alfred A. Knopf. She is a frequent contributor on Spanish food and travel to the *New York Times* and to other leading publications.

STEVE ETTLINGER (French cuisine) is the creator and editor of this book, and is a book producer and/or author of 15 popular reference books, photojournalism books, and novels, including *The Complete Illustrated Guide to Everything Sold in Hardware Stores* and *The Kitchenware Book.* He was sous-chef at Aesop's Tables (Wellfleet, Mass.) and lived in Paris for six years, where at one point his work as an interpreter took him to the best restaurants for every meal during one three-week period. He has travelled around the world, eating out more or less constantly. Ettlinger lives in New York City because of the restaurants.

MELANIE FALICK (Indian, Japanese, Thai, and Vietnamese cuisines) is the general editor of this book. She is a well-known researcher, writer, and editor who has credits with many different magazines, book publishers, and packagers for her freelance work covering the subjects of food, travel, and needlework around the world. She has traveled throughout Europe and spent extended periods studying in France, Kenya, Egypt, and Israel. She has held staff positions at ACCESS Press and *Chocolatier* magazine, and lives in Kripplebush, N.Y., because of the fresh air.

JOYCE JUE (Chinese cuisine) is the author of *Asian Appetizers*, *Wok and Stir-Fry Cooking*, and *The Cooking of Singapore*, and writes a biweekly column on Asian food for the *San Francisco Chronicle*. An Asian food consultant and expert, she travels internationally to teach cooking, and helped establish the Oriental Hotel's Thai Cooking School in Bangkok. She lives in San Francisco.

KATHY KINGSLEY (German cuisine) is a freelance food writer and researcher who most recently served as a food editor for a Reader's Digest cookbook series and as a national spokesperson and recipe developer for Nestlé foods. Her most recent book is *Chocolate Cakes* (Hyperion). She lives in Connecticut.

ROBERT SIETSEMA (Mexican cuisine) is a food columnist for the *Village Voice* and also the editor of the bimonthly food "fanzine," *Down the Hatch*. He lives in Greenwich Village, New York City, and eats in small, ethnic restaurants every chance he gets.

BONNIE SLOTNICK (American regional cuisine) is a food and nutrition writer and recipe editor in New York City, where she also runs the out-of-print cookbook department at Kitchen Arts & Letters Bookstore. She is a devoted collector of antiquarian cookbooks and does some serious baking for a Greenwich Village soup kitchen, where she is known as "Brownie Bonnie."

ISABELLE VITA (Middle Eastern cuisine) is a freelance food writer who develops, tests, and edits recipes for cookbooks and magazines. She is a frequent contributor to *Chocolatier* magazine. Her passion for Middle Eastern cuisine began when she majored in Middle Eastern history and religion at Barnard College. She misses Amir's Falafel on Broadway between 113th and 114th Streets in New York City.

N O MATTER HOW OFTEN ONE DINES OUT—AND, AS publishers of a series of restaurant and travel guides, my wife and I do so more than most people—one always has questions about foreign cuisines. In fact, that's part of the excitement of exploring unfamiliar foods—the adventure of discovering new tastes and styles. Unfortunately, that adventure can be a little intimidating, given the uninformative nature of most menus, coupled with the fact that most of us do not speak the languages associated with the cuisines we are sampling. But it needn't be that way.

Dining out should be a pleasurable experience, not a stressful one, and I appreciate any information that helps reduce the mystery surrounding foreign menus. I remember the first time that I was presented with *ossobuco* in an Italian restaurant; I had absolutely no idea what it was (let alone how to eat it properly). We all must have had similar experiences when we first started venturing out into the restaurant world.

Obviously, experience helps increase knowledge, but even though my wife and I now eat most of our meals in restaurants we don't know everything about each cuisine. For example, I'm no longer stumped by *ossobuco*, but I have a difficult time remembering that *gremolada* is the name of the garnish that's often sprinkled over it. Likewise, I'd be hard pressed to explain the differences among the myriad kinds of chilies encountered in dishes today, or to immediately recognize the Italian names for some of the more obscure pasta shapes. What's worse, people ask me to explain menu items all the time. I only know what I like, though I have always wished I had more information to share.

Now, to help make negotiating a foreign menu much easier, there is Steve Ettlinger's *Restaurant Lover's Companion*. Dining with it should be like dining with an articulate old friend who is world-wise, well-travelled, and delighted to share his or her experience.

From the moment I first heard Steve describe his book, I liked the idea. There has always been a need for easily accessed information of this type, and this book answers all those pesky, sometimes embarrassing questions raised by dining in ethnic restaurants—like the time I should have asked before ordering a dish with the French word for "cake" in its name. Imagine my surprise when I was presented with a plate of chicken livers instead!

With this book in hand, diners should be able to answer most of the questions that arise in any given restaurant, or by reading up beforehand, avoid having to ask any questions at all—and I've been in not a few restaurants where the waiters' limited knowledge of English made any kind of dialogue difficult. The information contained here is also much more extensive and accurate than what one could expect to hear from a beleaguered waiter (or from me, for that matter).

When it comes to understanding foreign cuisines, there's obviously no substitute for actual dining experience, but to familiarize yourself with the customs, ingredients, and cooking methods involved, no reservations are required—just *The Restaurant Lover's Companion*.

—Tim Zagat, publisher of the *Zagat Survey*

MANY FOOD PROFESSIONALS AGREED TO BE IN-
terviewed or to review the early versions of this
book. An extraordinary number of restaurateurs
helped us by sending menus or responding to specific questions. Though they are not listed here, we are most grateful
for the professional courtesy they extended. The editors and
contributors are especially thankful to the following people
who spent much precious time sharing their knowledge.
Though they offered many suggestions, and though the contributors were diligent, Steve Ettlinger, the editor, is ultimately responsible for the content and any errors that may
still be present or that might be the result of material that he
added. We wish to especially thank the following:

Restaurant Staff, Chefs, and Owners

(All restaurants in New York City unless otherwise noted)
Ismat Siddiqui, Chatkhara; Jaiya Thai; Marcel and Marie
Guélaff, La Petite Auberge; Gautam Mukerji, Nawab; Roland
Issa, Roland's of Lebanon, Danbury, CT; Josefina Howard,
Rosa Mexicano Restaurant; Lotus Café, Poughkeepsie, NY;
Rumba, Danbury, CT; San Martin's; Smith and Wollensky;
Arlecchino; Cent' Anni; Devra Dedeaux, Judy, and Randy,
Sugar Reef; Thai Chef; Dum, Krungthep City; Orhan Yeqen,
Turkish Kitchen; Zacateca's, Riverside, CA; Zarela Martinez,
Zarela; Yannick Cam, Washington D.C.; Cantler's Riverside
Inn, Annapolis, MD; John McBride, Enchilada Johnny's;
Christian N. Roula, Park Bistro; Salvador Farciert,
Albuquerque Eats; La Isla Bonita; Eli Akleh, Sido; Chef 28;
Andy Secular, Tortilla Flats; Sally McArthur, Anthony's,
Seattle, WA; Trois Jean; Alex Alejandro, El Parador; The Big
Enchilada; Kalustyan's; André Soltner, Lutèce

Other Experts

Amy Albert, Food & Wines from France; Cindy Krebs,
German Wine Information Bureau; Diane Bertolo and Tom
Darauer; James Arkema, Sayu Bhojwani, and Hesh

Sarmalkar, Dao Spencer, Asia Society; Sylvia Carter, *New York Newsday;* Irena Chalmers; Frances Houck; Curnonsky; Michelle Dunn; Steven Heiblim, Japan Society; Cathy Hymans; Bern and Franke Keating; Marcia Kiesel, *Food and Wine* magazine; Santushi Kuruppu; Aparna Lall; Doris and John Mason; Veronica Murashige; Bhanumathi Patil; Charlie Sahadi, Sahadi Importing Company; Gisela Weinland; Danai Karnpoj, Thai Consulate; Peg Rosen; Janie Hibler; Gary Goldberg, The Culinary Center of New York; Nicole Routhier; Vietnamese Mission to the U.N.; Lucio Caputo, Italian Wine and Food Institute; Rimonda Sofer

Special Mention

Editor Elizabeth Carduff, for enthusiasm and extra efforts; editor John Bell, for jumping in head first; production supervisor Pat Jalbert, for great spirit, unstinting devotion, and patience; designer Tilman Reitzle, for his talent and his bravery in taking on such a complicated manuscript; Evie Righter, for her extraordinarily accurate and thorough copy editing; Mike Donovan and Nancye Green, for generous support of the original concept; Carol Murashige, for administrative support and research assistance *extraordinaire;* Sharon Guskin; Betsy Chotin, for bringing Melanie and Steve together; Chris Whipple and Diana Waill, for their encouragement and adventurous appetites; Gusty Lange; Dylan Alexander Lange Ettlinger; Margery Ettlinger, for her crackerjack editing and culinary example; and Ralph Ettlinger (1917–1992), Chevalier de la *Chaîne des Rôtisseurs* and worldly gourmet companion, who, when confronted with his first hush puppies, exclaimed, "What the hell are those little brown balls?!" Yet another inspiration for a book.

To all of you, thank you. We couldn't have done it without you.

*The diners ponder, stutter, variously flaunting
their ignorance or their pretensions to knowledge.*
—M.F.K. Fisher, in *D is for Dining Out*

D ID YOU EVER WONDER WHAT TO ORDER OR HOW you were supposed to eat the "exotic" food served at an ethnic or regional restaurant? Not long ago, Steve was invited to dine at a fancy Indian restaurant by an important business contact. He ordered a dish new to him, a vegetable *thali*. When an enormous, gorgeous, intricately decorated silver platter arrived with rice in the center and small bowls of vegetables around it, he realized that he didn't know whether he should dump the little dishes onto the silver platter, spoon them onto his plate, or just eat straight out of them. No solution seemed right, and he didn't want to embarrass himself by asking what he thought was a dumb question, revealing his apparent lack of worldliness. He was familiar with many kinds of Indian food, but this particular serving style was new to him. He would have given anything to have known the right answer because being unsure made him nervous throughout the entire meal.

That's when he had the idea for *The Restaurant Lover's Companion*.

Dining in a restaurant, especially in an ethnic one, should be an enjoyable experience, but it can become a daunting one when one is confronted with an unfamiliar serving style, unusual ingredients, or foreign terms with little or no translation. That's not right.

Steve decided that what was needed was a book that would explain typical menus from the most common ethnic restaurants (as well as those featuring American regional specialties)—a sort of field guide—supplemented with commentary on how or what to eat as well as background on the dishes and ingredients. So he recruited veteran food writer and editor Melanie Falick to help hone the format, then with the help of numerous expert contributors and consultants (please read our Acknowledgments), we put together this book.

By the way, we found that there is no one way to eat Indian food from a *thali*. Because Steve was served his meal on his own *thali*, it would have been perfectly acceptable for him to eat directly from it, mixing the different dishes to his liking (see the chapter on Indian cuisine for more perspective). Knowing that is very liberating.

The Goal of The Restaurant Lover's Companion

This is not a definitive reference book or a complete glossary, but rather an introductory guide to make ordering easier and exploring new cuisines more fulfilling. *The Restaurant Lover's Companion* is meant to play the role of an erudite and well-travelled friend who dines with you and explains the meal as it progresses.

How This Book Was Researched

We checked menus, cookbooks, reference books, and magazine articles. We interviewed chefs, consultants, managers, and restaurant owners. Some had published their own cookbooks and were able to help us expeditiously; others didn't understand what we were doing, sometimes due to the lack of a common language, but, nonetheless, let us observe in their kitchens and learn by tasting. Collecting menus for research was easy, as so many Manhattan restaurants distribute copies of their menus to boost their delivery business. How many editors have research material shoved under their door every day?

Researching and checking this material was tremendous fun. No other book project in our experience has had such an impact on our daily lives, especially at lunchtime! We had never before realized the diversity of cuisines available within just one block of Steve's office: American Regional (New York deli and dairy as well as Tex-Mex), Caribbean, Chinese, French, German, Indian, Italian, Japanese, Mexican, Middle Eastern, Spanish, and Thai (well, okay, two blocks, in order to include the Spanish one). The only ethnic restaurants in this book not in the immediate neighborhood of Steve's office were Greek and Vietnamese (though there are some great Tibetan, Afghani, and Polish places). So whenever we needed firsthand perspective, or had a question that we wanted to answer ourselves (as opposed to calling on our team of experts) or a chapter we wanted to test, we ate lunch accordingly. It was a tough job, but then we're tough editors and researchers. A bit overweight and over budget, but tough.

Variations in the Field

On the menus you encounter you are bound to find dishes that are not quite the same as we describe them. That is to be expected, primarily because chefs are *supposed* to improvise, embellish, and otherwise individualize in respect to recipes (and budgets as well as availability of ingredients). Even classic French cuisine, which has been recorded in cookbooks since the 14th century, is subject to individual interpretation and continues to evolve. The information noted here is a guide to what you are likely to find on typical, traditional menus, not a record of every version of the dishes you will encounter.

Another reason for a discrepancy between what you might find on a restaurant menu and what you read here is spelling. In some cases, such as Thai and Indian, there is no standard English transliteration from the foreign language. In other cases, there is an official transliteration style (such as Pinyin for Chinese), but restaurateurs create their own spellings in ways that reflect their regional languages as well as their imaginations. Finally, the regional backgrounds of owners are often reflected in the language they use on their menus. We spoke to as many experts as we could and then made a decision that reflects as much as possible both academic accuracy and reality, which are not always the same.

Ordering Smart

Eating healthily is a matter of choosing individual dishes correctly. Though we were tempted to point out particularly healthful dishes in each chapter, we hesitated since such generalities are dangerous. Because recipes vary tremendously, even a generally lowfat dish might be made with a higher proportion than usual of high-fat ingredients, or it may be fried instead of broiled. Be sure to inquire as to how dishes are prepared if you need to limit the fat and calories you consume.

If you are especially concerned about eating food prepared only a certain way, such as without meat, salt, or alcohol, be sure to make your needs known to the waiter or cook before ordering. In general, it is possible to avoid rich, fat-laden foods by ordering intelligently and searching out broiled fish, steamed vegetables, grains, and so on. We have found that most restaurateurs are glad to explain how a particular dish is prepared or to modify a recipe so that the diner will be satisfied. The key is to ask.

Appetizers, Soups, and Main Courses

In many cultures, including Thai and Chinese, eating an appetizer or soup followed by a main course and dessert is uncommon. In others, what Americans consider typical main courses hold a different position. For example, Italians consider pasta a first course; Mexicans usually eat tamales and enchiladas as snacks rather than as part of the main meal of the day. In many cuisines meat is used in small quantities as a "condiment" to other ingredients such as vegetables, rather than being served on its own. The result is that some ethnic restaurants formulate their menus around American habits as a response to American expectations. Others combine the American and native way of eating. What this means, for example, is that a Thai restaurant may include a list of appetizers on its menu, usually foods taken directly from the "main course" section, and they may or may not reduce the size of the portions.

How to Use This Book

The format of *The Restaurant Lover's Companion* includes not only introductory information, but menus loaded with expert commentary. (The menus are explained in detail on page xx.)

Flip through *The Restaurant Lover's Companion* in your leisure time at home, not just when you are ordering in a restaurant. Read a particular chapter before going out to a restaurant so that you feel confident enough to try new foods and know how to put together a satisfying meal.

When you happen upon an ethnic restaurant that is dedicated to serving the traditional food in the traditional style of the country in question, prepare yourself for a surprise. It is likely to be quite different from what you might otherwise have imagined. Most cuisines are much more complex and developed—and better—than we've been led to believe by our encounters with Americanized versions. Also remember that many restaurateurs are more than willing to put together a traditional meal upon request. *The Restaurant Lover's Companion* gives you the information you need to know in order to request the real thing.

We hope you will find this book an invaluable dining companion that helps you explore new cuisines and enjoy familiar ones even more. But be warned: Reading this book is bound to make you hungry! *Bon appétit!*

— Steve Ettlinger and Melanie Falick

P.S.: Please write to us c/o Addison-Wesley, One Jacob Way, Reading, MA 01867, if you find alternative names or other information that pertain to the dishes listed here.

COURSE NAME

We arranged the food courses in the order in which they usually appear in restaurants, even if these dishes are eaten in a different order in their countries of origin. Thus, appetizers, soups, and salads appear towards the beginning of our menus; desserts and beverages (including alcoholic drinks) are at the end. Whenever possible we present the course names in the original language, as they may appear on the menus of more traditional restaurants.

Dish Name

We describe each dish's main ingredients and cooking method. If you see an **ingredient** in boldface, look for more information about it in the shaded section at the bottom of that page spread or of the page to which we refer you.

Whenever we have more to say about the history or variations of a dish, we add a note in italics. We hope this information will make you feel as if you are dining with a friend who knows the cuisine well.

WHEN FOREIGN dining customs differ from ours, we insert notes on how to eat traditionally. You don't have to follow these instructions, of course, but we hope knowing about them will make your meal more enjoyable, and perhaps make you feel more adventuresome.

We use boxed, shaded notes to elaborate on particular groups of dishes, cooking methods, types of wine, or other special aspects of an individual cuisine.

INGREDIENT NOTES

• We describe **ingredients** that may be new to you in the shaded section at the bottom of page spreads. Information in this section includes alternative names and descriptions of taste and preparation methods. Many ingredients that are significant in more than one dish are cross-referenced by page number.

*The
Restaurant Lover's
Companion*

CARIBBEAN
cuisine

★

ISLAND LINGO
Cheers–*Cheers, Mon* (cheers, mon)

SPANISH
Cheers–*Salud* (sah-**lood**)
Bon appétit–*Buen Provecho* (pro-**veck**-oh)
Thank you–*Gracias* (**grah**-see-us)

FRENCH
Cheers–*À votre santé* (ah **voh**-trih **sahn**-tay)
Bon appétit–*Bon appétit* (bone ap-ih-**tea**)
Thank you–*Merci beaucoup* (merr-**see** boh-**coo**)

THE CUISINE OF THE CARIBBEAN, A GARLAND OF OVER 7,000 islands stretching 2,600 miles between Florida and Venezuela, is a cultural patchwork. Each patch, or dish, represents the plentiful bounty of the islands' lush tropical vegetation, combined with the influence of one or more of the different groups of people that have lived there. The Amer-Indians who were living on the islands when Columbus and the Spaniards landed in 1492; the English, Portuguese, French, Dutch, Danish, and Swedish invaders who followed Columbus; the slaves the invaders brought over from West Africa; and the indentured servants from India and China who arrived when slavery was abolished—all of these groups played a role in shaping the fusion of cooking styles that has come to be known as Caribbean cuisine.

In general, Caribbean cuisine is based on foods that are high in carbohydrates and fiber. Meat, which is expensive in the Caribbean, is often used in small quantities—more as a flavoring than as a main component of a dish. Low-fat fish and shellfish naturally play an important role in this island cuisine.

Though most Caribbean restaurants in the U.S. attempt to recreate the region's authentic fare, many of the more commercially oriented restaurants use tropical foods as mere springboards for their own creativity. While these restaurants may call themselves Caribbean, they could more accurately be described as Caribbean-inspired or Ameri-Carib. What these restaurants lack in authenticity is often compensated for in such "tropical" trademarks as colorful rum drinks, island-inspired decorating, and calypso, reggae, and salsa music.

Principles of Flavor

Chilies of all shapes, sizes, and degrees of heat grow in abundance on the Caribbean islands and appear in many dishes. Among the kinds you will find in Caribbean restaurants in the U.S. are Scotch Bonnets, *wiri wiris*, and bird peppers. Because these fiery peppers cause perspiration, it's thought that eating them helps people to cool off, especially handy in tropical climates like the Caribbean. In the days before refrigeration, hot peppers may have also helped to mask the unwanted flavors of less-than-fresh foods.

Many different spices grow on the islands. Among the most commonly employed in island cooking are cinnamon, nutmeg, mace, allspice, and cloves. Other prevalent flavorings include ginger, garlic, coconut, and rum.

Foreign Influence

Before the arrival of Columbus, two main tribes of Native Americans occupied the islands of the Caribbean. These tribes were the peaceful Arawaks and the fierce Caribs. The Caribs were voracious meat lovers and frequently added an Arawak along with wild boars to their cookpots. Whatever (or whomever) they were eating, the Caribs seasoned their food generously with chilies, still the most prevalent seasoning on the islands today.

The Arawaks contributed a precursor to our modern barbecue, a grill made out of green wood sticks called a *barbacoa*; cassava bread (made from flour derived from a starchy root called cassava), which is still eaten throughout the islands; and *cassareep*, a mixture of cassava juice, sugar, and spices that is an integral ingredient in the pepperpots of Guyana, Trinidad, and Grenada.

Christopher Columbus brought sugarcane from the Canary Islands to the Caribbean in 1493, and it wasn't long before it was discovered that the cane juice could be fermented and distilled into rum, a product from which fortunes were made. Other European colonists in search of their own fortunes arrived shortly thereafter, and along with their mercenary desires and culinary customs, they brought to the islands such foods as breadfruit, bananas, oranges, limes, mangoes, rice, and coffee. Along with the colonists also came slaves from Africa, who carried from their homeland seedlings for okra, callaloo, taro, and ackee. Because the slaves were often fed bland, cheap foods unwanted by their masters, they learned to season their meals with intense flavors, a trademark of Caribbean cooking today. In the 19th century when slavery was abolished, indentured servants from India and China introduced curries and the stir-fry method of food preparation, respectively.

Ordering

Caribbean menus in the U.S. are divided into categories that include starters (soups, salads, and appetizers); main courses; side dishes of vegetables and sometimes chutneys; desserts; and beverages.

Service and Dining

Caribbean meals are served in courses, with each person ordering for him- or herself, though, of course, sharing is always an option. Appetizers such as fritters and coconut shrimp lend themselves to being enjoyed by everyone at the table, accompanied by a round of refreshing drinks.

Condiments

At least one bottle of hot pepper sauce is found on nearly every Caribbean table. Some sauces are chunky and others are smooth; some contain fruit (such as papaya) and/or vegetables, but the common denominator is that they are all made with chilies. Try dipping your food into a small amount of sauce at a time. If there is more than one type of sauce offered, mix them together to create your own favorite blend. Common brands include Pickapeppa (from Jamaica), Bonney Pepper (from Barbados), and Matouks (from Trinidad). Mango and other chutneys are also served, often with Indian-style curries.

Garnishes

Bright red or light green lantern-shaped Scotch Bonnet peppers are sometimes used as garnishes in Caribbean restaurants in the U.S. (Many Caribbean natives eat these peppers in large chunks with their food, but the average American will find them much too hot.) If desired, cut off a sliver, skewer it with your fork, and rub it on meat, fish, poultry, or fritters, or even drop it into soup. But don't even taste the sliver unless you are an aficionado of chilies—and have an asbestos-lined mouth.

Rice and Bread

Rice and beans accompany many a Caribbean meal, and each large island has its own favorite combination. In

Caribbean restaurants in the U.S. you are most likely to be offered the Jamaican rice and peas, in which rice is cooked with coconut cream and red kidney beans (note that "peas" is the generic term for dried beans in most of the Caribbean), or Cuban rice and beans, in which rice is matched with turtle or black beans. There are also the Dominican rice and brown beans, the Haitian rice and red beans, and Barbadian and Trinidadian rice with small yellow pigeon peas. In many cases the beans are so thoroughly cooked that they come to the table as a sort of stew, and with the rice they can often form a filling, inexpensive meal. Plain white rice and saffron rice also appear on many menus.

Cassava bread, which was originated by the Arawaks; Cuban bread, a soft and chewy, lard-enriched, soft-crusted bread; garlic bread; and unleavened, crepe-like *roti*, a "gift" from the indentured servants from India, are all found on Caribbean menus in the U.S as well. In some restaurants the bread is brought to the table automatically, at no additional charge.

Signature Dishes

Callaloo (soup made with callaloo greens, okra, and usually crab or pork; nearly as many variations as there are cooks); *Jerk Pork* (pork rubbed with chilies, herbs, and spices); *Pepperpot* (highly seasoned soup or stew that may include meat, seafood, and/or vegetables, often flavored with a bittersweet syrup called *cassareep*); *Roti* (unleavened, crepe-like bread wrapped around a curry filling); *Stamp and Go* (Jamaican fried codfish cakes)

Common Misconception

All Caribbean food is fiery hot. While Caribbean food can be spicy-hot on its own or with the addition of hot sauce, many restaurants temper the spiciness of their food for an American clientele. Much of the food of the Hispanic islands is mild, though it is often seasoned generously with garlic.

APPETIZERS

APPETIZERS Appetizers in a Caribbean restaurant can be simple little nibbles or almost the size of a main course. Many are representative of street foods in the Caribbean, such as meat patties and vegetable fritters.

Coconut Chicken or Shrimp
Chicken or shrimp fried in a light, sweet **coconut** batter

Conch or Vegetable Fritters
Conch or vegetables dipped in batter and fried; often served with a peppery dipping sauce or a chutney

In Puerto Rican restaurants fritters are made with codfish instead of conch and are listed as bacallaitos *on menus.*

Mariquitas de Plátano
Crispy **plantain** chips; often served with a dipping sauce, such as a black bean salsa

In some Caribbean restaurants a basket of plantain chips is brought to each table automatically, much as tortilla chips are served in Mexican restaurants.

INGREDIENT NOTES

• **Coconuts** and the palm trees on which they grow play an important role in Caribbean cuisine—and construction. The fronds and logs are used for building houses, and the coconuts themselves yield water, coconut oil, and meat, all of which are employed in cooking.

• **Conch** (pronounced conk) is a large mollusk, the flesh of which has a mild clam-like flavor. It has been popular in the Caribbean since the time of the Arawaks; Christopher Columbus reported that the Arawaks ate the meat and carved the spiral shells into tools, trumpets, and ceremonial objects. Today conch meat (often called *lambi*) is enjoyed throughout the Caribbean, especially in the Bahamas, where it is

known as hurricane ham. In Caribbean restaurants in the U.S., it is likely to be found in fritters, chowders, and salads, or sliced, marinated, and served raw.

• The **plantain** belongs to the same family as the sweet banana known well in the U.S., but is higher in starch and lower in sugar. In its unripe form it is like a potato. As it ripens—and its skin turns from green to yellow to dark brown—its flavor sweetens.

• **Annatto** or annatto seeds (called *achiote* in Spanish-speaking regions) are small, delicately flavored berries that give foods a yellowish orange color. They are used in the U.S. to color cheddar cheese, margarine, and smoked fish, and are sold in supermar-

Stamp and Go

Jamaican codfish patties fried in a heavy batter, often flavored with onions, **annatto**, and chilies

"Stamp and Go" was a command given to 17th-century English sailors when they had a task to do, such as haul on a rope. According to one tale about the origin of the name of these fritters, the Jamaicans on shore liked the sound of the command, so named these fritters after it. According to another theory, the name reflects how quickly passengers on rural bus routes can buy the little fritters at rest stops, get their tickets stamped, and then be on their way–or go.

Yuca Frita

Crisp fried **yuca** (cassava); often served with a flavorful dipping sauce

SALADS Salads on Caribbean menus in the U.S. often feature such "tropical" ingredients as hearts of palm and conch. They may also be seasoned in a creative way with a typical Caribbean flavoring. For example, a green salad may be topped with strips of chicken and croutons flavored with the Jamaican barbecue seasoning called jerk.

Hearts of Palm Salad

Chilled **hearts of palm** and **papaya** in a flavorful dressing, such as one made with scallion and coconut or simply lime juice

kets in a paste or powder form (combined with garlic, cumin, oregano, and food coloring).

• **Yuca**, also known as cassava or manioc, is a long, slim tuber (like a long potato) with bark-like skin and very starchy flesh that becomes nearly translucent when cooked. It is used to make *cassareep*, a bittersweet syrup, and tapioca, a common thickening agent. It is also ground into meal to make bread.

• **Hearts of palm** (*palmitos* in Spanish) are the tender, velvety, ivory-colored inner hearts of a small palm tree called a palmetto. Their mild flavor is reminiscent of artichokes. In the U.S., canned hearts of palm are most common because fresh ones are very rarely available.

• The **papaya** grows in bunches on top of a palm-like tree and can range in weight from 8 ounces to 20 pounds. It ranges in shape from round to pear-like to long and thin. The ripe flesh, which is sweet and refreshing, is a frequent ingredient in Caribbean-inspired salads.

Sweet Potato Salad
Diced **sweet potatoes** in a flavorful dressing, often based on lime

Conch Salad
Conch (•10) and chilies "cooked" in a marinade that is usually based on vinegar, lemon, or lime

SOUPS

Callaloo
Callaloo greens, crab, and pork in an **okra**-thickened broth flavored with chilies, garlic, and lime juice

Callaloo, in one form or another, is found on all the Caribbean islands. There are many different variations—the one described here hails from Tobago—but all seem to include the spinach-like callaloo leaves, which were first brought to the Caribbean by African slaves. Other variations of this soup might include salted codfish or coconut milk and omit the okra or lime juice. The word callaloo on a menu can refer to either this soup or simply the calloloo leaves themselves.

Sancocho (Puerto Rico and Dominican Republic)
Hearty soup/stew made with various root vegetables and squashes such as **yuca** (•11), yellow and green **plantains** (•10), yellow and green bananas, yams, *batatas* (a type of sweet potato), pumpkin, and pork or beef, seasoned with thyme and other herbs and spices

Sopa de Frijol Negro (Cuba)
Thick black bean soup; may be served with lemon wedges, chopped onion or hard-boiled egg, or white rice

Manish Water (Jamaica)
Highly seasoned goat soup

Reputed to promote fertility, this soup is a popular choice on wedding menus.

INGREDIENT NOTES

• The **sweet potato**, a member of the morning glory family, is not related to either the white potato or the yam. This highly nutritious vegetable with intensely sweet, pale white to deep reddish orange flesh grows on a perennial plant and, contrary to popular belief, has no more calories than a white potato.

• **Okra**, a green pod-shaped vegetable, is a member of the cotton family. Because okra releases a viscous liquid when cooked, it is often used as a thickening agent in soups and stews. It is one of the vegetables introduced to the Caribbean region by African slaves.

CHICKEN

Asopao

Soupy stew from Puerto Rico that features chicken (or meat or seafood) and rice, plus as many as 20 other ingredients, such as onion, tomato, bell pepper, ham, peas, olives, *sofrito* (see next page), and capers

The word asopao *means soupy in Spanish and that is how this dish, Puerto Rico's version of paella, is usually* described on menus, where it is often listed in the soup section. Soupy rice dishes are also popular on Dominican menus.*

Arroz con Pollo

Rice cooked with pieces of cut-up chicken on the bone and vegetables

Ginger Lime Chicken

Sautéed boneless chicken slices flavored with **ginger** and lime

MEAT

Sandwich Cubano (Cuba)

Half loaf of French bread filled with sliced roast pork, ham, cheese, pickles, mayonnaise, and mustard, grilled on a sandwich press until the cheese is melted and the meat is hot

Lechón Asado

Roast suckling pig

Curried Goat

Chunks of tender goat meat cooked in a spicy curry sauce

In Jamaica curried goat is served on holidays and other special occasions.

• **Ginger** arrived in the Caribbean via the Chinese indentured servants. It is used as a spicy flavoring in main dishes as well as in chutneys and ginger beer.

CARIBBEAN CURRIES

Although in India, where curries (or highly seasoned gravy-based dishes) originated, cooks prepare fresh spice mixtures for each curry and have traditionally looked down upon the use of prepackaged curry powder (a mixture of herbs and spices that usually includes coriander, cumin, turmeric, black and cayenne peppers, and fenugreek among its ingredients), many Caribbean cooks use these prepared mixtures all the time and unashamedly. In addition, Caribbean cooks commonly add allspice to their curries whereas it is unlikely that a traditional Indian cook would even consider the possibility.

13

SOFRITO: A PUERTO RICAN STAPLE

The exact recipe for *sofrito* varies from cook to cook, but among the basic components are cilantro, bell pepper, onion, garlic, tomato, and sometimes chilies, additional herbs, and salt pork that has been simmered in oil or lard that has been colored yellowish orange with **annatto** (•10). *Sofrito* is an integral ingredient in *asopao* as well as *arroz con pollo* and numerous other

 Puerto Rican soups, stews, and vegetable dishes.

Pepperpot

Highly seasoned meat or vegetable soup or stew

Pepperpot is found throughout the Caribbean in many different guises. In Guyana, Trinidad, and Tobago, it is a stew seasoned with cassareep, a bittersweet syrup derived from boiling down cassava root, sugar, and spices. In addition to flavoring the stew, cassareep

acts as a preservative, allowing cooks to reserve broth from one batch of pepperpot to use as a starter for the next. In Antigua, pepperpot is a vegetable soup. In Jamaica, it is a soup made with meat or poultry and vegetables.

Cook Down Oxtail

Pieces of **oxtail** "cooked down" with lima beans to form a thick stew

Jerk Pork (Jamaica)

Grilled, baked, or smoked pork, rubbed and marinated with chilies, herbs, and spices, such as thyme, allspice, cinnamon, nutmeg, and peppers

Pelau

Rice cooked together with meat, chicken, or seafood and vegetables; may also include pigeon peas (small yellow peas), saffron, raisins, or tomatoes

Like the Indian pullao *(or pilaf), this dish is made by cooking all of the ingredients in the same pot without a sauce or gravy.*

Roti

Unleavened crepe-like bread filled with or served alongside meat or vegetable curry

In India the word roti *refers to the unfilled unleavened bread alone, whereas in the Caribbean it often refers to both the bread and the accompanying curry.*

INGREDIENT NOTES

• Today, the term **oxtail** is commonly used to identify a cut of meat derived from a beef or veal tail.

Picadillo
Pork cubes in spicy sauce with green peppers, onions, pimiento, raisins, and olives

Ropa Vieja
Shredded beef (often leftover pot roast) in a spicy sauce; served with French fries or *tostones* (see page 17)

Ropa vieja *means "old clothes" in Spanish. This is a classic Cuban dish also found on Puerto Rican and Dominican menus.*

Jamaican Beef Patties
Baked pastry pockets filled with a peppery mixture of beef and spices

These savory pastries are said to be the Jamaican take on Cornish pasties, which are made with a mixture of beef and potato and are not usually spicy. In some Caribbean restaurants the beef inside the pastry is replaced with chicken, vegetables, or shrimp

FISH and SHELLFISH

Curried Shrimp or Chicken and Coconut
Shrimp or chicken sautéed with carrots, peppers, and coconut in a curry sauce; served with cal-abaza rice (see page 16)

Escovitch
Cooked fish pickled in a vinegar marinade

Escovitch is the Jamaican name for what residents of Spanish-speaking islands call fish prepared en escabeche.

• A **bouquet garni** is a small bundle of fresh herb sprigs tied with a string and added to soups, stews, and broths. The classic version combines parsley, thyme, and bay leaf, though cooks tend to improvise according to the flavoring needs of a particular dish.

Blaff
Firm white-fleshed fish, such as red snapper, marinated and poached with such ingredients as chilies, lime, garlic, allspice, and a **bouquet garni**; traditionally served in some of its cooking liquid accompanied by white rice

According to some food scholars, blaff, a classic from the French-speaking islands, is named after the sound made when the fish is dropped into its poaching broth.

Shrimp Creole
Fresh shrimp cooked with peppers, onions, and tomatoes; served over white rice

Ackee and Saltfish
Sautéed **ackee** and salt cod, often flavored with onions, chilies, and thyme

Ackee and saltfish is immensely popular in Jamaica, where it is eaten throughout the day.

SIDE DISHES In small, informal restaurants in urban areas in the U.S., many of these side dishes, especially the deep-fried ones, are served as snacks or appetizers.

Black Beans
Cooked black beans

Calabaza Rice
Rice flavored with **calabaza** squash and other seasonings

Pastelles
(Puerto Rico and Cuba)
Seasoned ground beef wrapped in *masa* (corn or grated plantain dough), wrapped in **plantain** (•10) leaves or parchment, and boiled

Rice and Peas
Rice and dried red kidney beans cooked with thyme, allspice, onions, garlic, and coconut cream

This bland Jamaican side dish goes well with the more spicy main courses. Note that "peas" is local jargon for dried beans.

INGREDIENT NOTES

• **Saltfish** (*bacalao* on Spanish-speaking islands; *morue* on islands where French is spoken) is saltwater fish that is salted and then dried. Most often saltfish is made with cod, but technically the term encompasses numerous fish species, including mackerel, herring, and haddock.

• **Ackee** is a reddish orange fruit that when ripe splits open to reveal shiny black seeds and edible, yellowish flesh that tastes similar to scrambled eggs. The scientific name for this fruit, which is poisonous when unripe, is *blighia sapida*, a reference to Captain Bligh, who in 1793 is believed to have carried the fruit from West Africa to Jamaica.

• **Calabaza** is a sweet, moist, pumpkin-like squash, in flavor reminiscent of Hubbard or butternut squash. In the Caribbean it is often used as the base for pumpkin soups and in vegetable dishes. It acts as a nice contrast with the fish or chicken combinations it usually accompanies.

Mango Chutney

A tart condiment made with pieces of mango and such ingredients as garlic, chilies, ginger, and **tamarind**

Mango chutney is a traditional accompaniment to curries, which are prevalent on islands where a lot of indentured servants from India settled, such as Guyana, Jamaica, and Trinidad and Tobago.

Maduros or Plátanos Fritos (Puerto Rico and Dominican Republic)

Deep-fried chunks of ripe (yellow) sweet **plantain** (•10)

Alcapurias (Puerto Rico)

Mashed green bananas or **yuca** (•11) filled with seasoned ground beef and vegetables, formed into flattened ovals, and deep-fried

Yuca con Mojo (Puerto Rico)

Chunks of boiled **yuca** (•11) in garlic sauce

Tostones (Puerto Rico and Dominican Republic)

Twice-fried (deep-fried) green **plantain** slices (•10) that are flattened between fryings and served with a chopped garlic and oil dipping sauce

Tostones are a favorite in Puerto Rico. A similar Puerto Rican side dish called mofongo de cerdo (mofongo *for short) is made by combining grated or mashed green plantains, pork cracklings, and garlic, and frying the mixture in a ball shape.*

Rellenos de Papas (Puerto Rico)

Lightly breaded, deep-fried mashed potato ball filled with seasoned ground beef and olives

D E S S E R T S Caribbean desserts run the gamut from cool, refreshing fruit platters and ice cream to cakes, pastries, and puddings. Many feature tropical fruits, spices, and rum.

Flan

Baked custard with a caramelized sugar topping

Fried Bananas and Rum

Sautéed sliced bananas flavored with rum

This dish is often flambéed. It may also be served with ice cream.

• **Tamarind** is the pulp of the brown pod of a tropical plant. It has a sweet-sour taste and is used as a flavoring in many dishes, including chutneys, jellies, candies, and beverages.

Jamaican Fruit Cake
Fruit cake flavored with rum
and allspice

Rice Pudding
Pudding made with rice, milk,
and sweet spices

BEVERAGES Rainbow-colored tropical fruit-
and rum-based drinks, many of which are given whimsical
names like Dark and Stormy, Joe's Island Relaxer, Surf Sider,
and The Hummingbird, are common offerings
in Caribbean restaurants and are often
presented in large glasses with festive swizzle
sticks. Strong espresso or American coffee is
frequently served at the end of meals. Some
Cuban restaurants feature espresso bars,
where patrons add a generous amount of
sugar to the strong brew.

Carrot Juice
Carrot juice sweetened with
coconut cream and sprinkled
with nutmeg; sometimes spiked
with rum

Ginger Beer
Tangy, spicy carbonated beverage
made from fermented ginger

Mango, Papaya, Passion Fruit, or Soursop Juice
Juice made from one or a
mixture of tropical fruits, such as
passion fruit and **soursop**

Batidos
Milk shakes made with a choice
of fruits, carrots, or puffed wheat

Shandy
Mixture of light lager beer,
ginger beer, angostura bitters
(a Trinidadian flavoring that
originated in Venezuela),
and nutmeg

*Thirst-quenching shandies—
as well as ginger beer and
planter's punch—were introduced to the Caribbean by the
British.*

INGREDIENT NOTES

• The **coconut cream** used to
make piña coladas and other
"island" drinks is very high in
fat. Consider yourself warned.

• **Soursop** is a large, oval, dark
green fruit with a thick skin that
can be spiny or smooth. Its pulp
is whitish-pink with a sweet,
mildly acidic flavor and a thick
custard-like texture. In the

Sorrel

Sorrel blossoms steeped in boiling water with other flavorings, such as cloves, orange zest, and ginger, then sweetened and combined with water and, sometimes, rum

Drinking this spicy-tart, dark red beverage is a Christmas tradition throughout many of the English-speaking islands. The blossoms from which it is made come from a plant in the hibiscus family, not the herb of the same name.

Piña Colada

Rum, **coconut cream**, pineapple, and ice combined in a blender

Puerto Rico is said to be the island where the piña colada (literally "strained pineapple") was invented. Some of the best piña coladas are made with chunks of pineapple rather than pineapple juice.

Daiquiri

Mixture of rum, lime juice, sugar, and sometimes ice and/or fruit, such as banana, mango, or papaya; often processed in a blender

Planter's Punch

Rum and fruit juice

Today any beverage featuring rum and fruit juice can be called planter's punch, but the name once meant a specific beverage made with lime juice, sugar, dark rum, water, ice, and sometimes a pinch of ground nutmeg.

Sangría

Wine punch with fresh fruit chunks floating in it

Curaçao

Orange-flavored liqueur from the island of the same name

Tia Maria

Sweet rum-based liqueur flavored with Jamaica's highly esteemed Blue Mountain coffee

Espresso

Strong black coffee

Café con Leche

Strong coffee mixed with a generous amount of hot milk

This is typically sweetened with lots of sugar and served with breakfast in the Caribbean. Sometimes it is made with more milk than coffee.

Caribbean it is made into juice, ice cream, desserts, and candy.

• **Passion fruit** is a sweet, small, egg-shaped fruit with a brittle rind (the most common variety has a dark purple rind) that protects edible, flesh-covered black seeds. Its flavor is sweet-tart, its aroma has been described as a blend of jasmine, honey, and lemon.

CHINESE
cuisine

★

Cheers–*Gan Bei* (gahn bay)
Bon appétit–*Man Chi* (mahn chur)
Thank you–*Xie Xie* (t**see**-eh t**see**-eh)

CHINESE HISTORY SPANS OVER 5,000 YEARS, AND FOR centuries China's geographic boundaries, diverse climates, and limited resources largely mapped out the development of Chinese cooking. From this vast land arose four distinct schools of cooking, each requiring of its chefs the ability to turn whatever there was to work with into a satisfying meal. As a result, a Chinese meal not only encompasses multiple courses but also provides an exciting spectrum of flavors, textures, fragrances, and colors. Achieving this harmonizing of opposites, this yin and yang, is second nature to good Chinese cooks.

The Chinese language as found on menus in the U.S. is difficult to translate accurately as restaurant owners often create their own phonetic spellings in ways that reflect their regional language as well as their imaginations. Pinyin is the official transliteration style, and in this chapter, as a compromise, it is used interchangeably with regional spellings, such as Cantonese, to reflect what is most commonly found on menus around the U.S.

Principles of Flavor

There are eight flavors or elements that Chinese cooks strive to cultivate and enhance. Five of them—salty, bland, sweet, sour, and bitter—can either be achieved in one dish or in the combination of dishes that make up a complete Chinese meal. A sixth flavor, called *gum* or golden, is a unique, almost euphoric taste that cannot be described in words but can be tasted in such Chinese delicacies as thousand-year-old eggs. The remaining two qualities are hot (as in spicy) taste and fragrance: Spicy Chinese foods should be not only pungent to the palate but should stimulate other senses in the body; the fragrance should stimulate the gastric juices.

CHINESE REGIONAL COOKING

The regional cooking of China encompasses four distinct schools within which there exists much local variation.

Southern School: Cantonese cooking, known for its light and savory qualities, is the most well-known form of cooking in the southern school and is also the most common form of Chinese cooking in restaurants in the U.S. Cantonese chefs are known for their stir-fry wizardry and mastery of seafood and dim sum cooking; lavish but prudent use of ginger and scallions; light hand with soy sauce; and use of only the freshest ingredients to promote natural and pure flavors. Cantonese cuisine is served in dim sum teahouses, banquet halls, and noodle houses as well as regular restaurants.

Northern School: Peking has been the center of China's political power and culture for centuries, and its cooking is the most well-known in the northern school. Wheat, not rice, is the main staple grain, and wheat flour is turned into breads and noodles. Northern cooks are known for their fondness for garlic and scallions, hoisin sauce, and "sizzling" foods with a sauce made with brown beans called *chiang pao*; interpretation of sweet-and-sour dishes, gravy-laden dishes, foods braised with soy sauce and soy paste (a thicker and richer version of soy sauce); and meat dishes, including ones featuring lamb or mutton.

Western School: Szechwan cooking, famous for its hot and spicy flavors, is the most well-known form of cooking within the western school (followed closely by the cooking of the neighboring province of Hunan, which features similar but even richer and hotter tastes). Szechwan peppercorns, hot bean paste, garlic, ginger, chilies, leeks, dried tree ear mushrooms, and preserved foods are among the favorite seasonings of this region. Seeds and peanuts, ground into paste or turned into oil and coupled with soybean paste, give Szechwan cooking its unique character. "Fish-flavored dishes" are made without fish, which is not available in the Szechwan basin, but with a sauce that contains a multitude of ingredients that go well with fish. They taste red hot, slightly sweet-and-sour, and savory all at the same time.

Eastern School: Shanghai is the culinary center of the eastern provinces of China, where the finest rice wine, called Shao Hsing wine, and another excellent product, Chinkiang black vinegar, are produced. In the Fukien province, one can find the best soy sauce, a must for red-cooking—cooking with soy sauce over a slow fire, a specialty of the eastern school. The region's food is thought to be refined and delicate, rich but not oily. Steamed breads, dumplings (northern-style dim sum), and noodles are trademark dishes of the eastern school.

Foreign Influence

There is evidence that foreign foodstuff has been adopted throughout the 5,000 years of Chinese civilization. Flour mills existed in China during the Han Dynasty (206 B.C.–A.D. 220), and it is speculated that the milling technique was borrowed from the West. Wheat came from western Asia during prehistoric times. Mutton was introduced by China's northern nomad neighbors, and today lamb is very much a part of the northern Chinese diet. Peanuts were brought from South America, and chili peppers, maize, and sweet potatoes accompanied the Western traders during the Ming Dynasty (A.D. 1368–1644). New World crops, such as tomatoes, sweet peppers, and chili peppers, dramatically altered southern China's cuisine.

Ordering

For a casual family meal, calculate one main dish per diner, including a poultry, fish, meat, seafood, and vegetable dish, plus a light soup, steamed rice, and, if desired, dessert. Choices should represent a variety of main ingredients and also diverse cooking techniques and contrasting sauces. Avoid the common error of ordering too many stirfried and deep-fried dishes, or too many dishes with the same main ingredient and sauces; flavors of the dishes should range from mild to rich and should offset each other. The Chinese typically order at least one or more steamed dishes, a braised dish, maybe a sizzling platter for a festive occasion, a clay pot casserole dish, plus a light soup. Ordering is customarily done by the host or the organizer of the group. Traditionally, he or she also picks up the tab.

forFor tips on "ordering" in a dim sum restaurant, turn to page 50.

ORDERING LIKE A PRO

Chinese menus are almost always separated into categories according to main ingredients, such as poultry, seafood, meats, and vegetables. These ingredients are cooked using numerous cooking techniques and a host of sauces. Most of the sauces are interchangeable with various main ingredients and styles of preparation; rather than ordering straight from the menu, most Chinese aficionados have their dishes "cooked to order," by specifying the main ingredient, the style of cooking, and the type of saucing. See descriptions of cooking styles and sauces on pages 25–28.

Also, think twice before ordering something Szechwanstyle in an undoubtedly Cantonese restaurant—more than likely it will be disappointing. Find out what the restaurant's specialties are, stay within those boundaries, and you are likely to have an enjoyable meal.

THE OTHER CHINESE MENU

In Chinese restaurants in communities with large Chinese populations there are most definitely different menus for the Chinese clientele. These menus feature authentic, family-style Chinese cooking, a less oily, less rich, generally healthier cuisine than is represented on the English-language menu. Broken down into price-fixed dinners, called *woh choy*, these menus include a balance of meat, fish, and poultry, and a variety of cooking methods, such as steaming, braising, and clay pot cooking. If you would like to be served this type of meal but do not read Chinese, try explaining your desire to the waiter or order by pointing to the food being enjoyed by Chinese patrons.

CHINESE COOKING METHODS

Stir-frying, one of the most popular restaurant cooking methods, is done over extraordinarily high heat in a large, round spun-steel pan called a wok. Often in a restaurant setting, the meats to be stir-fried are first poached in vegetable oil, which keeps them from toughening and allows them to be held longer, but also adds fat. Peanut oil is the preferred cooking oil in better Chinese restaurants because of its high smoking point and neutral flavor.

Dry-frying produces dishes that do not have a "wet" gravy-like sauce. The ingredients are usually stir- or deep-fried, then the liquid seasonings are reduced until they are "dry"—like a glaze.

Deep-frying is a technique mastered by the Chinese cook. Many foods are deep-fried in pieces with or without a batter. Large ingredients, such as fish, shellfish, and poultry, are often deep-fried whole to preserve their flavor. Deep-fried foods should be crisp and clean-tasting, not oily.

Steaming is used for all types of meat, fish, poultry, and vegetables. If steamed foods do not appear on the English menu, they may be ordered anyway; simply ask the waiter.

Poaching is used for meat, fish, and poultry, and especially for preparing cold-cut style dishes that are served as appetizers for banquet-style meals, such as sliced pork and sliced chicken.

Braising, or red cooking, is similar to stewing. Red refers to the sauce in which the food has been braised, which is actually reddish brown in color. Common ingredients used for braising are soy sauce, star anise, dried shiitake mushrooms, garlic, ginger, scallions, stock, and wine. The finished dishes are hearty and full-flavored.

Clay pot cooking refers to braised dishes finished in a clay pot, which bolsters the flavors of the ingredients. The pot is brought to the table and the food is served from it.

Sizzling platter dishes are partially cooked in the kitchen, then brought to the table and poured into a sizzling hot cast-iron platter, where the cooking process is completed in front of the diners. It is customary for all the diners to lift their napkins to shield their faces and clothing from the splatter of the food hitting the hot platter.

CHINESE COOKING SAUCES and STYLES OF PREPARATION

Black bean sauce is a mildly piquant but highly aromatic savory sauce made from pungent fermented salted black beans. Sometimes ginger but always garlic is mashed with black beans. Sliced or cubed onions and peppers are cooked with the main ingredient. Dishes prepared with black beans are most often stir-fried, braised, or steamed.

Lobster sauce is an enriched black bean sauce enhanced with chopped pork and beaten eggs, but not necessarily lobster. This fancy version of the basic black bean sauce was developed for lobster—the dish became known as lobster Cantonese—thus its name. Crab and shrimp can also be made with "lobster" sauce.

Oyster sauce, actually oyster extract reduced to a thick rich concentrate, is a cooking and table condiment used for many stir-fried dishes. It does not taste fishy, but rather like a rich savory stock. Most oyster sauce dishes are made with a cornstarch-thickened gravy-like sauce.

Fish-flavored sauce (often referred to as garlic sauce) is a Szechwan-style sauce that neither contains fish nor has a fishy taste. It is rich and aromatic and hot, sweet, and tart all at once, and counts among its ingredients ginger, garlic, scallions, vinegar, chili oil or chili paste, soy sauce, and sesame oil. Often, chopped water chestnuts and tree ear mushrooms are added, and sometimes Szechwan peppercorns, white pepper, or sugar.

Capital sauce, also known as Peking sauce, is a rich, thick sauce made with hoisin and brown bean sauces, garlic, and scallions when served with noodles or with Worcestershire sauce, ketchup, garlic, ginger, sugar, and vinegar when served with pork chops and spareribs.

Kung pao is the name for dishes cooked in a sauce made with charred dried red chilies, peppers, roasted peanuts, soy sauce, wine, garlic, and ginger. Its flavor is spicy, sweet, sour, and savory all at the same time.

Sweet-and-sour sauce, made with sugar, vinegar, ketchup, and sometimes fruit juice, is thick and syrup-like and is poured over battered deep-fried foods. Sometimes it is used with what the Chinese consider old meat—that is, meat that is more than a day or so old.

Hot-and-sour sauce is made with vinegar, hot chili peppers or hot chili oil, sesame oil, and black or white pepper. Garlic, ginger, scallions, and sesame oil are often added.

Hot bean sauce (also called Szechwan bean sauce) is a cooking condiment. It has a spicy, rich, savory flavor and is often enriched with garlic, ginger, scallions, vinegar, soy sauce, and sesame oil.

Mu shu is a northern style of preparation: dishes prepared with scrambled eggs, shredded cabbage, bamboo shoots, lily buds, wood ear or tree ear mushrooms, and shredded meat, fish, or poultry. *Mu shu* dishes are napped with hoisin sauce, wrapped in Mandarin pancakes, and topped with slivered scallions.

Sub gum is not a sauce. *Sub gum* dishes are either cooked, garnished, or topped with a mixture of meat, fish, and poultry, or a medley of vegetables. Many noodles and won ton preparations come with *sub gum*.

Service and Dining

All of the components of a Chinese meal are traditionally shared among everyone in a dining party. A large tureen of soup is set on the middle of the table first (and in a home setting is left on the table throughout the entire meal) and the remaining dishes follow. The meal commences when the head of the household or the host raises his or her chopsticks and invites everyone to join in. Rice is served throughout the meal.

SERVING ETIQUETTE: According to Chinese custom, it is improper to lift up the serving platter in order to serve yourself or to take more than you can consume in one bite. Instead, reach as far as is necessary with your chopsticks and take one biteful of whatever you desire (or use a serving spoon if one is provided), then place the biteful on your rice and eat the two together. Repeat this process until you are finished eating.

Condiments

Generally speaking, if dishes are meant to be eaten with condiments, such as duck sauce, hot mustard, or hot chili oil, the condiments will be brought to the table in small jars or saucers. Use the serving spoon to transfer a small amount of a condiment from a jar onto your plate or dip your food directly into a condiment in a saucer. (For descriptions of condiments served with dim sum, see page 51.)

Light soy sauce is very often placed on the tables at Chinese restaurants in the U.S., but grudgingly so because Chinese chefs are insulted when it is used (just as American chefs are insulted when diners slather ketchup on their food). Soy sauce is not even meant to be sprinkled on rice (as many Americans choose to do) because the rice is there to absorb the flavors of the main dishes. In Szechwan restaurants, however, soy sauce (in addition to hot chili oil and white vinegar) is placed on the table to be used as a condiment for dumplings and other dishes, such as noodles and cold poached meats.

Soy sauce comes in many varieties and grades. The two most common varieties are light and dark. Light (sometimes referred to as thin) is more delicate but a bit saltier than dark.

Garnishes

Large chunks of ginger, garlic cloves, chili peppers, star anise, and cinnamon bark are often left in a dish, but are not meant to be eaten.

Rice

The majority of Chinese restaurants in the U.S. represent the southern school of cooking, where rice is the main source of starch. Rice is meant to be eaten directly out of a rice bowl, not from the dinner plate. Hold the bowl up near your mouth to catch any rice that might fall. If you are not given a rice bowl in a Chinese restaurant, ask for one. Brown rice is considered too flavorful to accompany most Chinese foods (rice is present to absorb, not add, flavor). Still, some Chinese restaurants in the U.S. make brown rice available to diners who prefer it.

Utensils

A standard Chinese place setting includes a rice bowl, a small plate (the size of a luncheon plate), blunt-ended chopsticks (Japanese chopsticks are pointed at one end), a porcelain soup spoon, and a tea cup. The plate is used to hold a small serving of food, condiments, and discarded bones and shells. A diner should eat directly from his or her bowl of rice.

HOW TO USE CHOPSTICKS
WITH THE RICE BOWL

How to Hold Chopsticks Hold one chopstick about one-third of the way down from the top (the fatter end) between the thumb and index finger and brace it against the inside edge on the pad of the third finger. Place the second chopstick above the first, about an inch away, holding it almost like a pencil with the top chopstick resting against the inside pad of the middle finger. Angle the top chopstick toward the bottom one so that the tips meet. The hand should only occupy the top third of the chopsticks. Use only the index and middle fingers to move the top chopstick up and down to grasp and hold food.

How to Hold the Rice Bowl Hold the rice bowl in the opposite hand of the chopsticks. Place the thumb on the top edge of the rice bowl and rest the bottom of the bowl on the fingertips.

CHOPSTICK ETIQUETTE:

Use the top end of the chopsticks (not the end you have been eating from) when serving others a piece of food.
Do not stab or poke food with chopsticks.
Do not cross chopsticks.
Do not point with chopsticks.
Do not leave chopsticks sticking out of the rice in the bowl.
When you have finished your meal, set the chopsticks parallel to each other across the top edge of the dinner plate.

Using the Chopsticks and the Rice Bowl Together To serve yourself, if necessary, reach across the table with chopsticks to the desired dish and select a small piece of food. Transfer the food to the rice bowl and eat it with a small amount of rice by lifting the bowl to your lower lip. (With chopsticks, tactfully "shovel" a bite of rice and food into the mouth.) Treat the next desired entrée in the same fashion until you are full. If there is a dipping sauce, mustard, or other condiment available, the food may be dipped into it en route to the rice bowl.

Signature Dishes

Won Ton Soup (delicate dumplings in broth); Spring Rolls (shredded meat and vegetables wrapped in a thin dough and deep-fried); Pot Stickers (brown, crusty dumplings filled with meat and vegetables); Hot-and-Sour Soup (shredded meat and vegetables in spicy seasoned broth); Kung Pao Chicken (stir-fried boneless chicken, peanuts, and peppers in a spicy, sweet, sour sauce); Peking Duck (crispy-skinned duck); Mandarin Pancakes (pancake for wrapping food); Sweet-and-Sour Pork (deep-fried pork cubes drenched in a sweet-and-sour sauce); Mu Shu Pork (shredded pork, vegetables, and scrambled eggs wrapped in Mandarin pancakes); Lobster Cantonese (stir-fried lobster in the shell with pungent black bean sauce); Egg Foo Yung (pan-fried meat, seafood, and vegetable omelet); Chow Mein (crispy pan-fried noodles); Eggplant with Garlic Sauce (braised eggplant strips in a spicy-hot sauce)

The MSG Question

Some Chinese restaurants—usually the lower-quality ones—continue to use MSG in their cooking as a flavor enhancer. Although you may ask that no MSG be added to the food you order, often the stocks with which they are made have already been "seasoned."

Common Misconceptions

Mandarin is a style of Chinese cooking. There really is no such thing as mandarin cooking. The mandarins were the high officials and aristocrats of China during the Ching Dynasty (A.D.1644–1911). They did enjoy the best and finest cooking of China, and restaurateurs seem to use the word mandarin to give the impression that they are serving high-quality food. The word "mandarin" is properly used in certain dish names, such as Mandarin pancakes, in which case it implies that the dish is from northern China.

Rice is the main source of starch for all Chinese people. In northern China, where wheat is the predominant grain, bread and wheat-flour noodles are the main source of starch in the diet.

Chinese food is high in fat, sodium, and cholesterol. Recently, a highly publicized report accused Chinese restaurants of serving food with high levels of sodium, fat, and cholesterol. It is important to understand that the 15 dishes that were analyzed (which included *kung pao* chicken, lo mein, *mu shu* pork, and orange beef) are rarely cooked at home in China and are definitely not part of the daily Chinese diet; rather, they are reserved for special occasions, and even then, are eaten in small portions. To maintain a healthy diet in a Chinese restaurant, simply order the way the Chinese do, leaning toward steamed and poached dishes and concentrating on fewer meat and more vegetables entrées. And remember that each dish in a Chinese restaurant is meant to be part of a multiple-course meal shared among four to eight people.

CHINESE BANQUETS

Banquets are an expression of luxurious entertainment reserved for honored guests and business associates as well as for festive celebrations. A banquet menu consists of expensive delicacies, exotic foods, and symbolic extravagant dishes, such as shark's fins, bird's nest (made out of the saliva that birds use to make their nests), "dragon and phoenix" (lobster and chicken), abalone, and duck. Because of the host's display of affluence and good fortune, rice is considered a filler food and is served gratuitously at the end of the meal. As a courtesy to the host's graciousness, the diner should not eat more than a few bites of rice, nor should he or she ask for rice before it is served. Polite, gracious guests eat what is served to them even if they can't identify it (particularly if they want to close a business deal successfully).

Chinese **MENU**

APPETIZERS Appetizers and salads are not part of a standard Chinese meal. However, to kick off a banquet, two appetizer-like courses are served: a cold one followed by a hot one. Traditionally dim sum items are not part of a dinner menu either; however, the trend in the U.S. is to include popular ones, such as pot stickers, spring rolls, and scallion pancakes. Salads, which are a new concept in Chinese cooking, are made with cold shredded meats and vegetables, not leafy greens. The custom of placing duck sauce (really plum sauce made with plums, apricots, and sugar), hot mustard, and fried noodles on the table at the beginning of a meal is not at all Chinese but was invented to satisfy American diners. Fried noodles that are wide and flaky are homemade; the narrower, harder ones are factory-bought, and there is no comparison in taste or texture between them.

Spring Rolls (or Egg Rolls)

Shredded pork, shrimp, celery, onions, **dried shiitake mushrooms**, bean sprouts, and scallions, wrapped in thin dough and deep-fried until crisp

There are subtle differences between spring rolls and egg rolls. Usually the wrappers used to make spring rolls are made out of wheat flour and water while the wrappers used to make egg rolls are made out of wheat flour, water, and beaten egg, making them a bit heavier. Also, some chefs make their spring rolls smaller than their egg rolls. The name "spring roll" comes from the tradition of serving these small savory pastries on the first day of the Chinese New Year, which occurs in the early spring.

INGREDIENT NOTES

• **Chinese dried shiitake mushrooms,** also known as dried black mushrooms, are a staple of Chinese cooking; they are used not only as a vegetable but also as a seasoning ingredient to infuse a hearty flavor into stocks and sauces.

• In Chinese cooking **sesame oil** is used primarily as a seasoning and for marinades but seldom for cooking. The strong nutty flavor and aroma of Asian sesame oil comes from toasting the seeds before pressing them for oil.

• **Hot chili oil** is an infusion of dried red chilies in vegetable oil. It is used as a dipping sauce and seasoning oil.

Pot Stickers
Pan-fried and steamed dumplings filled with minced pork, cabbage, ginger, scallion, and **sesame oil**; served with a dipping sauce of vinegar, soy sauce, and **hot chili oil**

Fried Won Ton
Deep-fried shrimp or pork-filled dumplings; served with a sweet-and-sour dipping sauce

Bon Bon Chicken Salad
Szechwan shredded cold poached chicken and julienne cucumber napped with a spicy sesame seed paste, garlic, ginger, vinegar, and **hot chili oil** dressing; served over **glass noodles**

Scallion Pancakes
Pan-fried slightly crisp and chewy pancakes speckled with minced scallion

Cantonese Roast Chicken Salad
Shredded **Cantonese roast chicken**, scallion slivers, **Chinese parsley**, sesame seeds, and shredded iceberg lettuce tossed with Chinese mustard, soy sauce, and **sesame oil** dressing

Szechwan Sesame Chicken
Cold sliced boneless chicken tossed with a spicy dressing made from **sesame seed paste**, **Szechwan peppercorns**, ginger, garlic, vinegar, sugar, **sesame oil**, and **hot chili oil**

The dressing used for Szechwan sesame chicken is sometimes referred to as strange-flavored or odd-flavored sauce. This dressing is also used with noodles and other meats, such as pork.

• **Glass noodles**, also known as mung bean, clear, transparent, and cellophane noodles, are made from mung beans (which in their sprouted form are called bean sprouts).

• **Cantonese roast chicken** is made by filling a chicken's cavities with chicken stock, scallions, ginger, garlic, and such spices as star anise, five-spice powder, and sometimes cinnamon, then roasting the bird in a tall oven.

• **Chinese parsley** is also known as cilantro. The pungent leaves are used as a seasoning and garnish.

• **Sesame seed paste** is a creamy butter made from roasted sesame seeds.

• **Szechwan peppercorns** are tiny, reddish brown peppercorns that are not at all spicy but have a distinctive and lasting flavor and aroma. They are not related to black or white peppercorns.

Barbecued Pork

Sliced pork fillets marinated in soy sauce, **hoisin sauce**, rice wine, honey, ginger, and **five-spice powder** (•39), then barbecued

S O U P S In most restaurants in the U.S., either a large tureen of soup is brought to the table and servings are dished out into individual soup bowls or the soup is ladled into soup bowls in the kitchen and then distributed at the table. In Chinese homes the soup is set on the table and left there for diners to eat, sometimes directly out of the tureen, throughout the meal.

Won Ton Soup

Light delicate dumplings of minced shrimp and pork, bamboo shoots, and scallions, in a clear, light chicken broth

Although it is common for Chinese restaurants in the U.S. to serve won ton soup at dinnertime, the Chinese serve it and noodle dishes as lunch entrées. The soup is served in a large bowl as a one-dish meal, with such toppings as barbecued pork or shrimp with bok choy (a leafy vegetable from the cabbage family); chopped roast duck; beef stew; or sub gum, a mixture of meat, seafood, and vegetables. These toppings may also be offered in Chinese restaurants in the U.S., even if they are not mentioned on the menu. Discuss the possibilities with your waiter.

HOLD THE SOUP SPOON in your hand with half of the length of the index finger resting in the groove of the spoon's handle. The thumb and middle finger support the bottom of the spoon.

INGREDIENT NOTES

• **Hoisin sauce** is a thick, reddish brown table and cooking condiment made with soybeans, garlic, chili peppers, vinegar, and sugar. It is often incorrectly referred to as duck sauce or plum sauce. It is served with Peking duck and *mu shu* pork.

• **Tree ear mushrooms** are small dried black fungi (about ½ inch across when dried). They are prized for their chewy and crunchy texture and ability to absorb other flavors. A larger variety (about 1 to 2 inches across when dried) are called wood ears.

Soup

A spicy Szechwan-style soup made with pork or other meat, **tree ear mushrooms**, **lily buds**, bamboo shoots, and bean curd, seasoned with white pepper, vinegar, sesame oil, and **hot chili oil** (•34)

Egg Drop or Egg Flower Soup

A light, clear chicken broth garnished with shredded or minced chicken or pork, dried shiitake mushrooms, bamboo shoots, bean curd, and lightly beaten eggs

Szechwan Cabbage and Shredded Pork Soup

A piquant and savory chicken soup seasoned with sautéed shredded pork and crunchy shredded **Szechwan preserved vegetable**

Minced Chicken and Corn Soup

A creamy corn and chicken soup topped with minced chicken, peas, and finely shredded ham

TO DRINK SOUP FROM a tureen placed in the middle of the table, dip your soup spoon into the communal soup bowl and, without swishing your spoon in the soup, draw up a spoonful and bring it directly to your mouth.

Sizzling Rice Soup

Chicken soup with assorted seafood, diced dried shiitake mushrooms, bamboo shoots, peas, and scallions, topped with **sizzling fried rice crackers**

West Lake Soup

Chicken soup topped with egg drops (sometimes called egg flowers), marinated minced beef, crabmeat, and chopped Chinese parsley (cilantro)

in salt and pickled with ground chilies, it boasts a salty, spicy taste and crunchy texture and is used as a seasoning vegetable for stir-fried, steamed, and braised dishes throughout China.

• **Lily buds,** also known as golden needles and tiger lily buds, are the dried unopened flowers of orange day lilies. They add a subtle sweet flavor and interesting texture to vegetable dishes.

• **Szechwan preserved vegetable** is made with a vegetable reminiscent of mustard cabbage and kohlrabi. Preserved

• **Sizzling fried rice crackers** are made by breaking the crust of rice left in the bottom of the rice cooker into small pieces, drying the pieces, then deep-frying them, at which point they puff up. The puffed crackers are removed from the oil and immediately dropped into the hot soup, which results in a sizzling sound upon contact.

POULTRY

Poultry featured on a Chinese menu can include chicken, duck, squab, quail, goose, or any number of tiny game birds, but chicken and duck are the most popular.

Minced Squab in Lettuce Cups

A light stir-fried mixture of finely minced squab, water chestnuts, dried shiitake mushrooms, bamboo shoots, and scallions; served in a chilled lettuce cup and napped with **hoisin sauce** (•36)

Crispy Skin Chicken

Crisp deep-fried whole chicken chopped into bite-size pieces; served with lemon wedges to be squeezed over the chicken and a roasted salt and Szechwan peppercorn dip

Kung Pao Chicken

Stir-fried cubes of chicken, peanuts, peppers, and chilies in a sweet, sour, garlicky sauce

Shrimp or other meats may be ordered cooked in kung pao *style.*

General Tso Chicken

A spicy Hunan-style dish of deep-fried chicken cubes tossed with a garlicky hot-and-sour sauce

Lemon Chicken

Deep-fried chicken breast glazed with a sweet and tangy lemon sauce

Cashew Chicken

Stir-fried boneless chicken cubes with snow peas, **straw mushrooms**, carrots, onions, water chestnuts, and cashews

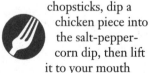

TO EAT CRISPY SKIN CHICKEN with chopsticks, dip a chicken piece into the salt-pepper-corn dip, then lift it to your mouth and bite off some of the meat. Return the remaining piece to your rice bowl or dinner plate. Repeat until all the meat is freed from the bone and eaten. Discard the bone onto the dinner plate.

INGREDIENT NOTES

• **Straw mushrooms**, which taste similar to button mushrooms, are small, stemless, and oval-shaped. They are only available canned in the U.S.

PEKING DUCK is served with the prized crispy skin separated from the meat. To eat, slip a piece of skin (and if the meat is boned, add that too), a smear of hoisin sauce, and scallions into the bun, or wrap the pancake around the filling. Eat with your hands. If the meat is not boned, eat it like tea-smoked duck.

Peking Duck

Paper-thin crispy duck skin; served with Mandarin pancakes or steamed buns (see page 46), **hoisin sauce** (•36), and feathery scallion brushes

A banquet dish, Peking duck may not appear on the regular dinner menu, though it can often be special-ordered 24 hours in advance. Some restaurants specialize in Peking duck; at those establishments it need not be special-ordered.

Tea-Smoked Duck

Szechwan-style duck marinated and steamed in rice wine, Szechwan peppercorns, ginger, and **five-spice powder**, air-dried, then smoked over rice, tea, brown sugar, **star anise**, and cinnamon; served with steamed buns or Mandarin pancakes (see page 46)

TEA-SMOKED DUCK comes to the table chopped into bite-sized pieces with the skin and often the bone intact, accompanied by steamed buns (lotus buns) or Mandarin pancakes and a hoisin sauce or roasted salt and Szechwan peppercorn dip.

If the duck comes with the bone, use your chopsticks to hold a piece of duck and dip it into the sauce or dip, then lift the piece to your mouth and eat the meat off the bone. Discard the bones onto your dinner plate. Eat the bread separately.

If the meat comes boned, dip your chopstick into the sauce or dip (unless there is a spoon, in which case you should use it to first transfer the sauce or dip to your plate or rice bowl), smear the sauce in the split bun or on the pancake, then stuff the meat into the bun or wrap the pancake around it. Eat with your hands.

• **Five-spice powder** is a pungent spice blend of five spices (more or less), usually including cinnamon, clove, Szechwan peppercorns, star anise, and fennel or anise seed.

• **Star anise** is an eight-pointed seed pod from a tree belonging to the magnolia family. It has a strong anise flavor.

FISH and SHELLFISH The Chinese are sticklers for fresh seafood, and many Chinese restaurants specializing in seafood proudly exhibit tanks filled with live fish and shellfish. The style of preparation most popular among the Chinese is whole live fish steamed and served simply with ginger, scallions, and Chinese parsley (cilantro). When ordering seafood in a Chinese restaurant, ask the waiter what is freshest and what style of preparation best suits it.

Steamed Fish with Ginger and Scallion Slivers

Fresh whole fish steamed with ginger, scallions, Chinese parsley (cilantro), rice wine, and soy sauce, and singed with sizzling hot oil

Sweet-and-Sour Fish

Whole deep-fried rock cod or snapper; served with a thickened glaze-like sauce made with sugar, vinegar, ginger, bell peppers, onions, and carrots

Hunan Crispy Fish

Whole fish deep-fried and topped with a spicy, garlicky, sweet-and-sour sauce

One Fish Two Ways

One whole fish prepared in two ways: the fish fillet is sliced and stir-fried with *choy sum*, ginger, and salt, and the remaining fish is steamed with ginger, scallions, and **brown bean sauce**, and garnished with Chinese parsley (cilantro)

Live steelhead out of the tank is commonly used for One Fish Two Ways. However, catfish, rock cod, and striped bass are also popular.

Shrimp Egg Foo Yung

Lightly browned omelet of beaten eggs, small shrimp, peas, bean sprouts, and onions; served napped with a thickened chicken stock gravy

In China pan-fried egg omelets are made in the same manner but are not served with the gravy.

INGREDIENT NOTES

• *Choy sum* is the young and flowering heart of bok choy.

• **Brown bean sauce** is a prepared condiment of fermented soybeans. It is used throughout China and in particularly large amounts in Peking-style dishes.

Lobster or Crab Cantonese

Stir-fried chunks of lobster or crab in the shell, bell peppers, and onion in a garlicky black bean sauce, enriched with minced pork and beaten eggs (known as lobster sauce)

> TO EAT LOBSTER or crab from the shell, pick out all the meat you can with your chopsticks, then use your fingers to finish the job.

Honey-Glazed Walnuts and Prawns

Plump stir-fried prawns coated in **"special sauce"** and garnished with crispy sweet walnuts

Shrimp and Asparagus with Black Bean Sauce

Stir-fried shrimp, sliced asparagus, onions, bell peppers, ginger, garlic, soy sauce, and **salted black beans**

This dish can also be prepared with chicken, beef, or pork, and without the black bean sauce, which gives it a lighter flavor.

Braised or Roasted Crab with Ginger and Scallions

Stir-fried crab in the shell with a reduced sauce of fresh ginger chunks and scallions, soy sauce, and rice wine or dry sherry

Stir-Fried Clams and Scallops in Black Bean Sauce

Clams and scallops in the shell stir-fried with onions, garlic, ginger, soy sauce, and black bean sauce

The Chinese order this dish steamed instead of stir-fried for equally delicious flavor.

Prawns or Scallops in Garlic Sauce

Spicy prawns or scallops, **tree ear mushrooms** (•36), and water chestnuts stir-fried in a garlicky sauce made with **hot bean sauce**, ginger, scallions, soy sauce, sugar, and vinegar

• The **"special sauce"** is a sweetened mayonnaise dressing.

• **Salted black beans** are small black soybeans that are salted and fermented. They are used sparingly (about 1 to 2 tablespoons at a time) in meat, fish, poultry, and strong-flavored vegetable preparations.

• **Hot bean sauce** is the Szechwan version of **brown bean sauce,** with an infusion of crushed chili.

MEAT   Meat consumption is minimal in China, where a single portion is usually limited to three ounces or less. Pork is the primary meat; beef has always been considered a luxury since cows were traditionally used as work animals and couldn't be spared to the table.

Sizzling Beef
Beef slices stir-fried with **brown bean sauce** (•40), chili peppers, ginger, garlic, and scallions; finished on a sizzling hot platter at the table

Orange Beef
Beef slices stir-fried over high heat with garlic and dried chili peppers and a spicy orange sauce

Ginger Beef
Stir-fried beef slices with a piquant sauce made with lots of finely shredded ginger

Oyster Sauce Beef
Stir-fried beef slices, ginger, and scallions with **oyster sauce**

Mongolian Beef
A northern Chinese dish of marinated beef slices stir-fried with chili peppers, scallions, soy sauce, sugar, and sesame oil; served over crispy **glass noodles** (•35)

Dry-Fried Shredded Beef
A spicy, aromatic dish of crispy beef shreds cooked together with finely shredded carrots, celery, and ginger, and seasoned with **Szechwan peppercorns** (•35) and sesame oil

Sweet-and-Sour Pineapple Pork
Deep-fried pork cubes with onions, green peppers, tomatoes, carrots, and pineapple cubes, glazed with a thick sauce of sugar, vinegar, and ketchup

Peking Pork Chops
Pork chops marinated in rice wine and soy sauce, then deep-fried and tossed with a rich thick sauce of Worcestershire sauce, ketchup, vinegar, sugar, garlic, and ginger
   This dish is also prepared with spareribs, in which case it is called **Spareribs in Capital Sauce.** *Among Chinese diners, capital sauce is a popular alternative to sweet–and–sour sauce.*

INGREDIENT NOTES

• **Oyster sauce** is a popular Cantonese table and cooking condiment made by reducing oysters, water, and salt to a thick rich concentrate. It has a savory flavor that neither tastes nor smells fishy.

Mu Shu Pork

Stir-fried combination of scrambled eggs, shredded cabbage, bamboo shoots, lily buds, **wood ear mushrooms** (•36), and shredded pork; this mixture is napped with **hoisin sauce** (•36) and wrapped in a Mandarin pancake (see page 46)

Twice-Cooked Pork

Szechwan-style sliced pork with scallions in a hearty rich sauce made with garlic, ginger, soy sauce, sugar, **hot bean sauce** (•41), and sometimes **hoisin sauce** (•36)

This dish is called twice-cooked because it is made using two cooking techniques: the pork is first simmered in water, then sliced and braised in the hearty, rich sauce. On some menus twice-cooked dishes are called double-cooked.

VEGETABLES   Though vegetables are the main ingredients in the dishes that follow, vegetarians should note that some of them count small amounts of meat or seafood among their ingredients.

Water Spinach with Fu Yu Sauce

Stir-fried fresh **water spinach** with *fu yu* and garlic

Pea Shoots

Stir-fried **snow pea shoots** with peanut oil, ginger, and salt

Stuffed Bean Curd (Tofu)

Steamed fresh bean curd stuffed with minced shrimp and scallions

Stir-Fried Chinese Broccoli

Chinese kale stir-fried briefly with peanut oil, sesame oil, ginger, and salt

---

• **Water spinach** boasts large leaves and a watercress-like flavor.

• *Fu yu* is a wine-fermented soybean curd that tastes like well-aged cheese.

• **Snow pea shoots** are the edible leaves, stems, and tendrils of the pea plant.

• **Chinese broccoli**, more appropriately called **Chinese kale**, boasts large leaves but few florets, and an earthy, slightly bitter flavor.

Stir-Fried Bok Choy

Chinese cabbage stir-fried briefly with peanut oil, sesame oil, ginger, and salt

Ants Climbing a Tree

Spicy **glass noodles** (•35) braised with hot bean sauce, chopped pork, garlic, ginger, chilies, scallions, and sesame oil

Supposedly, the name of this dish refers to the resemblance between the noodles and the branches of a tree, with the specks of pork as ants climbing a tree.

Ma Po Bean Tofu

Braised fresh bean curd cubes with chopped **tree ear mushrooms** (•36), water chestnuts, ground pork, garlic, ginger, **chili paste**, and scallions

Dry-Fried String Beans

A rich, aromatic dish of deep-fried string beans with a mixture of chopped pork, **Szechwan preserved vegetable** (•37), **dried shrimp**, garlic, ginger, rice wine, and soy sauce

Asparagus in Crab Sauce

Stir-fried asparagus in fluffy light cream sauce enriched with crabmeat and lightly beaten egg whites, garnished with minced ham

Crab sauce is also served with Chinese napa cabbage and broccoli.

Stir-Fried Mixed Chinese Vegetables

A seasonal mixture of celery, bamboo shoots, snow peas, water chestnuts, dried shiitake mushrooms, and broccoli in a thickened chicken stock flavored with **oyster sauce** (•42)

Eggplant with Garlic Sauce

Braised eggplant strips, Szechwan-style, with garlic sauce (see fish-flavored sauce, page 27); cooked and served in a clay pot

INGREDIENT NOTES

• **Chili pastes** are made by grinding up salted and fermented chilies. Additional ingredients, such as oil, garlic, black beans, ginger, and soybeans, may be added.

• **Dried shrimp**, which have a pungent flavor and aroma, are a common ingredient in Chinese vegetable dishes, soups, dumpling fillings, and *congee* (rice porridge).

NOODLES Although noodle dishes appear on dinner menus in Chinese restaurants in the U.S., they are only there to satisfy non-Chinese patrons. The Chinese traditionally eat these dishes for lunch, as a snack, or for a late-night meal, but rarely for dinner. For birthdays, a plate of "long-life" noodles is served at the end of the meal, like the Western birthday cake. In the past these wheat-flour birthday noodles were made extra long, but at the modern Chinese birthday party, any noodle will suffice.

Beef Chow Fun with Black Bean Sauce

Stir-fried fresh rice noodles in black bean sauce (see page 26) with sliced beef, bell peppers, and onions

Chow fun *may be prepared "dry," without the "wet," gravy-like black bean sauce.*

Singapore-Style Chow Mai Fun

Stir-fried *mai fun* combined with barbecued pork, shrimp, chicken, and shredded vegetables, and seasoned with curry powder

Sub Gum Chow Mai Fun

Stir-fried *mai fun* with a mixture of seafood and vegetables

Barbecued Pork Lo Mein

Egg noodles lightly tossed with soy sauce, **oyster sauce** (•42), sesame oil, shredded barbecued pork, bean sprouts, and scallions

Vegetarian Lo Mein

Egg noodles lightly tossed with soy sauce and **oyster sauce** (•42), then combined with a shredded vegetable mixture of **dried shiitake mushrooms** (•34), **wood ear mushrooms** (•36), **Szechwan preserved vegetable** (•37), carrots, cabbage, scallions, and ginger

Combination Chow Mein

Crispy pan-fried egg noodles topped with a mixture of chicken, shrimp, celery, onions, bean sprouts, and scallions

• *Mai fun*, or dried rice vermicelli, are also known as rice stick noodles. These wiry thin dried rice noodles are reconstituted in water before they are stir-fried or boiled. They are very versatile and can be prepared with many different toppings. When these noodles are made fresh they are called *chow fun* or *ho fun*.

Anise-Beef Soup Noodles

Small cubes of beef braised with **five-spice powder** (•39), cinnamon, and **star anise** (•39); served over noodles in broth

Noodles Peking Style

Boiled egg noodles and shredded cucumber topped with a rich, piquant sauce made with ground pork and **hoisin** (•36) and **brown bean** (•40) sauces

RICE AND BREAD

Steamed White Rice

Yang Chow Fried Rice

Fried rice with diced chicken, small shrimp, barbecued pork, eggs, and scallions

For dinner the Chinese prefer plain steamed rice over fried rice, which they feel interferes with the flavors and sauces of the entrées. They reserve fried rice (which is made with precooked cold rice, sometimes left over from a previous meal) for lunch, snacks, and occasionally breakfast. Fried rice dishes are included on dinner menus in the U.S. to please the non-Chinese clientele.

Mandarin Pancakes

A chewy Chinese-style crepe made with wheat flour and water; used as a wrapper for other foods

Fried Rice with Salted Fish and Chicken

Chiu Chow-style delicately seasoned fried rice with flecks of salted dried fish and diced chicken

Chiu Chow is a lesser-known branch of Cantonese cooking.

Salted dried fish, redolent of anchovy, has a taste that may need to be cultivated. However, for anchovy lovers this is a delicious version of fried rice.

Steamed Buns

Steamed fluffy, slightly sweet white buns made with wheat flour

Mandarin pancakes and steamed buns (also known as lotus buns) accompany many Chinese dishes, particularly those from north China. The slightly sweet flavor of steamed buns soothes the fiery flavors of Szechwan cooking.

DESSERTS The Chinese eat desserts at banquets, but at family or other casual meals seldom finish with anything other than fresh fruit. The custom in Chinese restaurants in the U.S. of serving fortune cookies at the end of a meal is not practiced at all in China; in fact, a Japanese-American living in San Francisco is credited with inventing these amusing cookies.

Almond Float
A chilled, silky-smooth gelatin made with almond extract, milk, and sugar, topped with **lichee** or fruit cocktail

Eight Jewel Rice Pudding
Steamed **glutinous rice** pudding dotted with blanched almonds, **lotus seeds**, **red dates**, cherries, and **red bean paste**

Spun Apples
Battered, deep-fried hot apple wedges, glazed with sugar syrup and black sesame seeds, the outsides hardened in ice water at the table

INGREDIENT NOTES

• A **lichee** is a small oval fruit with jelly-like, grayish white, delicately sweet pulp, spiny red or brown skin, and a large pit. Most Chinese restaurants serve canned, skinned lichees.

• **Glutinous rice** is a short-grain rice often used for stuffings and desserts. When cooked, it becomes moist and sticky; it is also known as **sticky rice** or **sweet rice**.

• **Lotus seeds**, the small, pale yellow seeds of the lotus plant, are somewhat bland and starchy. Chinese cooks add them to desserts, soups, and herbal preparations.

• **Red dates**, also known as *jujubes*, are an important fruit in China, where several different varieties from sweet to sour are cultivated. Only sweet varieties are commonly available in the U.S.

• **Red bean paste** is made by mashing together boiled azuki beans and water, then cooking the mixture until thick and dry.

BEVERAGES Clear, light soup is considered the main beverage at a Chinese family meal. Warmed rice wine may be served on more formal occasions. Cognac and whisky have become Chinese favorites for banquets. Tea is served at the end of all meals and throughout the meal at dim sum restaurants. Some non-dim sum restaurants in the U.S. serve a pot of tea as soon as diners sit down and replenish it throughout the meal; this is a custom designed to please non-Chinese clientele who want to drink something with their food but do not consider soup a beverage as the Chinese do.

CHINESE TEA
There are three general categories of Chinese tea: green, black, and oolong. The Chinese do not add milk to their tea. The only time they add sugar (usually rock sugar) is when they are drinking a combination of *bo lei* (see Black tea below) and chrysanthemum tea.

Green tea is made with leaves that are plucked young (when they are still green), then quickly dried.

Black tea (called red tea by the Chinese) is made with green tea leaves that are toasted, rolled, and fermented, a process that turns the leaves black (though the infusion is actually reddish in color). *Bo lei*, a black (red) tea thought to aid digestion, is rich and mellow in taste, perfect after a meal.

Oolong tea, which is made with partially fermented tea leaves, combines the best of the green and black (red) teas. Oolong is infused with jasmine flower petals to make jasmine tea.

Rice Wine
Warm Shao Hsing rice wine (also known as Shaoxing)
Shao Hsing is an area in eastern China.

Beer
Tsing Tao, a relatively heavy and dry lager with a light bouquet
Beer has become the accepted beverage among non-Chinese for casual Chinese meals. It goes particularly well with hot and spicy dishes.

DIM SUM Dim sum is a Cantonese
specialty of hot, appetizer-size entrées (dumplings,
fritters, and other small dishes) served at tea houses
that are open, in China as well as the U.S., only for lunch
and sometimes breakfast. In addition to appetizer-size
entrées, dim sum restaurants may serve noodle dishes and
fried rice as well as rice gruel, or *congee*, a thickened porridge-like rice soup that is considered the morning oat-
meal of China. Tea is served throughout the meal.
To get the best selection at a dim sum restaurant,
arrive early, before the noon crowd (dim sum makes
for an especially satisfying brunch), and take
your time as the dim sum is paraded out
of the kitchen.

HOW TO "ORDER" IN A DIM SUM RESTAURANT

There is no menu and no orders are taken for dim sum. Instead, waiters push carts or carry trays filled with the freshest cooked items from the kitchen, singing out in Chinese what they have. When the waiter passes your table, you literally point at what you want and the waiter gives it to you. In traditional dim sum restaurants the plates or baskets are left on the table until you ask for the check, at which point the dishes are cleared and the check is tallied (with few exceptions, there is a fixed price per plate). More modern establishments provide a check at the beginning of the meal and as each item is served the check is hand-stamped; empty plates are cleared during the course of the meal.

If you would like a noodle or rice dish, place your order with the waiter at any time during the meal.

If you would like more hot water for your teapot (most Chinese teas taste better—more mellow and fragrant—with the second and third brewing), set the pot's lid ajar. As an appropriate thank-you gesture to the waiter for replenishing the water, tap the table with your four fingers; no eye contact needed.

ETIQUETTE: Most plates or baskets of dim sum include three or four dumplings, buns, or rolls meant to be shared around the table, not consumed by one person alone. Proper etiquette dictates reaching with your chopsticks for a single item (never more) and bringing it to your plate, stretching across the table if necessary (many restaurants outfit each table with a lazy susan to simplify the process). If desired, dip your portion into a condiment, then bring it to your mouth and begin again with the next piece of food.

CONDIMENTS FOR DIM SUM

Each place setting at a dim sum restaurant usually includes a condiment saucer for each diner,
but if yours does not, it is acceptable to spoon or pour condiments from the main jar or bowl in the center of the table
onto your plate (pouring or spooning condiments directly
over food is not encouraged). Either dip a piece of food into
the condiment or dip a chopstick into the condiment and
smear or tap the seasoning over the food. Use condiments
sparingly; they are not meant to overpower the natural flavors of the food.

Hot mustard (*gai lot*): Colman's dried mustard powder
combined with water to make a paste

Hot chili oil (*lot yau*): combination of peanut and sesame
oils and dried red chilies

Scallion oil (*chung yau*): hot peanut oil poured over shredded scallions and strained; used on its own and to make
other dipping sauces

Sweet scallion oil (*tiem chung yau*): dipping sauce made by
heating scallion oil with soy sauce and sugar

Soy sauce (*see yau*): dark, salty sauce made with fermented
and boiled soybeans, salt, and roasted wheat or barley

Vinegar soy sauce (*see cho yau*): mixture of soy sauce, white
vinegar, and hot chili oil

Ginger soy sauce (*geung chung yau*): slightly sweet and salty
sauce made with sugar, soy sauce, peanut and sesame oils,
shredded ginger, and scallion

STEAMED DIM SUM

Siu Mai (Shumai)
Steamed, basket-shaped minced pork dumpling wrapped in fresh egg-flour pasta

Ngau Yuk Siu Mai
Steamed, basket-shaped ground beef dumpling wrapped in egg-flour pasta

Ha Gow
Steamed bonnet-shaped shrimp dumpling enclosed in a **wheat starch** wrapper

Fun Gau
Half moon-shaped dumpling filled with minced shrimp, pork, mushrooms, and bamboo shoots, enclosed in a **wheat starch** wrapper

Pai Gwat
Steamed pork sparerib nuggets with black bean sauce (see page 26) or sour plum sauce

Cheung Fun
Steamed fresh rice-flour roll filled with barbecued pork, shrimp, or marinated beef; served topped with sweet scallion oil (see page 51)

Cha Siu Bau
Steamed bun filled with barbecued pork

Siu Loon Bau
A Shanghai dumpling filled with gelatinized soup and minced pork and shrimp; served with finely shredded young ginger and red vinegar dipping sauce

Nor Mai Gai
A steamed **lotus leaf** packet of **glutinous rice** (•47), chicken, sausage, shrimp, pork, and black mushrooms

---

INGREDIENT NOTES

• **Wheat starch** is wheat flour from which the gluten has been removed. Wrappers made with wheat starch have a somewhat gummy texture.

• **Lotus leaves** are the dried leaves of the lotus plant. They are used as wrappers for dim sum in the same way that Mexican cooks use corn husks for tamales. They are not meant to be eaten.

DEEP-FRIED DIM SUM

Yung Dau Fu
Fresh bean curd stuffed with shrimp

Yung dau fu *may be prepared in four ways: steamed, deep-fried, pan-fried, or braised, all of which are delicious.*

Woo Gok
An egg-shaped, deep-fried "croquette" of mashed **taro root** stuffed with a minced mixture of pork, shrimp, mushrooms, and bamboo shoots

Cheun Guen
Crispy spring roll with meat and vegetable filling

Jien Dui
Chewy sweet sesame seed ball filled with **red bean paste** (•47)

Shrimp Toast
Minced shrimp purée spread on toast and deep-fried

Hom Soi Gok
Chewy glutinous rice flour dumpling filled with minced pork, shrimp, bamboo shoots, and black mushrooms

• **Taro root**, a tuber with a flavor reminiscent of bland sweet potatoes, is thought to have been a staple in the diet of prehistoric man.

PAN-FRIED DIM SUM

Lo Bok Goh
Pan-fried squares of radish **pudding cake**

Mah Tai Goh
Pan-fried squares of sweet water chestnut **pudding cake**

Scallion Pancakes
Pan-fried crisp and chewy pancakes flecked with minced scallion

Lah Jiu
Pan-fried bell peppers stuffed with minced shrimp

Pot Stickers
Pan-fried dumplings filled with minced pork, cabbage, ginger, and scallion; served with a dipping sauce of white vinegar, soy sauce, and hot chili oil

"Pot and stick" is the literal translation of the Cantonese name for these dumplings, which are sometimes made with a technique that requires that they stick to the pot, at least momentarily.

BAKED or BARBECUED DIM SUM

Don Tot
Sweet egg custard in a flaky pastry crust

Cha Siu
Sliced barbecued pork

Cha Siu Goh
Barbecued pork in a flaky pastry crust

Guk Cha Siu Bau
Baked bun filled with barbecued pork

INGREDIENT NOTES

• **Pudding cake** is made by steaming a giant white radish (the Chinese call it a turnip) or water chestnut until softened, then mashing it with scallions and minced barbecued shrimp and pork.

CONGEE Also known as *jook*, *congee* is a thick rice porridge that the Chinese eat for breakfast and sometimes at other times during the day. Bland on its own, *congee* is usually either garnished with meat, seafood, pickled vegetables, or other seasoned toppings, or eaten with Chinese fried *cruller*, a baguette-like donut that is sliced and dunked into the *congee*, much as donuts are dunked into coffee. Soy sauce is not considered an appropriate seasoning for *congee*. (If you must add it, do it discreetly.) A few drops of sesame oil, some chopped scallions, and a dash of white pepper are perfectly acceptable.

Fish Congee
Hot rice *congee* topped with thin slices of seasoned fresh raw fish

Beef Congee
Hot rice *congee* topped with seasoned beef meatballs or thinly sliced raw beef

Preserved Egg and Pork Congee
Hot rice *congee* topped with preserved egg wedges and marinated minced pork

FRENCH
cuisine

★

Cheers–*À votre santé* (ah **voh**-tr **sahn**-tay)
Bon appétit–*Bon appétit* (bone ap-ih-**tea**)
Thank you–*Merci beaucoup* (merr-**see** boh-**coo**)

FOR MANY DINERS FRENCH COOKING IS THE STANDARD against which all other cuisines are measured. Certainly the French have established a worldwide reputation for fine and expensive restaurants that in many diners' minds are synonymous with haute cuisine—the ultimate in culinary art.

The high status of French cuisine can be attributed to numerous factors, including the abundance of written materials (dating back hundreds of years) that define classic French dishes and cooking techniques as well as the highly regarded professional training schools and associations that use these same recipes and techniques as the basis of their curricula. The underlying belief throughout much of the Western world is that mastery of French culinary techniques is crucial no matter what route a student of cooking ultimately chooses to follow. No other country has such an established system for training professionals to perpetuate a distinct culinary tradition.

Principles of Flavor

Flavorings in French cooking tend to be subtle and wine-based, either wine with herbs or wine with butter, cream, eggs, and/or stock. Much of the flavor comes from sauces as well as cooking juices and stocks.

Foreign Influence

It is undisputed that the use of sauces and seasonings can be traced to the ancient Romans, but the fact that Catherine de Médicis (the Italian wife of King Henry II) introduced haute cuisine (along with the fork) to the French court in the mid-1500s is a pill most French people find hard to swallow. As in most countries, France shares certain characteristic ingredients and preparations with its neighbors, such as the Germanic dishes of Alsace that feature cabbage and pork products, and the Mediterranean/Italian-influenced dishes of Provence that feature olive oil and tomatoes.

Ordering

French meals consist of small portions of food served in a definite sequence of courses, at the very least two: an appetizer and a main course accompanied by vegetables (never *just* a main course!). In the most opulent of settings a meal may include as many as six courses.

Many restaurants offer a prix fixe menu, consisting of a series of courses (for example, a choice of appetizer, main course, salad, and dessert) from a set menu at a set price, and/or a *menu dégustation*, a tasting menu consisting of small samples of many dishes, served in courses, at one special price. Ordering a variety of dishes also gives the chef more opportunities to display his or her art.

Service and Dining

The style of service in a French restaurant varies somewhat predictably depending on the type of restaurant, but a meal in a top-rated French restaurant is a memorable experience that delights all the senses, not just taste.

Types of French Restaurants

French restaurants can be divided into two general categories:

Restaurant or grand restaurant: The most traditional, well-staffed, elaborate, and expensive place, where dining is a real event featuring the most exquisite food, elegant decor, perfect service, and prices to match. You will be served by a team of waiters, some of whom merely oversee the service.

Bistro and brasserie: The word *bistro* implies that a restaurant is informal, and though it can still feature fabulous, classic food and fairly stiff prices, *cuisine bourgeoise* (see page 63) is more common. A *brasserie* ("beer hall") is similar to a *bistro* but is generally open at all hours and serves from the same menu at all times.

Restaurant names often include two words that are not descriptive at all:

Auberge: Though in French the word *auberge* means a country inn with lodging, in a restaurant name in the U.S. it only implies an eating establishment with a picturesque decor and a country atmosphere that may be informal or formal.

Café: While cafés in France generally limit their menus to inexpensive snacks, Americans use the term *café* in the names of all kinds of restaurants, including some very expensive ones.

Condiments

French food is almost never eaten with condiments, probably because most dishes are prepared with sauces. Exceptions to the rule include certain homey meat or sausage dishes, such as pot-au-feu (see page 77) for which a pot of hot Dijon mustard and other condiments are placed upon the table. Dijon mustard is also placed on the table in some informal restaurants, where diners tend to spread it on bread as a snack prior to a meal, though it is intended for use with steaks or cold sausage.

Garnishes

The French use the term *garnish* to refer to vegetables, seafood, fruit, pastry, foie gras, sauces, or stuffings that accompany a dish rather than the small sprigs of parsley or lemon zests that may decorate plates. The garnish, which is usually indicated in the dish name (such as *sole florentine* [sole with spinach] or *à la florentine*), plays the essential role of blending the tastes of the main component, such as the meat, with the other ingredients.

COMMON FRENCH GARNISHES

Clamart dishes are served or stuffed with green peas, either whole or puréed. (Clamart is a small district that used to be famous for its peas.)

Dijonnaise dishes are made with hot mustard, a specialty of Dijon, or a mustard-flavored mayonnaise. Some dessert dishes with black currants are also called *à la dijonnaise*.

Financière dishes are served with chicken or veal dumplings, truffles, mushrooms, and olives, or a sauce with Madeira wine and truffles. ("Financier's" style means rich in ingredients.)

Florentine dishes are served or stuffed with spinach. (Florentine refers to Florence, Italy, from where spinach may have been introduced to France in the time of Catherine de Médicis.)

Forestière dishes are served or stuffed with wild mushrooms or mushroom sauce (so named because mushrooms are gathered in the forest).

Parmentier dishes are served or made with potatoes (named after the man who popularized the potato in French cuisine, Antoine Parmentier).

Bread

All authentic French restaurants will bring crisp, fresh bread to the table soon after you sit down, either slices of long, thin loaves (called baguettes) or small rolls, but usually no butter (buttering one's bread is an American habit the French have not adopted). The bread, which generally boasts a thick, tasty crust and a substantial, chewy interior, is meant to be eaten throughout the meal and to be used to push food onto your fork, to absorb sauces, and as a foil to soft cheeses.

Utensils

In the most formal French restaurants, tables are set with a remarkable array of specialized flatware. If in doubt about which fork or knife to use, as a general rule, start with the outermost, which is generally the smallest, and work your way in toward the plate over the course of the meal.

Signature Dishes

Foie Gras (fatted goose liver), *Pâté Maison* (slice of a loaf of ground, seasoned meat); *Truite Meunière ou aux Amandes* (lightly floured trout sautéed in butter and garnished with lemon and parsley or sautéed almonds); *Bouillabaisse* (Provençal seafood stew); *Cassoulet* (sausage, smoked ham, duck confit, and bean cassserole); *Coq au Vin* (chicken stewed in red wine with mushrooms); *Entrecôte Marchand de Vin* (sautéed rib steak garnished with butter mixed with shallots and red wine); *Boeuf Bourguignon* (beef stew made with red wine); *Mousse au Chocolat* (rich, airy chocolate pudding-like dessert); assorted cheeses; assorted pastries; and assorted fine wines, liqueurs, and brandies

Common Misconceptions

All French restaurants are fancy and snobby. Not at all! Many bistros feature and even foster an informal atmosphere, and the host or hostess can usually be seen displaying his or her joie de vivre in lively exchanges with the guests.

Traditional French restaurants serve only heavy, rich, fattening meals. Only bad chefs put heavy sauces on everything. Certainly some dishes are flavored with vegetables or herbs and are not sauced, such as roast chicken or poached fish, and it is easy to choose a light soup. Note that *nouvelle cuisine* dishes can be quite high in fat or calories, though a healthful derivative of this style, called *cuisine minceur*, features dishes without fat or cream.

Styles of French Cuisine

French restaurants tend to feature one of three kinds of cuisine, though some are noted as featuring "contemporary cuisine," which is a blend of the new and the old, or in any case allows the chef to interpret standard recipes in an individualistic, creative manner. Many new restaurants feature this kind of cuisine, which by its very nature cannot be described in our sample menu.

Haute, classic, or grande cuisine is the richest and most elaborate of all cuisines, and is found in the most sophisticated and expensive traditional French restaurants. It was developed by the Renaissance royalty and aristocracy and refined by professionals who codified it in numerous books and culinary schools. Haute cuisine features complex recipes with numerous ingredients and intricate cooking techniques as well as generous servings of rich, velvety sauces (usually served over the food). Its critics bemoan its tendency toward heaviness and lack of inventiveness, though these days many chefs bend the rules and blend, change, and otherwise try to surprise diners with new ingredients, sauces, techniques, and garnishes. When done to perfection, this is one of the world's great arts.

Cuisine bourgeoise, which can be complex or simple, has its ancient origins in the homes and farms of ordinary citizens who cared deeply about gastronomy. It is found today in restaurants (and homes) of all kinds. It is based on hearty dishes (some of which demand very long cooking times) that often highlight ingredients from a particular region served in their natural juices. Copious portions are the norm.

Nouvelle cuisine, introduced in the 1970s, focuses more attention on the chef's inventiveness with lighter fare and cooking styles, such as slightly undercooked vegetables and fish. A rebellion in part against the basic flour-heavy classic sauces and established, complex recipes, it features flourless and even vinegar- or fruit-based sauces or reductions (generally placed artfully on the plate prior to the food), purées, and fresh ingredients, though it still can be very rich; some sauces are made with cream or butter or egg yolks instead of flour. (*Cuisine minceur*, a derivative style, features nonfat sauces and dishes; contemporary cuisine is a term used to describe interpretations of classic dishes with lighter sauces,

---

FRENCH REGIONAL CUISINE

Regional (or provincial) cuisine is important to French chefs, and some design their menus to feature at least a few dishes from their native region. This is often reflected in the name of the restaurant. Though there are 10 or 11 regions, depending on who's counting, only the following three tend to be featured in restaurants in the U.S.

Provence/Southern (à la Provençale): Features olive oil, tomatoes, herbs, and garlic.

Normandy (à la Normande): Features cream, butter, apples, and derivative products, as well as brandy, white wine, and champagne.

Alsace (à l'Alsacienne): Features pickled cabbage, white wines, and pork products.

a sort of fully evolved *nouvelle* approach). *Nouvelle cuisine* is also known for its odd juxtapositions of exotic ingredients, such as calf's sweetbread in sea-urchin cream, and is generally served in small portions in relatively upscale restaurants. Its detractors bemoan the tendency toward pretentious presentation and high prices for very small portions, but when done well *nouvelle cuisine* can surprise and delight the palate and the eye.

FRENCH SAUCES

Sauces are the most distinctive aspect of French cooking. There are three major types—brown, white, and emulsified—from which chefs devise hundreds of others, creating a complex family tree. A few common examples are listed here; others are noted in the menu section. Almost all are velvety and rich, and all take a lot of time, equipment, and devotion to make.

Brown sauce is made from a browned mixture of flour and butter, called a roux, and concentrated stock made with meat that is slightly browned in a skillet. (Sometimes a plain, concentrated brown sauce, called *demi-glace*, is used alone). The following are among the many sauces based on brown sauce:

Sauce Bordelaise ("Bordeaux sauce," also known as bone marrow sauce): Brown sauce, red wine, shallots, herbs, and beef bone marrow

Sauce chasseur ("hunter sauce"): Brown sauce, tomato sauce, white and Madeira wines (or cognac), wild mushrooms, shallots, and herbs

Sauce Périgueux ("Perigord sauce"): Brown sauce, truffle essence, chopped truffles, and sometimes Madeira wine; if the truffles are sliced, it is called *Sauce Périgourdine* (name derived from the Périgord region, a major source of truffles)

Sauce Robert: Brown sauce, white wine, chopped onions, and mustard (named after its inventor, as recorded by Rabelais in 1552)

White sauces are based in part on a lightly cooked mixture of flour and butter, called a roux. The two basic white sauces are *béchamel* (roux mixed with milk and/or cream) and *velouté* (roux mixed with veal, poultry, fish or mushroom stock). They are used to make the following sauces, among many others:

Sauce Bercy: Fish stock *velouté*, white wine, shallots, and parsley; named after a wine market area in Paris

Sauce cardinal: Fish stock *velouté*, cream, and lobster butter; named after the red color of cooked lobster, like a cardinal's robes

Sauce Mornay: Béchamel sauce, cream, and Swiss and Parmesan cheeses; named after either the eldest son of the inventor, a Parisian chef, or a 16th-century Huguenot leader

Sauce Nantua: Béchamel sauce, crayfish stock, and crayfish butter; named after a small town in the Alps

Sauce Normande: Fish stock (and/or mushroom stock) *velouté*, egg yolks, and thick cream; named after the region of Normandy, famed for its cream

Emulsified sauces include hollandaise (made from a blend of melted butter, lemon juice, and egg yolks) and mayonnaise (made with oil instead of butter, and sometimes a bit of mustard). They are used to make the following sauces, among others:

Sauce Béarnaise: Hollandaise sauce, tarragon, vinegar, wine, and shallots; named after Béarn, the birthplace of Henri IV

Sauce Chantilly or mousseline: Hollandaise sauce and whipped cream; named after Chantilly, the château where whipped cream was popularized

Sauce Choron: Hollandaise or Béarnaise sauce and tomato purée; named for a famous chef in the late 1800s

Other minor groups of sauces are simpler but distinctive. They include:

Butter sauces, in which melted butter is mixed with cooked ingredients. *Beurre blanc* (also known as white butter, or *beurre Nantais*), made with shallots, white wine, and vinegar, is the most common and is usually used with fish. It is also the basic sauce for many variations.

Compound butters (*beurres composés*) in which cool butter is mixed with seasonings such as herbs, blanched shallots, garlic, or wine. *Maître d'hôtel* (made with finely chopped parsley and lemon juice) is the most common.

Dessert sauces (*crèmes* or *coulis*), in which sugared fruit purées, chocolate, and many custards figure prominently. Among the custards, *crème Anglaise* ("English cream"— basic custard cream of egg yolks, sugar, and milk) and sabayon (frothy egg yolk, wine, and sugar mixture) are the most common.

OTHER COMMON MENU TERMS

Chaud-froid: Refers both to a sauce and to a dish, either of which is prepared hot but served cold, either as an aspic itself (a savory jelly) or something glazed with a cream and gelatin mixture incorporating either brown or white sauce. Often quite decorative; used extensively in cold buffets

Coulis: A concentrated, liquid purée of vegetables, fruit, or shellfish used both as a sauce or as an ingredient in a sauce or soup

Duxelles: A paste-like flavoring, stuffing, or garnish made from mushrooms, onions, shallots, and herbs cooked in butter

En papillote: Food cooked in a paper packet (usually parchment paper)

Fricassée: Meat or fish cut into small pieces and cooked in butter, then lightly stewed with mushrooms, onions, and a cream and egg yolk sauce

Glace de viande ou poisson: A super-reduced and concentrated meat stock or fish poaching liquid; also called a glaze

Mignonette: Although almost all menus use this term to describe a small, round, flat piece of lamb fillet (also known as a medallion), the term *mignonette* actually means coarsely ground white pepper in French

Salmis: A method of cooking game or poultry that combines roasting (dry) and braising (wet) with brown sauce to create a stew

Timbale: Small, deep, round receptacle (porcelain, metal, or edible pastry) that any kind of food, including fancy desserts, can be baked and/or served in

French **MENU**

HORS D'OEUVRES (APPETIZERS) and ENTRÉES (FIRST COURSES)

After you have settled in at a French restaurant, a waiter may approach your table with the question, *"Pour commencer?"* (To start with?), which is a request for your appetizer order.

Appetizers are essential to even the simplest French meal, and many restaurants offer a large array. Some French menus list their hot appetizers or small second courses under the heading "Entrées."

Foie Gras en Brioche
Portion of **foie gras** (fatted goose liver) that is marinated, seasoned, and cooked, then baked a second time in an airy pastry shell

Saucisson Chaud de Lyon en Croûte
Moist, dark red sausage with small cubes of fat, baked in a pastry crust; served warm

The tradition of putting a seasoned meat dish or pâté in a pastry shell, or croûte, *dates back to Roman times.*

Coeurs de Palmiers
Hearts of palm served with a light mustard vinaigrette

Pâté Maison et Rillettes, Pain de Campagne
Slice of a loaf of coarsely ground, seasoned meat, alongside a scoop of potted meat; served with chewy country bread

Each restaurant (maison) *features different types of pâtés and* rillettes *(potted meats). Pâté can be smooth or coarse; both can be made from any meat, poultry, game, fish, or vegetables, though the tradition-*

INGREDIENT NOTES

• **Foie gras** is made with goose liver, but sometimes duck liver is used in complex, cooked dishes described as having foie gras as an ingredient. Goose liver is considered superior in taste and texture when served on its own and is more expensive; duck liver, with a slightly lighter and finer texture, generally holds up better in cooked dishes and

items such as liver *mousses* (light loafs). *Pâté de foie gras* is not pure liver, and is defined by French law as puréed goose liver combined with up to 20 percent pork liver, truffles, eggs, or other foods; *mousse de foie gras* contains up to 45 percent other foods. An item identified as just "pâté" is made of meat and perhaps some offal (variety meats), but not pure liver.

al recipes call for pork, duck, or goose meat with a fair amount of fat and usually peppercorns and wine or cognac. An extra-fine or smooth pâté is called a mousse, *while a coarser one is called a* pâté de campagne.

Rillettes *are made with shredded meat cooked with sea-soned fat that is pounded into a paste-like consistency and packed into a small pot.*

Terrine de Légumes aux Herbes de Provence
Slice of ground vegetable loaf seasoned with **Provençal herbs**

The words pâté *and* terrine *are used interchangeably to refer to ground and seasoned meat (including some organ meat), vegetables, seafood, or fish baked in a loaf mold called a* terrine, *and usually served cold, although terrines are supposedly served directly from the terrine itself, as opposed to pâtés, which are removed from the mold before serving and often have crusts. They both differ from American meat loaf in the fineness of the grind and the lack of bread-like fillers, as well as the seasoning.*

Galantine de Canard
Slice of boned duck loaf stuffed with forcemeat (ground seasoned meat), pistachio nuts, olives, or **truffles**, and glazed with aspic made from its own cooking juices; served cold over greens

A ballottine *is a cylindrical galantine that is wrapped in a cloth before it is cooked.*

Ratatouille
Provençal vegetable stew of eggplant, tomatoes, onions, bell peppers, zucchini, garlic, herbs, and olive oil

Ratatouille may be served hot or cold, either as an appetizer, vegetable dish, or main course.

Brandade de Morue
Hearty purée of salt cod, olive oil, milk, and sometimes potatoes and garlic from the Provençal-Languedoc region in the south of France

Brandade may also be served as a fish or main course.

• *Herbes de Provence* is the phrase used for an aromatic mix-ture of herbs that may include basil, bay leaf, fennel seed, laven-der, marjoram, rosemary, sage, summer savory, and thyme.

• **Truffles**, wild fungi that grow underground near the roots of oak, chestnut, hazel, or beech trees, are among the rarest and most expensive foods in the world, and are, therefore, used very sparingly; luckily, it takes only a small portion to impart flavor to a dish.

Céleri Rémoulade

Shredded **celery root** in tangy, creamy mayonnaise dressing flavored with mustard, garlic, and pepper

Macédoine de Légumes

Vegetable mixture of peas, carrots, turnips, and green beans, diced into ¼-inch cubes and bound with mayonnaise or aspic

Macédoine de légumes is also served hot, as a garnish, in which case it is bound with butter, cream, and herbs. Fruit macédoines *(diced fruit in syrup and rum or kirsch) are used as a cold garnish. The term* macédoine *is derived from Macedonia, the ancient kingdom assembled from the Balkan states by Philip II, the father of Alexander the Great.*

Pissaladière

Provençal onion and anchovy open-faced tart with olives; served hot or cold

Salade Niçoise

Mixed Provençal salad with tomatoes, cucumber, fresh green or fava beans or small artichokes, green bell peppers, onions, hard-boiled eggs, anchovy fillets or tuna, black Niçoise olives, olive oil, garlic, and basil

In France, salade Niçoise *is eaten as a main course.*

*Often salads made with meat, poultry, or cheese (*salades composées*) and listed as appetizers on menus in the U.S. were created in response to American demand.*

Fromage de Tête Vinaigrette

Head cheese in mustardy oil and vinegar dressing

Tian de Saint-Jacques et Légumes Provençaux

Sliced sea scallops on a bed of chopped vegetables seasoned with Provençal herbs, baked in a shallow earthenware pot (called a *tian*), **au gratin**

INGREDIENT NOTES

• **Celery root** is also known as celeriac or celery knob. It is grown just for its root, and has a stronger taste than the more familiar branch celery.

• *Fromage de tête* (head cheese) is a sausage product made from meaty bits of calf or pig head that are cooked in a seasoned, gelatinous meat broth, then poured into a mold to cool. It is also called *museau de porc*.

• **Au gratin** indicates that a dish is topped with grated Gruyère or Parmesan cheese, bread crumbs, and butter, then baked.

Saucisson à l'Ail Tiède, Salade de Lentilles Vertes
Slice of warm garlic sausage; served on a green lentil salad

Saucisson sec, *dried sausage, is commonly used instead of garlic sausage in this dish.*

Oeufs à la Russe
Hard-boiled eggs; served cold with diced vegetables in a thick tomato mayonnaise

Poireaux Rémoulade ou Vinaigrette
Blanched leeks; served cold with rémoulade sauce (mayonnaise with mustard, garlic, and pepper) or Dijon mustard vinaigrette

Escargots de Bourgogne
Snails Burgundy-style: baked and served in garlic butter (usually in their shells); also served as a main course

Saumon Fumé
Extra-thin slices of smoked salmon; usually served with toast

Saumon Froid, Sauce Verte
Cold poached salmon with a green mayonnaise sauce that has been colored and flavored with a purée of spinach, watercress, parsley, chervil, and tarragon

POTAGES (SOUPS) French soups come in a wide range of styles, including *consommés* (clear, concentrated stock garnished in a variety of ways), *soupes* (hearty, peasant-style), *bisques* (smooth, rich, and creamy with seafood), and *potages* (thickened, often with potatoes; also, confusingly, the general word for soup).

The *potages* are made in three styles: *crème* (with basic white sauce and puréed ingredients); *purée* (with puréed ingredients, such as potatoes and vegetables, and a basic meat stock); and *velouté* (with the basic *velouté* sauce [see page 65] and eggs).

Potage du Jour
Soup of the day

Consommé de Volaille, Julienne de Légumes
Light chicken broth with julienned vegetables

Soupe à l'Oignon Gratinée
Hearty, dark onion soup with a thick layer of bread topped with Gruyère cheese that is lightly browned under an open flame

Soupe de Poissons
Seafood soup, including any of a variety of fish and shellfish, such as red snapper, monkfish, crab, shrimp, mussels, and clams, as well as tomatoes, leeks, fennel, white wine, herbs, and olive oil

Soupe au Pistou
Provençal vegetable soup of green beans, white beans, onions, potatoes, tomatoes, and thin noodles, flavored with a mixture of crushed basil, garlic, and olive oil called *pistou* (known in Italy as pesto)

Bisque de Homard
Creamy soup made with puréed lobster, white wine, cognac, and fresh cream plus diced lobster meat

Vichyssoise
Cold potato-leek soup, thickened with cream and garnished with chopped chives

Any cold soup made with potatoes and another vegetable, such as zucchini, may be called vichyssoise.

POISSONS et FRUITS DE MER (FISH and SHELLFISH)
At formal French meals, seafood is usually eaten as a separate course, prior to the main course. However, on simple menus seafood dishes are listed along with meat dishes as main courses.

Truite Meunière ou aux Amandes (ou Amandine)
Lightly floured trout sautéed in butter, garnished with lemon and parsley (*meunière*) or sautéed almonds (*amandes*)

The word meunière *means "miller's wife," a reference to the flour with which the fish is prepared. Sole often replaces the trout in these classic, simple preparations.*

Coquilles Saint-Jacques
Jumbo sea scallops; usually served with a heavy cream or white wine sauce on a scallop shell

Saumon de l'Atlantique Grillé Sauce Béarnaise
Grilled Atlantic salmon with béarnaise sauce (see page 65)

Darne de Saumon aux Tomates Rôties et Fenouil Confit
Thick salmon steak with roasted tomatoes and fennel

Moules Marinière

Large bowl of mussels steamed in white wine with onions, shallots, herbs, and butter, then garnished with chopped parsley

Other seafood may be cooked à la marinière ("sailor's style"), which means cooked in white wine and herbs and garnished with mussels. Marinière sauce is a Bercy sauce (see page 65) made with mussel cooking juices.

Raie au Beurre Noir

Skate in a sauce of browned butter flavored with capers and lemon juice

Quenelles de Brochet Truffées, Salpicon de Homard

Delicate pike dumplings with bits of truffle; served with a cream sauce studded with diced lobster

The term salpicon *in the name of a dish implies finely diced food bound with sauce (for savory dishes) or syrup or cream (for sweets). A* salpicon *can be used to fill or garnish and may be hot or cold.*

Cuisses de Grenouilles Sautées, Beurre d'Ail et Tomate (à la Provençale)

Frog's legs sautéed in garlic butter with tomatoes

Homard Froid à la Parisienne

Cold lobster meat garnished with diced vegetables in a thick mayonnaise; served under aspic and with deviled eggs

Bouillabaisse

Seafood stew from Marseilles made with a wide variety of fish and shellfish plus onions, tomatoes, leeks, white wine, olive oil, saffron, fennel, herbs, and lots of garlic; cooked rapidly and served over garlic-flavored croutons accompanied by *rouille* ("rust"), a piquant pepper-garlic-and-oil sauce; served as a main course

A Provençal dish similar to bouillabaisse is bourride, *a strained fish soup enriched with egg yolks, flavored with orange peel, and bound with* aïoli *(a garlic mayonnaise sauce). It may be served over bread or* en croûte *(in a crust), often with the fish on the side.*

INGREDIENT NOTES

• **Skate**, a kite-shaped fish also called ray, is sometimes listed as *aile de raie*, or ray fin. Its firm, white flesh is similar to that of scallops.

ENTRÉES ou LES PLATS
(MAIN COURSES)
Les plats is the generic term for the main course, or meat course, on most French menus in America, but on traditional French menus these categories may be identified differently, such as *"grillades"* (grilled meats) or *"viandes et volailles"* (meat and poultry) or *"spécialités"* (specialties). On a very formal French menu, the term *entrée* is likely to designate a light second or third course that follows the hors d'oeuvre or soup and fish courses and precedes the main course.

Choucroute Garnie à l'Alsacienne
Alsatian dish of finely shredded, mildly salted, fermented cabbage (a sort of sweet sauerkraut) cooked in white wine and seasoned with herbs and spices, such as juniper berries, peppercorns, or garlic; served with boiled potatoes and a variety of fresh and smoked pork products, such as lean, thick-cut bacon, pork shoulder, pork loin, and sausages

Quiche Lorraine
Savory tart made with eggs, cream, bacon, and onions

On some menus this may be found under the listing Tourte du jour, *or savory pie of the day.*

Côtes d'Agneau Vert-Pré
Broiled lamb chops with watercress on the side and a pat of *maître d'hotel* butter (compound butter made with chopped parsley, lemon juice, and possibly mustard) on top; served with deep-fried matchstick potatoes

Filet de Boeuf Bordelaise
Beef fillet in red wine sauce made with bone marrow and shallots

Entrecôte Sautée Marchand de Vin
Sautéed rib steak with red wine sauce ("wine merchant sauce") made with red wine, cream, beef stock, and shallots

Steak au Poivre, Gratin Dauphinois
Steak cooked in a sauce of coarsely crushed peppercorns, cognac, reduced pan juices, and shallots; served with scalloped (sliced) potatoes baked in cream sauce

If the cut of steak for steak au poivre *is not specified, it is likely to be a sirloin or fillet. Ask to be certain.*

Escalope de Veau Chasseur
Sautéed veal scallop in "hunter" sauce that features mushrooms, shallots, tomato sauce, and white wine

Tartare de Boeuf, Pommes Frites

Steak tartar (raw chopped beef mixed with spices and Worcestershire or Tabasco sauce, accompanied by chopped onion, parsley, shallots, and cornichons (pickles), raw egg yolk, and capers as well as ketchup, olive oil, and Worcestershire sauce) mixed by the waiter tableside; served with French fries

The serving of raw eggs has been discontinued in most restaurants in the U.S. because of the risk of salmonella poisoning. Some restaurants will make an exception and serve an egg yolk in a broken half-shell with tartare de boeuf *if a diner makes a specific request for it.*

Pot-au-feu

Traditional peasant or family-style soup/stew—really a boiled dinner—of beef pot roast poached with root and leaf vegetables, such as turnips, clove-studded onions, parsnips, leeks, carrots, and celery; served with condiments such as coarse salt, pickles, horseradish, mustard, and an herb mayonnaise; served in courses beginning with the broth, followed by the bone marrow on toast, then the sliced meat and vegetables

---

FRENCH FRIES
Even the classiest French restaurant makes sure that its fries are cooked to perfection—thin, crispy, and golden—as French diners traditionally use the quality of the fries as a gauge of the chef's ability. The rationale is that if the chef pays attention to the fries, then he or she is serious about all details.

Magret et Confit de Canard

Roast duck breast (with thick layer of fat on top) sliced thin and served with shredded, preserved duck meat (confit)

Confits of various meats and fowl are made from cooked, shredded meat that is preserved in its own fat. When applied to a vegetable, it means cooked down to a jam-like consistency.

Boudin Noir, Grillé

Large grilled blood sausage (also known as black or blood pudding) made from pork, pig's blood, and fillers; served with mashed potatoes and applesauce

Fillers and flavors used to make blood sausage vary widely, but typically include onions, herbs, white wine, and allspice. Boudin blanc, *or white pudding, is a less common, lighter, delicately spiced sausage made from chicken, veal, rabbit, or pork.*

Canard à l'Orange
Roast duck cooked with a sweet and slightly sour orange sauce

Foie de Veau Grand-mère
Sautéed calf's liver with *grand-mère* (grandmother) garnish of fried bacon, small brown-glazed onions, sautéed mushrooms, and fried new potatoes

The terms grand-mère, *as well as* bonne femme *("good wife"),* à la ménagère *("housewife"),* à la paysanne *("peasant"), and* en cocotte *(casserole), imply uncomplicated, home-style, family favorites that are usually garnished or made with vegetables.*

Râble de Lapin Rissolé
Crisp sautéed saddle of rabbit with white beans and baby fennel

Rabbit may be listed on a menu as lapereau *(young rabbit) or* lapin, *and saddle as* râble *or* selle. Râble *is the loin of the rabbit;* selle *(French for saddle) refers to a fillet cut from two undivided loins of any meat. (*Selle *is used more often to refer to lamb.)* Rissolé *means fried until crisp and brown.*

Noisettes de Veau Poivre Vert
Sautéed slices of veal loin in green peppercorn sauce

Rognons de Veau Moutarde
Veal kidneys in mustard cream sauce

Ris de Veau Braisé Forestière
Sweetbreads (calf thymus gland) braised in white wine with fresh mushrooms

Médaillons de Venaison Grand Veneur
Small slices of venison loin with *Grand Veneur* sauce; served with chestnut purée

The word médaillon *in a dish title usually refers to a small, flat, round piece of meat but can be used for any food.* Noisette *(which means hazelnut in French) is an alternative term that is sometimes used to refer to small slices of tender lamb, beef, or veal, usually cut from the rib or loin. If the meat is not identified, it is usually lamb.*

Coq au Vin
Chicken stewed in a red wine sauce made with mushrooms, onions, and diced bacon

INGREDIENT NOTES

• *Grand Veneur* sauce is a rich, dark pepper sauce (*poivrade*) mixed with cooking juices, red currant jelly, and cream.

Feuilleté de Petits Légumes et Asperges à la Nage de Persil

Puff pastry stuffed with baby vegetables and asparagus; served in a parsley broth (*à la nage* means swimming)

Foie de Veau Lyonnais

Sautéed calf's liver with glazed chopped onions cooked in pan juices and vinegar

The term lyonnais ("*from Lyons*") *in a dish title indicates a food cooked with onions. Lyons has been known as a gastronomic center since antiquity, and local onions are featured in the region's cuisine.*

Caille Farcie en Croûte Lucullus

Quail stuffed with fat goose liver and truffles

Lucullus *refers to the Roman general who became famous primarily because of the elaborate and expensive feasts he hosted. Any dish that is notable primarily for the richness or rareness of its ingredients (and foie gras and truffles most certainly are rich and rare) can be called* Lucullus.

Selle d'Agneau aux Épinards

Saddle (loin) of lamb stuffed with spinach

Suprême de Chapon Grillé

Grilled capon (young castrated-chicken) breast with artichoke, asparagus, **morels**, and garlic

Though the word suprême *usually means breast (and wing, sometimes) of chicken or game and also a fillet of fish, with no particular recipe, the connotation is that the recipe will include a delicate or extraordinary garnish, such as truffles or, as above, an unusual combination of ingredients. The word is also but more rarely applied to luxurious dishes (such as foie gras) and to a rich cream sauce that is often served with poultry.*

Tripe à la Mode de Caen

Casserole from the city of Caen in Normandy made with beef tripe (stomach lining), vegetables, cider, and Calvados; cooked for 10 hours and served with boiled potatoes

Carré d'Agneau aux Herbes

Roast or broiled rack of lamb, generously seasoned with herbs (usually Provençal, such as rosemary and thyme) and garlic; cut into chops for serving

• **Morels** are rare, wild, honeycomb-patterned mushrooms that have a slightly smokey, earthy flavor. They are of the same species as truffles.

Boeuf Bourguignon (à la Bourguignonne)

Beef stew in which the beef is braised with red wine, butter, bacon cubes, onions and mushrooms; served with boiled potatoes

The term à la Bourguignonne *(Burgundian) refers to food cooked in red wine and garnished or cooked with small onions, button mushrooms, and pieces of fatty bacon. A similar country stew of braised meat from another region in France is usually called a* daube *and has the name of the region it derives from following it. In other cases, it is just* daube de boeuf *(or whatever the main ingredient is). Some* daubes *have the word* fendant, *or melting, added to the name because of the extreme tenderness of the meat.* Ragoût *is yet another name for stew.*

Navarin d'Agneau au Romarin, Petits Légumes

Brown, light, lamb stew with pearl onions, turnips, new potatoes, mixed baby vegetables, and rosemary

This dish is often served à la printanière, *or with spring vegetables.* Blanquette de veau *is a similar but white stew made with an egg yolk and cream sauce.*

Tournedos Rossini

Slices of filet mignon and **foie gras** (•70); served with *sauce Périgourdine,* a rich brown sauce made with *demi-glace,* sliced truffles, and **foie gras**; served over large croutons

The name Rossini *in a dish title suggests that the recipe includes foie gras and truffles, and usually a demi-glace sauce. This is indeed a reference to the famous composer, a big haute cuisine fan who once said, "To eat, to love, to sing, and to digest; in truth, these are the four acts in this* opéra bouffe *that we call life, and which vanishes like the bubbles in a bottle of champagne."*

Cassoulet Toulousain

Traditional country casserole from southwestern France (around Toulouse) made with sausage, smoked ham, garlic, and white beans, plus possibly duck confit (preserved duck; see page 77), goose confit, or mutton

Cassoulet *is the most argued over of all French dishes, with each southwestern town or micro-region swearing that its version is the only authentic one. Some towns swear by duck preserves, others by goose, still others by mutton. Some use different beans, others different finishing techniques (crust vs. no crust), ad infinitum.*

GRILLADES (GRILLED or BROILED MEATS)

Some restaurants place their grilled meats in a separate section of the menu, and even though they have another section labeled "Entrées," diners are expected to order only one dish from either section, not one from each. In French cooking, the word "grilled" means "broiled" unless specified as "charcoal grilled." In any case, dishes listed here have only herbs for flavoring, and any sauce is served on the side.

Paillarde de Poulet ou Veau
Grilled pounded chicken breast or veal scallop

The word paillarde *generally means a thin, flattened piece of meat, but is sometimes applied to fish fillets, too. The term originated at a famous 19th-century restaurant owned by a man named Paillarde.*

Coeur de Filet, Béarnaise
Broiled filet mignon with béarnaise sauce (see page 65)

Chateaubriand
Thick, long filet mignon grilled with herbs; served with béarnaise sauce (see page 65) and château potatoes (small potato balls sautéed in butter)

Chateaubriand is always served for two. The recipe was named after a 19th-century French statesman and author.

LÉGUMES et PATES ALIMENTAIRES (VEGETABLES and PASTA)
Vegetables and pasta are often served as an automatic accompaniment (garnish) to a main course and are not usually ordered separately, though some menus do list them separately as a convenience for diners who prefer to make their own choices. They are generally cooked with a small amount of butter and seasoning, varying according to the chef's style.

Carottes Glacées
Carrot slices braised in butter

Épinards en Branches
Leaf spinach

Haricots Verts
Green beans

Champignons des Bois en Saison Sautés ou à la Crème
Wild mushrooms, in season, sautéed or in cream sauce

Nouilles Fraîches Maison
Homemade fresh pasta

SALADES (GREEN SALADS)

It is the French custom to serve a simple green salad after the main course in order to refresh the palate.

Salade Mélangée (or Panachée)

Mixed greens, usually dressed with house vinaigrette (oil, vinegar, herbs, and mustard)

FROMAGES (CHEESES)

A cheese course, which follows the salad course, is a unique and world-famous aspect of French meals. The opportunity to taste a few portions from the vast French repertoire—there are approximately 400 different types of French cheeses, and many are exported—should not be missed. In France cheese is not eaten prior to a main course, and figures in only a limited number of dishes, such as *soupe à l'oignon gratinée* (see page 73).

> CHEESE: In the better restaurants, the waiter will present the cheese tray to you and then cut small portions of the three or four cheeses you select by pointing. You do not need to name them, though sometimes they are labeled. Cheese is usually eaten by placing a small piece on a bite-size piece of bread, but it can be eaten with a knife and fork (follow each bite with a nibble of crusty bread). Butter the bread if you want, especially when you are eating sharp cheese. Place pieces of soft cheese on bread but do not spread soft cheese as if it were peanut butter. Some strong cheese goes better with fruit than bread. Wine is excellent with all cheeses but especially the creamier ones.

Plateau de Fromages

Selection of cheeses from the cheese tray

Served from a tray or cart, this assortment may include cheeses of the following types: chèvre *(goat),* soft-ripened *(including ultra-rich double and* triple crème*), semi-soft (or* "monestary"), semi-hard, *and* bleu *(blue-veined) cheeses. Within each group tastes ranges from mild to sharp. Be sure to select several different types with contrasting tastes and textures.*

LES DESSERTS (DESSERTS)

Desserts (sometimes called *entremets* if made with a lot of cream or milk) are a close second to sauces in defining the creative genius of French cuisine. They range from light to very rich. Many of the most popular ones were developed for the French royal court during the Renaissance, but most good chefs include on their menus at least one of their own unique creations, sometimes listed as a *Délice du Chef.*

Mousse au Chocolat

Airy (*mousse* is French for foam), light, soft blend of chocolate, beaten egg whites, and egg yolks; served with whipped cream or vanilla sauce

While chocolate mousse is the classic, there are many flavor variations, including lemon (citron) *and raspberry* (framboise). *Savory versions of mousse, such as fish or even chicken, are sometimes served as appetizers or main courses.*

Soufflé au Grand Marnier ou au Chocolat

Baked, airy, egg-based dessert flavored with orange liqueur (Grand Marnier) or chocolate, and served directly from the oven, puffed up well above the height of the baking dish

This complex culinary invention must be ordered in advance and eaten immediately upon being served. It is found in many different flavors and in chilled or frozen versions, usually with a sauce over or around it.

Crème Brûlée

Vanilla custard with caramelized brown sugar topping

Crème Caramel (ou Renversée)

Caramel custard; served inverted, with a layer of caramel glaze and sauce to cover

Pyramide au Chocolat

Different types of chocolate sauces and soft chocolate pieces blended with whipped cream and butter, inside a chocolate-walled pyramid surrounded by fresh raspberries

Marquise au Chocolat

Glazed loaf of bittersweet chocolate mousse made extra-smooth with butter; served chilled with vanilla custard cream

The term marquise *can refer to any of a variety of delicate chocolate desserts, including chocolate filled and frosted almond cakes as well as frozen creations. In loaf form, a marquise such as the one described here may also be called a* terrine.

Profiteroles
Tiny cream puffs filled with pastry cream, whipped cream, or ice cream, and topped with warm chocolate sauce

Succès Maison
Layers of almond-studded meringue and praline-flavored buttercream, decorated with slivered almonds, sugared hazelnuts, and marzipan

Tarte Tatin
Traditional extra-sweet, upside-down caramelized apple tart; served warm with fresh cream

Tarte au Fruit
Open-faced fruit pie in a shell of tender butter pastry crust brushed with melted jelly glaze

Tarts can be made with different fruits, such as pommes *(apples),* citrons *(lemons),* poires *(pears),* pêches *(peaches), or* framboises *(raspberries), and often a frangipane (almond cream) or custard filling. Tarts are considered showcases for the fruit, which is artfully arranged.*

Sélection de Crèmes Glacées et Sorbets
Assorted ice creams or sorbets

Sometimes ice cream is listed under the heading Glaces *or* Glaces Crémeuses. *At the finest restaurants it will be made on the premises by the pastry chef.*

Pêche Melba
Poached, pitted peach halves sauced with raspberry purée; served over vanilla ice cream

Pêche Melba is one of several dishes dedicated to Dame Nellie Melba, a famous 19th-century Australian opera singer. This dessert was created in 1892 by the great chef Escoffier for a dinner in her honor at the Savoy Hotel in London.

Coupe aux Marrons
Vanilla ice cream topped with candied chestnuts and/or chestnut purée

Crêpes Flambées
Large, sweet, thin pancakes finished tableside by cooking in flaming brandy

Pâtisserie du Jour
Selection of any number of fresh pastries of the day, such as *Opéra* (layered sponge cake with chocolate sauce and buttercream; *Millefeuille* (thin layers of flaky puff pastry alternating with layers of vanilla pastry cream; the individual pastry is called a *Napoléon*); *Concorde* (chocolate meringue and chocolate mousse); Raspberry Charlotte (sponge cake with raspberry custard filling); or *Paris-Brest* (large ring-shaped éclair filled with praline cream and topped with slivered almonds)

BOISSONS (BEVERAGES)

Let's face it: The most important beverages on a French menu are the wines. If you do not wish to drink wine with your meal, by all means order only mineral or tap water, or beer to go with the Alsatian sauerkraut dish, *choucroute* (see page 76). Otherwise, it is nice to start your meal with an apéritif (usually an herbal or sweetened wine) to stimulate your appetite, and to finish your meal with a strong coffee and *digestif* of brandy to aid digestion.

Café filtre, espresso, thé
Coffee drip-brewed by the cup, espresso coffee (served in a demitasse, a small cup), and a selection of teas

VINS (WINES)

Better French restaurants offer a separate menu for wines and spirits, called a *carte des vins*. Some are quite detailed, listing every bottle; others may contain the labels of each wine, or details from each label; and some note only the color (red, white, or rosé). Most group them by region and color (see pages 88–91). If you need help choosing a wine that fits your budget and taste and suits the food you have ordered, ask the waiter or, if there is one, the sommelier (wine steward) for a recommendation. It is definitely worthwhile to try a fine wine if at all possible.

Included here are some very basic guidelines, over which the experts can argue while the rest of us go ahead and enjoy the meal with whatever fine wine happens to grace our table.

Vintage (harvest year) is not a great concern for most diners—only for those with impeccable memories, detailed personal notebooks, or the unflagging desire to impress others. Unless you know the particular wine well, the vintage is only a very general guide.

When drinking more than one kind of wine with a meal, your best bet is to order wines from the same region as the cuisine you are sampling; enjoy light and dry wines before heavier ones; less important and younger before noble and older; dry white before red; and sweet wine only with (or for) dessert.

Matching (some use the term *marrying*—but it's not that serious) food to wine is a good idea, much as the right spice is chosen to season a dish. The fuller-bodied, heavier red Burgundies and Bordeaux are best for hearty meats and game, while white or light red wines are commonly suggested for more delicate dishes, such as fish and fowl. Try to order a red wine if something is cooked in red wine, and the same for white; a wine from the same region as the recipe is best. Lighter fruity reds, such as Beaujolais or those from the *Vin de Pays* category, are the most versatile wines and are suitable if you need one kind of wine to go with a wide variety of dishes. If in doubt, the experts say, just order what you like and don't worry too much about it. For once, the experts keep it simple.

WINE ETIQUETTE

In the best restaurants, the appropriately shaped glasses will be placed on your table after you have ordered wine. When the sommelier (wine steward) or waiter brings your wine bottle to your table, he or she will present it to the host to check the label. The cork will be placed at the host's place; it should be ignored unless it smells or looks like an old cigar stub, in which case the wine should be refused, of course. A small amount of wine will be poured for the host, who should sip quickly and casually, and accept the wine unless it tastes like vinegar, nuts, or cork, or, in the case of white wine, if it is not chilled. (Bits of cork floating in a glass cause no harm to the wine but should be removed by the sommelier or waiter.) Once the wine is accepted, the waiter or sommelier will serve everyone at the table. When you need more wine poured, either do it yourself or ask the waiter or sommelier to do it for you.

FRENCH WINE LABELS

There are four general, legal categories for French wines:

***Vin de Table* (table wine):** The broadest category and the lowest quality wine; it should also be the least expensive. Certain brands have loyal drinkers, but many table wines do not inspire loyalty.

***Vin de Pays* (country wine):** No indication of quality or taste beyond the average, just an indication of what part of the country the wine came from.

***Vin Délimité de Qualité Supérieure*, or *VDQS* (delimited superior quality wines):** Better local wines made according to strict standards; a good value, but not many wines are in this relatively new category.

***Appellation d'Origine Contrôlée*, or *AOC* (controlled place of origin):** The best wines, though there is a wide range of quality and price within this category. For example, the label will read, "Appellation Haut-Médoc Contrôlée." Generally, the more limited the size of the vineyard, village, sub-region, or region indicated, the better the quality and higher the price; Haut-Médoc is a small village within the large region of Bordeaux, so if the label had said Bordeaux instead of Haut-Médoc, it would have been indicating a wine of lesser quality.

FRENCH WINE REGIONS

Wine lists are usually broken down by region of origin and color according to the *Appellation d'Origine Contrôlée* labeling system, and though there are ten so-named regions, many lists include wines from only the most popular regions or combine some of the smaller ones inaccurately.

All kinds of wines are produced in each region (red, white, and rosé; simple and complex; light and hearty; cheap and pricey; forgettable and fabulous); some of each region's best-known wines are listed here.

Alsace

This region is known for its dry, white, aromatic, strong but fruity and sometimes spicy wines named after the grapes with which they are made: Pinot Blanc, Pinot Gris (Tokay d'Alsace), Riesling, Muscat, Gewürztraminer, and Sylvaner. The best wines are labeled *Grand Cru*.

Bordeaux

Some of the world's most famous and rarest wines (along with some unimpressive, everyday table wines) are produced in Bordeaux, which produces more wine than any other region in the world. The most famous and most commonly represented districts and sub-divisions, called *communes* (parishes or villages), include Pauillac, Saint-Estèphe, Saint-Julien—these first three are the most famous—Margaux (wines with great finesse and vigor that age beautifully); Saint-Émilion and Pomerol (full, round red wines); Graves (crisp, dry whites); Médoc and Haut-Médoc (aromatic wines that age beautifully); and Sauternes (sweet, golden white wines). The finest wines are bottled where the grapes are grown (labeled *mis en bouteille au château* or similar), and some of the still finer of these finest estate-bottled wines are labeled with one of several even more superior grades of *crus classés* (classified growths). All of these distinctions are, of course, reflected in the price—and, one hopes, the taste.

Bourgogne (Burgundy)

Burgundies are available as hearty, rich reds and dry whites in a wide variety, some of which are among the world's finest (on par with the most famous Bordeaux wines). The better wines belong to either a *Grand Cru* (best) or

Premier Cru classification of a land unit, not a château.

Burgundy's principal sub-regions include Côte de Nuits, Côte de Beaune, Chablis (dry white wines made from the Chardonnay grape), Côte Chalonnaise, and Mâconnais (dry whites such as Pouilly-Fuissé). Many of the better-known wines of the two Côtes regions are Gevrey-Chambertin, Nuits-Saint-Georges, Beaune, Pommard, Meursault, Puligny-Montrachet, and Chassagne-Montrachet. (Burgundian wines are labeled by the vineyard and its commune, hence the hyphenated names).

Beaujolais is a popular and major sub-region of Burgundy that is so well known that its wines are often listed in their own category. They are medium-bod-ied, fruity, almost all red, and sold under the following four group-ings, in ascending order of basic quality: Beaujolais, Beaujolais Supérieur (with 1 percent higher alcohol content), Beaujolais-Villages (a fuller-bodied blend from any of 38 villages), and 10 *crus*, or villages. The *crus* are, from the lightest to the most full-bodied: Chiroubles, Brouilly, Côte de Brouilly, Saint-Amour, Fleurie, Chénas, Morgon, Juliénas, Régnié, and Moulin-à-Vent.

Some non-*cru* Beaujolais is sold right after harvesting as Beaujolais Nouveau or a bit later on as *primeur*. It is released with much fanfare on the third Thursday in November each year. It is especially fruity and light, as well as inexpensive.

Languedoc-Roussillon

Simple wines and some with strong bouquets, fruity round fla-vor, full body, and a slight spici-ness. This region is known for its enormous vineyards that produce large quantities of table wine, though in recent years it has begun to develop some higher quality wines as well as some *vins doux naturels* (naturally sweet wines).

Champagne

Vins mousseux is the name given to all sparkling wines made in France, and there are about 20 of them, but the ones pro-duced in the Champagne region are literally in a class by them-selves. Made according to very specific and legally defined meth-ods, grown and made only in the Champagne region, and sold by brand name rather than vineyard or grape type, they have justifi-ably become world-famous. Non-sparkling wines made in this region include the usually white Coteaux Champenois and Rosé des Riceys. For more on ordering Champagne see page 90.

Provence-Corsica
(usually combined with Côtes du Rhône)
Strong, aromatic white, red, and rosé wines, such as Bandol, Bellet, Cassis, Palette, and Côtes de Provence. Provence is best known for dry, fruity rosé wines. Corsica produces good, young, fresh and fruity rosé and white wines but is better known for its robust and slightly effervescent reds.

HOW TO READ A CHAMPAGNE LABEL

A champagne label always indicates which of the three basic taste categories the wine in the bottle falls into: *brut* (extra dry with almost no sugar); *extra dry* (less dry); *sec* or *dry* (sweet); and *demi-sec* (sweetest). The most popular Champagne is *brut*, which is of course a bit more expensive. The *secs* and *demi-secs* are good dessert choices.

Other label terms are *Blanc de Blancs* (made solely from Chardonnay grapes, which are white); *Blanc de Noirs* (made solely from Pinot Noir and/or Pinot Meunier grapes, which are black); *Rosé* (colored pink, usually by mixing in a little red wine); and *Cuvée spéciale*, *prestige cuvée*, or *de luxe cuvée* (the most expensive version of a particular brand). Also, the bottling company is noted as either a *négogiant manipulant* (large merchant), abbreviated NM, or a *récoltant-manipulant* (grower), abbreviated RM. No vintage is listed because Champagne is usually made by blending wines from different years; hence the designation on the label of non-vintage, or NV, on a wine list. Occasionally, during an exceptional year a single wine will be used, in which case the year is noted prominently on the label and the price is a bit higher.

The well-known and well-advertised brand names, not particular châteaux, are your assurance of a top-quality drink. Some other wonderful regional wines have a slight effervescence—they may be labeled "sparkling wine" or *"méthode champenoise"*—but if they are not made in the Champagne region they are not substitutes for the real thing.

Côtes du Rhône (Rhône Valley)

Rich, full-bodied, spicy red wines and well-aged white wines. Gigondas and the extra-strong Châteauneuf-du-Pape are the best known reds; Tavel and Lirac are the best-known rosés.

Sud-Ouest (Southwest)

A small region affiliated with Bordeaux, producing similar intense and full-bodied wines, such as the powerful Cahors and the fruity or sweet Bergeracs.

Jura and Savoie

Known for its unusual *vins jaunes* (yellow wines) and *vins de paille* (straw wines) that are specially made to develop strong aromas and flavors. Others are dry or fresh and fruity.

Val de Loire (Loire Valley)

Crisp, light wines, usually white and dry but also plenty of rosés and some reds. Better-known types are Sancerre, Pouilly-Fumé, Vouvray (both still and sparkling), Saumur, Reuilly, Anjou rosé, reds from Chinon and Bourgueil, and Muscadet.

APÉRITIFS The French tend to eschew strong cocktails prior to eating and begin their meals (perhaps at the bar) only with an apéritif, an alcoholic beverage meant to stimulate the appetite. Popular choices include light scotch and water or soda, a sweet or bittersweet wine fortified with brandy, spirits flavored with herbs and plants (the most popular of which is the anise-flavored *pastis*, which is mixed with up to five parts water). Other choices include vermouth or white wine with *cassis* (red currant liqueur), which is called a *kir*, and Champagne, sometimes mixed with *cassis*, called a *kir royale*.

BRANDIES, LIQUEURS, and CORDIALS

Sold by the glass, which varies in size and shape depending on the type of drink, these strong, distilled spirits have delicate flavors that are meant to be savored at room temperature and slowly (beginning with the aroma) after a meal. Almost all brandies are made from white wines and are aged in oak casks that give them their characteristic colors and flavors (a little caramel is added for color, in some cases). Menus often list their regions of origin as a way of indicating their taste and quality to connoisseurs.

Cognac X.O.

Twenty-five-year-old, double-distilled, top-quality, 80-proof brandy blend from the Cognac region north of Bordeaux

Cognac quality is designated by the age of the youngest brandy in the blend: Trois Etoiles *(Three Stars)—minimum 30 months;* VO *(Very Old),* VSOP*(Very Superior Old Pale), and* Réserve*—minimum 4½ years, but usually* 7 *to* 10; Extra, XO, Napoléon, *and* Grande Réserve*—the oldest, 6½ to sometimes 50 years but 25 to 40 is best. The brandy starts out clear and acquires color (and taste) as it ages in special oak casks; it does not age at all once bottled.*

One of six geographical subregions is also noted on the label. They have the following improbable names, of which the first three are considered tops: Grande Champagne, Petite Champagne, Borderies, Fins bois, Bons bois, *and* Bois ordinaires; *Fine Champagne is a blend of* Grande *and* Petite Champagne *cognac, which contains at least 50 percent* Grande Champagne. *These each have slightly different tastes, but not different quality per se. The word* Champagne *as used here has absolutely nothing to do with the famous bubbly wine.*

An important note: While all cognac is brandy, not all brandies are cognac, though they may so aspire!

Armagnac V.S.O.P.

Five-year-old, slowly distilled, 80-proof, dry brandy from the Armagnac region south of Bordeaux

Armagnac, like cognac, may be sold by age. Usually it is blended and placed in one of two categories determined by the youngest vintage in the blend, as follows: Trois Étoiles *(Three Stars)—aged at least 1 year;*

VO, VSOP, *or* Réserve—*aged at least 4 years (10 is excellent);* Hors d'age—*aged more than 10 years.*

Any of three sub-regions of origin is also noted on the label: Bas Armagnac, Ténarèze, *and* Haut Armagnac. *A blend of these is simply labeled* Armagnac *and no mention is made of sub-regions.*

> The custom of drinking Calvados between courses as a palate cleanser is known as *le trou Normand* (the Norman hole). The American equivalent to Calvados is applejack.

> The taste difference between cognac and armagnac is slight and subject to much interpretation. However, cognac, because it is double-distilled, is somewhat more complex, subtle, and fine than armagnac, which is slightly more robust, or fleshier, thanks in part, perhaps, to being distilled only once. Prices and qualities overlap, but older, finer, and more expensive cognacs are more common than are similar armagnacs.

Calvados
Double-distilled cider, with a distinct apple aroma, from Normandy; aged in oak casks that give it a golden color

Eaux-de-vie
Colorless brandy made from distilled fruit juice; choices include *Poire William* (Williams Pear), *fraise* (strawberry), *framboise* (raspberry), *kirsch* (cherry), *mirabelle* (yellow plum), and *prunelle* (purple plum)

Though the term eau-de-vie *(water of life) is commonly used to describe only these clear fruit brandies, it is a correct French term for all brandy. These fruit brandies usually come from Alsace, and are sold in extremely tall and thin clear bottles.*

Marc
Particularly strong, woody brandy made from distillation of whatever is left after grapes have been pressed for wine, mostly *de Bourgogne* (from Burgundy) and *de Provence*

Liqueurs
Sweetened cognac, eaux-de-vie, or other distilled spirits flavored with fruit, plants, seeds, herbs, or spices, and sold by brand name

GERMAN
cuisine

★

Cheers–*Prosit* (prost)
Bon appétit–*Guten Appetit* (**goo**-ten uppa-teet)
Thank you–*Danke* (**dan**-keh)

G ERMAN CUISINE IS SIMPLE, ROBUST, AND SUBSTAN-
tial fare designed to go with that popular German
thirst-quencher, beer. The atmosphere at German
restaurants is generally casual and festive—almost as if you've
dropped in at a party that has been going on for hours.

Principles of Flavor

Characteristic German flavors come from combining herbs
and spices such as dill, sorrel, thyme, juniper berries, caraway seeds, and mustard seeds. The distinctive sweet-and-
sour flavor is obtained with vinegar and sugar or fresh or
dried fruit. The most commonly used vinegars are apple
cider and wine, although nowadays many German chefs are
experimenting with berry- and herb-flavored vinegars. Also
common is pickling or preserving foods in a brine or vinegar solution, as for such dishes as sauerkraut, pickled herring, and pickled cucumbers (pickles).

GERMAN REGIONAL COOKING

A discussion of German cooking is not complete without addressing the significance of its well-established regional cuisines. Many German restaurants in the U.S. specialize in the cooking of a particular region, while others limit themselves to what may be considered the clichés of German cooking, such as Wiener schnitzel, bratwurst, and sauerbraten.

Bavaria: A southern region known for its beer, sausage, and schnitzel (veal or pork cutlets).

Black Forest (or *Baden*): Another southern region; known for its game, especially venison, a bountiful supply of cherries and plums, and Spätzle, one of Germany's favorite noodles or dumplings.

Rhineland (or northwestern Germany): Best known for its first-rate wines and potato and pot roast dishes.

Saxony: In what used to be East Germany; home to a variety of sweet yeast cakes and dishes made with calf's liver.

Berlin and surrounding area: Especially noted for dishes made with ground beef, such as beef tartare (*Schabefleisch*), the famous *Deutsches Beefsteak*, which Americans call hamburger, and its hearty soups, such as pea with bacon.

Westphalia: Famous for its hearty and robust foods, including Westphalian hams (which are cured, then smoked), stews, and pumpernickel bread.

Foreign Influence

Germany's cuisine has been greatly influenced by its neighbors. For instance, in East Prussia there is widespread use of sour cream and caraway seeds, which are distinctive characteristics of both Polish and Czechoslovakian cuisines, and paprika, from Hungarian cuisine. Other influences include the baking of yeast pastries and the presence of creamy horseradish sauce from Scandinavia, cheese and bacon from Austria and Switzerland, and the use of juniper berries in sauerkraut, a technique borrowed from Alsatian cooks.

Ordering

A traditional German meal includes an appetizer, soup or salad, entrée accompanied by a vegetable or other side dish, and dessert. Meat dishes may also come with a fruit compote such as apple, pear, prune, or raisin—a tradition that began when fresh produce was unavailable in Germany during the winter.

Many German restaurants offer a prix fixe menu *(Gedeck)*, which means that you pay a preset price for a complete meal. These menus usually include the chef's specialties and prove to be a good value. The daily specials at a German restaurant are listed as *Tagesgericht*.

Condiments

The three most popular condiments in German restaurants are mustard, horseradish, and applesauce, although applesauce is also considered a side dish. They can be either spread directly onto foods or used as a dip. German mustard, served with sausages, pork, or beef, comes in three basic strengths—mild, medium-hot, and hot—and in different flavor combinations, such as horseradish-mustard or wine-mustard. Horseradish, served with boiled beef and roasts, may come freshly grated, bottled, or in a creamy sauce. Applesauce, homemade or from a jar depending on the restaurant, is served with potato pancakes and baked ham.

Garnishes

Dill pickles are frequently used as an edible plate garnish. Other common garnishes include fresh chives and nuts, such as pistachios and almonds.

Breads

Full-flavored and textured breads are served with almost every meal. The traditional breads are black bread, which is not black but rather a dark brown rye bread; pumpernickel, a coarse dark bread flavored with molasses; light rye bread; and poppy seed rolls. On some restaurant tables you may also find a basket of soft pretzels to snack on.

Germany is also noted for its sweet yeast breads, which you may find in German restaurants in the U.S. during the holidays. Most famous are Christmas *stollen*, rich loaves studded with dried fruit, and *Kugelhupf*, light yeast cakes with dried and candied fruit baked in a specially designed fluted ring mold.

Signature Dishes

Kartoffelpuffer (potato pancakes); *Rollmops* (pickled herring rolls); *Sauerbraten* (pot roast); *Wiener Schnitzel* (breaded veal cutlets); *Spätzle* (tiny dumplings or noodles); *Wurstplatte* (German sausages and cold cuts); *Sauerkraut* (fermented cabbage); *Schwarzwälder Kirschtorte* (Black Forest cake)

Common Misconception

German food consists of only heavy meat-and-potatoes fare. Although meat and potatoes are the cornerstones of German cuisine, most menus include light seafood and poultry selections. In addition, many young chefs are working to lighten some of the heavier dishes to suit the modern palate.

German MENU

VORSPEISEN (APPETIZERS)

In most German restaurants in the U.S., appetizers are served à la carte, but occasionally you will find a restaurant that serves them buffet-style, offering a wide selection of delicacies, including fresh shrimp, mussels, relishes, salads (such as cucumber salad and coleslaw), pickled herring, sausages, and marinated and pickled vegetables (such as cabbage and green beans).

Marinierter Hering
Pickled herring fillets; served with bread or flatbread

Rollmops or Rollmöpse
Pickled herring rolls stuffed with dill pickles and onions; sometimes served in sour cream

Rollmops are a favorite snack in Germany, where they are eaten at any time of day. They are also a popular remedy for hangovers.

Sahnesauce Hering
Pickled herring marinated in sour cream and onions; served with bread

Champignon Schnitte
A slice of bread topped with **mushrooms** in sauce, then browned under the broiler

Kartoffelpuffer or Reibekuchen
Potato pancakes made of shredded **potatoes** (•102) mixed with onion, flour, sometimes egg, and salt and pepper, then fried in oil until golden brown and crunchy; served with applesauce or sour cream to be spread over the pancakes or used as a dip

Small potato pancakes, called Kleine Kartoffelpuffer, *are often made for appetizer portions. Larger potato pancakes are sometimes served as a light meal or as accompaniments to schnitzel (cutlets) and* Braten *(roasts).*

INGREDIENT NOTES

• **Mushrooms**, both wild and domestic, grow plentifully in Germany and are employed often in cooking. The most cherished varieties include chanterelles, morels, porcini, and brown champignons.

Leberpastete (Pâté)
Calf's liver cooked with onions and apples and made into a spread; served with dark bread

Leberkäse
Spiced liver and fat pork sausage; served hot or cold

Rindfleisch
Raw ground beef fillet or sirloin steak tartare shaped into a small patty; served with such condiments as raw onion, capers, horseradish, gherkins (small, crisp, tart pickles), and sometimes raw egg yolks

In the U.S., it is unlikely that beef tartare will be served with raw egg yolks because of the concern among health authorities that eating uncooked eggs can cause salmonella poisoning.

Schwarzwälder Bauernschinken
Smoked **Westphalian ham** atop pumpernickel or light rye bread

Cocktail von Hummerkrabben
Fresh jumbo shrimp cocktail; served with a horseradish-tomato dipping sauce

Heringssalat
Salad of bite-size pieces of skinned marinated herring fillet, hard-cooked eggs, onions, pickles, mayonnaise, and sometimes apples, pickled beets, or potatoes; served with bread

Geräucherter Lachs
Paper-thin slices of smoked salmon; served with slices of dark bread and sweet (unsalted) butter

GERÄUCHERTER LACHS: Spread the dark bread with sweet butter, then top with a slice of smoked salmon.

• **Westphalian ham**, which is cured, then smoked over beechwood and juniper branches, is dark, dense, and mildly smokey. It is the product of pigs that have been raised on acorns in the Westphalia forest and is considered a delicacy among ham aficionados.

SUPPEN (SOUPS)

German soups can be thick and hearty, creamy, or clear. The clear soups *(consommés)* are often enriched with dumplings made from semolina, a coarsely ground wheat flour.

Tagessuppe
Soup of the day

Gurkensuppe
Cucumber soup traditionally seasoned with fresh **dill**; served either hot or cold

Cucumber soup is often served with croutons, which are meant to be sprinkled over the top. The better restaurants will make the croutons themselves.

Gulaschsuppe
A hearty beef-based soup with vegetables and **potatoes**, seasoned liberally with paprika

Hausgemache Fleischbrühe mit Griessnocken
Beef consommé with semolina dumplings

Kartoffelcremesuppe
Cream of **potato** soup made with chicken stock, onion, and cream, usually garnished with fresh chives

Krautsuppe
Cabbage soup made with chicken or beef stock plus cubed meat (such as beef, lamb, or pork) and vegetables

When made with kale, this soup is called Grünkohlsuppe.

Erbsensuppe
Thick, porridge-like pea soup that often contains bits of frankfurter or smoked bacon

When pea soup is made with meat, it is called Erbseneintopf *and is served as a main course.*

INGREDIENT NOTES

• **Dill**, a feathery herb, is used fresh, dried, and in seed form in German cooking (the seed is actually the herb's dried fruit).

• Today **potatoes** are a featured ingredient in many a German dish, including salads, soups, pancakes, and dumplings. When the tubers were first introduced to 16th-century Europe, however, they weren't popular at all. In fact, the Germans did not begin to cook with them until after 1744, when Frederick the Great had seedlings distributed to the peasants and stationed armed soldiers on their farms to make sure they planted them.

SALATE (SALADS) Green salad is usually offered as a first course in German restaurants to satisfy the American clientele, but in Germany it is traditionally eaten as a side dish. Salads often come with creative dressings, such as potato or hazelnut vinaigrette. In some upscale restaurants, composed salads (in which the components are artfully arranged on a plate) are also offered, again as a first course. Heartier salads, such as those made with sausages, are considered a main course.

GERMAN SAUSAGES

Sausage *(Wurst)* is the foundation of German cuisine and appears on German menus in the U.S. under many categories, such as appetizers, salads, and entrées. Of the countless varieties the best known and most popular are the following:

Bratwurst: "the roasting sausage" made with pork

Knockwurst: smoked sausage made from either beef or a combination of veal and pork

Weisswurst: a mild white sausage made with veal

Mettwurst: a mildly smoked pork sausage good for spreading on crackers or bread

Frankfurter Würstchen: lightly smoked pork and beef sausage; ancestor to the American hot dog

Leberwurst: liver sausage

Bayerischer Wurstsalat

Bavarian sausages sliced and marinated with vinegar, onion, and mustard; served with dark bread

Krautsalat

Shredded white cabbage (either raw or lightly braised) mixed with bacon drippings or a vinaigrette and flavored with **caraway seeds** and sometimes chopped walnuts

• **Caraway seeds** come from a plant in the parsley family and are used in German cooking in rye breads as well as with beets and in sauerkraut and other cabbage-based dishes. The seeds have a nutty anise-like flavor with a peppery undertone.

Rote Beete Salat
Shredded red beets tossed with a vinaigrette; often seasoned with fresh horseradish and **caraway seeds** (•103)

Gurkensalat
Thinly sliced cucumbers in a creamy dressing (such as sour cream or yogurt) seasoned with **dill** (•102) and mustard seed

Kartoffelsalat
Warm potatoes tossed with bacon drippings and vinegar and combined with chopped onion and herbs, such as parsley or chervil

German potato salad can be prepared with a variety of dressings, including the classic warm bacon drippings and vinegar; mayonnaise and bacon drippings or oil; or oil and vinegar.

RIND (BEEF)
Beef in Germany is most often braised or pot-roasted, methods that are appreciated for their ability to turn inexpensive cuts into tender entrées and to produce delicious gravies to serve with potatoes and dumplings.

Sauerbraten
Wine-marinated braised beef; served with a sweet-and-sour gravy and sometimes dried fruit

To make sauerbraten, the German pot roast (literally "sour roast"), a piece of beef is first placed in a sweet-and-sour marinade for several days. Next the meat is braised (browned and then cooked slowly in a tightly covered pot, which renders the meat extremely tender and develops its flavors). This German specialty is commonly accompanied by boiled potatoes, dumplings, or noodles.

Rindsrouladen
Thinly sliced, rolled beef fillets (beef roulades) stuffed with pickles, onions, and bacon; served with gravy

Gekochtes Ochsenfleisch
Boiled beef; usually served with a horseradish sauce or grated fresh horseradish

Boiled potatoes and cabbage are traditional accompaniments to this dish.

Fleischklösschen
Meatballs poached in beef stock

This dish is called Pfälzer Fleschkepp *when the meatballs are made with a combination of pork, veal, and beef.*

KALB (VEAL)
No cut of meat is more loved in Germany than the veal cutlet. Pounded with a meat mallet to tenderize, veal cutlet is a standard on German menus in the U.S.

Wiener Schnitzel
Breaded veal cutlets sautéed in butter; served with lemon wedges

Rahmschnitzel
Sautéed veal cutlets in cream sauce

Jägerschnitzel
Breaded sautéed veal cutlets; served with sour cream and mushrooms

Naturschnitzel
Veal cutlets sautéed without breading and often served with a pan sauce

Schnitzeltopf
Veal stew with onions, mushrooms, herbs, and cream; served with *Spätzle* (small dumplings or noodles)

Kalbshaxen
Braised veal shanks in creamy gravy

Kalbsschnitzel mit Käse und Schinken
Sautéed veal cutlets topped with smoked ham and **Emmentaler cheese**

Schnitzel à la Holstein
Sautéed breaded veal cutlets topped with a fried egg and anchovies

Schnitzel à la Holstein *is named after Baron Friedrich von Holstein, a German diplomat of the Imperial days, who liked to be served many different delicacies on one plate. When prepared in its grandest style, the meat is accompanied by very small portions of smoked salmon, caviar, mushrooms, truffles, and cooked crayfish tails, then topped with a fried egg, anchovies, capers, and a sprig of parsley. In most restaurants, however, the cutlet is not served in such a luxurious manner.*

INGREDIENT NOTES

• **Emmentaler cheese** is named after Switzerland's Emmental Valley, where it is believed to have been made as early as the 15th century. A cow's milk cheese, it has a mild, slightly sweet, nut-like flavor and marble-size "eyes," or holes, that develop while it is ripening.

GEFLÜGEL (POULTRY)

Entenbrust mit Schwarzwälder Kirsch
Duck breast glazed with dark cherries and **kirsch**

Gänsebraten
Roast goose stuffed with apples, raisins, herbs, **juniper berries**, and other spices, such as coriander, cloves, and ginger

Goose was being stuffed with apples in Germany as early as the Middle Ages and it is still very popular. It is traditionally served on Christmas and on Martinmas, the November 11th holiday that honors St. Martin.

Gebratene Ente
Roast duck commonly filled with an apple-sausage stuffing; served with boiled potatoes, *Spätzle* (small dumplings or noodles)

Mandelschnitzel
Boneless chicken breast lightly coated with ground almonds and sautéed with raisins

SCHWEIN (PORK)

Schweinebraten
Roast pork loin; served with sauerkraut and *Semmelknödel* (bread dumplings) or mashed potatoes

Zigeuner Schnitzel
Sautéed lightly floured pork cutlets; served with onions, peppers, and mushrooms in a creamy paprika sauce

Ripple mit Linsen
Smoked center-cut pork chops; served with lentils

INGREDIENT NOTES

• **Kirsch** is a clear brandy made from cherries.

• **Juniper berries**, dark purple pungent berries, are used by German cooks to season everything from sauerkraut to venison. They give gin its distinctive taste and are also used as a flavoring for a kind of schnapps called *Steinhäger*.

WILD (GAME)

WILD (GAME) Germany's magnificent forests and mountains are filled with an enormous variety of game, and German cooks have traditionally made full use of this natural bounty. Because game is not terribly popular among Americans, it is not widely represented on menus in the U.S., though at least a few dishes are usually included during the autumn hunting season.

Gebratener Rehrücken
Roast saddle of venison, larded and flavored with **juniper berries** and black pepper

The saddle, the unseparated loin from both sides of the animal, is a very tender and expensive cut of meat.

Rehfilet
Roasted tenderloin of venison

Hasenragout
Rabbit stew seasoned with such ingredients as wine, vinegar, **juniper berries**, bay leaf, peppercorns, and cloves

FISCHGERICHTE (FISH and SHELLFISH)

Fish and shellfish are most likely to appear on the menu of restaurants that feature the cooking of Northern Germany. This is the only region in Germany that borders the ocean, specifically the North and Baltic seas. On these menus you are likely to find pike, perch, trout, salmon, sole, flounder, cod, eel, crayfish, shrimp, and mussels.

Fisch-Klösschen
Baked fish dumplings; often served with **sorrel** sauce

Tiefsee-Garnelen
Jumbo shrimp lightly breaded and deep-fried

Lachsschnitzel
Pan-fried salmon fillets in a cream sauce

Grüner Aal
Tender chunks of eel in a green sauce made with watercress, spinach, or **sorrel**

Bachforelle mit Äpfeln und Gerösteten Mandeln
Pan-fried brook trout topped with apples and toasted almonds

Angelschellfisch in Senfsauce
Poached haddock in a mustard sauce

• **Sorrel**, also called **sour grass**, is a perennial herb used frequently in German cooking, especially in soups and green sauces, for its sour, tangy flavor.

GEMÜSE (VEGETABLES and OTHER SIDE DISHES)

As a general rule, vegetables and other side dishes are not listed separately on German menus but are included automatically with an entrée. In fact, most vegetables hold a rather humble status in German cuisine. Exceptions include mushrooms, asparagus (especially the tender, buttery white variety), cabbage, and potatoes, all of which are quite popular.

Rotkraut
Red cabbage braised with vinegar, apples, bacon bits, onion, and cloves; served as an accompaniment to meat and poultry dishes

Geschmortes Weisskraut
Braised green cabbage, typically flavored with vinegar and **caraway seeds** (•103); served as an accompaniment to meat and poultry dishes

Rotes Sauerkraut
Sauerkraut that has been reddened with shredded beets; served as an accompaniment to venison, pork, or poultry

Blumenkohl
Sautéed cauliflower drizzled with **brown butter** and topped with bread crumbs

Sauerkraut
Shredded white cabbage fermented with apples, salt, and a mixture of spices that usually includes **juniper berries** (•106); the traditional accompaniment to German sausages and pork

Though sauerkraut (literally "sour plant") is a signature dish of the cuisine of Germany, the Germans did not invent the method for making it. It was the Romans who first recorded the technique of salting shredded cabbage and letting it ferment, and they are believed to have gotten the idea from the Orient.

Spätzle
Tiny dumplings or noodles made from flour, eggs, and milk, flavored with nutmeg

Spätzle, literally tiny sparrows, are served in place of potatoes and usually with dishes that contain a gravy, such as sauerbraten and roulades.

INGREDIENT NOTES

• **Brown butter**, also called nut butter, is butter that has been cooked over low heat until golden brown and fragrant. It is commonly drizzled over potatoes and vegetables.

Grüne Spätzle
Green *Spätzle* (made with spinach) in a cream sauce

Käse Spätzle
Tiny dumplings or noodles layered with **Emmentaler cheese** (•105); served as is or baked in a casserole

Kartoffelklösse Gekochte
Potato dumplings made by boiling a mixture of mashed **potatoes** (•102), flour, and egg

Potato dumplings are the classic accompaniment to sauerbraten.

SALZKARTOFFELN: Never cut boiled potatoes with a knife; always break them with a fork.

Salzkartoffeln
Potatoes boiled in salted water

Kartoffelpuffer
Potato pancakes (see Appetizers, page 100)

Kartoffelbrei
or Kartoffpüree
Mashed potatoes

Zwiebelkuchen
Cheese, onion, and bacon tart made with a yeast dough; also served as a snack or small main course

NACHSPEISEN (DESSERTS)

Apfelpfannkuchen
Large pancake filled with thinly sliced spiced apples; served plain, sprinkled with confectioner's sugar, or drizzled with vanilla custard sauce

When dessert pancakes are made with cherries, they are called Kirschpfannkuchen.

Bayrischer Apfelstrudel (Bavarian Apple Strudel)
Thin layers of pastry filled with sliced apples, then rolled and baked until golden brown; served warm or at room temperature

• **Cheese** is presented in a host of ways in German cooking—typically in sauces, vegetable tarts, and as a topping for schnitzel. The most popular cheeses include Emmentaler, Münster, Tilsiter, Blauschimmelkäse (blue cheese), Camembert, and Quark (reminiscent of a sharp cottage or ricotta cheese).

Schwarzwälder Kirschtorte (Black Forest Cake)

Moist chocolate cake layers filled with **cherries** soaked in cherry brandy, frosted with whipped cream, and garnished with chocolate shavings

Haselnusstorte

Light **hazelnut** torte made of sponge cake filled and frosted with sweetened whipped cream

Zwetschgenkuchen

Plum tart

Arme Ritter

Batter-dipped bread sautéed in butter; served with vanilla sauce on top or applesauce on the side (to be used as a spread)

This German classic, a cousin to French toast, is sometimes served for breakfast or as a light dinner.

INGREDIENT NOTES

• **Cherries** (in addition to mushrooms) grow in abundance in the Black Forest in southern Germany.

• **Hazelnuts** have a hard brown shell and gold-colored flesh covered by a thin brown skin. The nuts have a rich, buttery flavor favored by German bakers.

GETRÄNKE (BEVERAGES)

GERMAN BEER

Beer-drinking, both with food and by itself, is one of the oldest and best-known German customs, and over 5,000 varieties are brewed by over 1,000 breweries. Distinguished as light *(helles)* or dark *(dunkles)*, German beers are further classified by their hop content, whether they are top or bottom fermented, how long they are stored, and their alcohol content (2.5 to 7 percent). Government regulation of quality dates back to a 1516 law stating that only malt, hops, yeast, and water may be used in beer production—no artificial ingredients. German beer goes especially well with sausages, but can also be enjoyed with almost any German food. German beer is properly served at a slightly warmer temperature than American beer. Following are some of the German beers most commonly found in restaurants in the U.S.:

Weizenbier (or Weissbier): a light, snappy, foamy wheat beer with a spicy aroma

Berliner Weisse: a delicate light, top-fermented white (wheat) beer that is traditionally spiked with a shot of raspberry syrup and may be served in a bowl-like goblet

Bock: a dark, strong, malty-tasting beer *(Starkbier)* with more than 6 percent alcohol by volume

Maibock: a high-quality bock beer (see above) that is pale in color

Märzenbier: a medium-strong, slightly sweet beer, between light and dark in color

Pils or Pilsner: a slightly bitter, pale golden light beer often served with schnapps

Malzbier: a sweet, dark, non-alcoholic malt beverage

Wine

Selected mid- and top-level
wines from various regions of
Germany

GERMAN WINE

A flourishing top-rate wine industry exists in
southern and western Germany along several
of the main rivers, the best known of which is the Rhine.
Although there is some red wine production, most wine produced is white. In general, German wines are light, dry, and
fresh-tasting with nuances of fruit and flowery bouquets.
Most are drunk young.

Many German wines are known by the grape variety.
The king of German white wines is the refreshing and crisp-
tasting Riesling. When choosing a German Riesling, look
for wines from the growing regions of Mosel-Saar-Ruwer,
Rheingau, Rheinpfalz, and Rheinhessen. These regions produce some of the best-quality Rieslings. Other good varietals include the mild Silvaner, Weissburgunder (Pinot
blanc), Grauburgunder (Pinot gris), Scheurebe, and the new
Riesling-like crossing, Kerner. Other popular wines include
Liebfraumilch, a lightly sweet white wine; Sekt, a sparkling
white wine that can range from extra dry to sweet (Germany
is the world's largest producer and consumer of sparkling
wine, most of it made from French and Italian grapes); and
Weissherbst, a rosé wine. German wines harmonize well
with most German food, though a waiter should be able to
suggest a particular match. German white wine should be
served well chilled and German red wine slightly chilled.
Crystals in the neck of the bottle or even in your glass are a
sign of long fermentation of superior wines made from
mature, sweet grapes of a certain acidity. They do not affect
the taste of the wine.

GERMAN WINE LABELS

German wine labels provide detailed information on growing region, vineyard, vintage, grape variety, and quality category. As a basic guide, keep in mind that only two major categories of wine are exported in any quantity: the mid-level *Qualitätswein b.A.* (QbA) and the top level *Qualitätswein mit Prädikat*. All but the sweet dessert wines noted below are available in a level of dryness noted as either *Trocken* (dry) or *Halbtrocken* (semi-dry).

The top-quality wines, *Qualitätswein mit Prädikat*, are further classified in ascending order of sweetness, based on how ripe the grapes were at harvest time (they sweeten as they age): *Kabinett* (the lightest of all), *Spätlese* (full-bodied), *Auslese* (usually but not always sweet), and sweet dessert wine rarities, *Beerenauslese* (BA), *Eiswein*, and *Trockenbeerenauslese* (TBA).

Schnaps

Schnaps *is the generic term for a popular distilled dry spirit made from grains or potatoes; it can be flavored in a variety of ways, including with fruit, peppermint, juniper berries, or caraway.*

Coffee

Coffee, not tea, is the hot beverage of choice among most Germans.

GREEK
cuisine

★

Cheers–*Eis eiyean* (**eas** e **yee** an)
Bon appétit–*Kalle orexi* (**kall**-ee or-**ecks**-ee)
Thank you–*Efharisto* (eff-har-is-**tow**)

THE COOKING OF GREECE, WHICH CAN BE TRACED
back to earliest classical times, has always relied on
pure, simple ingredients: olive oil, a product of the
olive trees that cover the Greek countryside, said to be gifts
from the ancient gods; fish and shellfish from the Mediterranean and Aegean seas, which are frequently marinated,
seasoned with olive oil and oregano, and broiled; honey and
nuts, such as walnuts, almonds, and pistachios, which are
highlighted in Greek desserts; and lamb, not surprising
considering that sheep have grazed on this land since prehistoric times.

Principles of Flavor

Except for garlic, which is used generously in many dishes,
Greek food tends to be subtly seasoned with such herbs and
spices as oregano, dill, parsley, mint, bay leaf, cloves, cinnamon, and marjoram. Olive oil is incorporated into marinades, sauces, and dressings. Honey sweetens many desserts.

Foreign Influence

Greece was a conquering nation that, in turn, was con-
quered, and its cuisine reflects the inevitable blending of cultures that occurs under such historical circumstances. When
the Huns invaded Corinth around A.D. 500, they introduced

115

butter. In A.D. 1200 the Venetians introduced the lemon seed. Around A.D. 1300 pasta was introduced by the Italians, Serbs, and Franks. The most significant influence was the Turkish occupation of the Greek mainland and islands, which occurred from 1453, with the fall of Constantinople, until 1922, with the mass exodus of the Asia Minor Greeks, called the *mikrasiates*, from Turkey. Among the dishes brought back to Greece by the *mikrasiates* was moussaka, the ever-popular meat and vegetable casserole (see page 126). Many dishes that are referred to as *à la politika*, such as *anginares à la politika* (artichokes marinated in olive oil and lemon juice) come from the Greeks from Constantinople, who referred to Constantinople as Polis or Poli.

Ordering

G reek menus conform to the traditional style of American menus, starting with appetizers and continuing on to soups, entrées, and desserts. It is a good idea to order an assortment of appetizers when you place your drink order, then order additional appetizers (be sure to try both hot and cold offerings) and/or the main meal once you have had more time to review the menu.

Except in some of the higher-priced restaurants, a salad, plus often a vegetable side dish, rice, and potato, are included in the price of the entrée. The traditional Greek salad (made with greens of the season, tomatoes, peppers, olives, a hefty sprinkling of feta cheese, oregano, and an olive oil and vinegar dressing) may be served as a first course (common in formal restaurants) or as an accompaniment to the main course.

Informal restaurants sometimes encourage patrons, before ordering, to look over the array of uncooked foods displayed in a refrigerated case near the cooking area, which may include fresh snapper, squid, or lamb or pork chops. Meats may be roasting nearby. Prepared dishes may also be displayed, such as stuffed peppers or tomatoes. In some restaurants, instead of or in addition to a printed menu, the waiter may provide an informal explanation of the foods available, first inquiring as to whether diners would prefer something from the grill, *tis skaras*, or baked, *mayerefto*.

Service and Dining

The waiters at the more casual restaurants may seem hurried and frenzied, but this should not deter the diner from eating in a relaxed manner. Eating is a slow art to the Greeks, and waiters, regardless of the hustle and bustle, usually expect diners to take their time and savor their meals.

Some of the more relaxed restaurants do not include any desserts on their menus. Instead the waiters suggest that diners visit a Greek pastry shop, called a *zaharoplastio*, where a wide assortment of both Greek and continental desserts, along with American coffee, demitasse (espresso), and tea, are served. The restaurants that do offer desserts usually make them on the premises and display them on a large tray. Servings tend to be large; often one dessert can easily serve two people.

Condiments

Aside from olive oil and vinegar to add to a Greek salad, no special condiments are set on a Greek table.

Garnishes

The Greeks tend to keep garnishes simple: Fresh sprigs of parsley and lemon wedges are the most common choices.

Rice and Bread

Plain, simple white crusty bread (sometimes enriched with olives or made with semolina flour) or pocketless pita cut into triangles is always served in a plentiful manner in Greek restaurants. Rice, which is usually cooked in chicken broth (sometimes enhanced with bits of onion), is one of the staples of Greek cuisine, and is served with most main courses, often accompanied by potatoes. Instead of rice, some restaurants serve orzo, a small rice-shaped pasta.

Utensils

Filled appetizers made with phyllo, called *bourekakia*, can be picked up with the hands. Dips, such as *tzatziki*, *taramosalata*, and *skordalia* (see page 122), are meant to be eaten with bread. Either transfer some of the dip onto your plate and dip the bread into it (or spread the dip on the bread with a knife) or place the dip in the center of the table and have each diner dip bread into it.

Signature Dishes

Spanakopita (spinach phyllo puffs); *Avgolemono* (egg-lemon chicken soup with rice); *Horiatiki Salata* (country-style salad; also known as Greek Salad); *Psari tsi Skaras* (grilled fish); *Souvlaki* (pieces of lamb, beef, chicken, shrimp, or swordfish on a skewer with vegetables); *Dolmades* (grape leaves stuffed with rice or meat); *Moussaka* (meat and vegetable casserole); *Baklava* (nut-filled layered phyllo pastries)

Common Misconceptions

Greek food is very oily. Olive oil is an important ingredient in many Greek dishes; however, in recent years, because of concern about fat consumption, there has been an effort to use it more sparingly. In addition, many dishes that used to be deep-fried are now broiled instead.

Greek desserts are too sweet. Most Americans are familiar with the Greek pastry baklava, which is made with layers of nuts and honey and is indeed sweet. There are many less sweet choices, including *ravani*, a farina cake, and *pasta flora*, a lattice-topped tart filled with apricot purée.

Greek wine tastes like turpentine. Years ago the only wine imported from Greece had a resin flavor that most Americans found unpleasant. More recently there has been redevelopment and refinement in Greek wine production—resinated wines are not even popular in Greece anymore—and as a result many delicious, inexpensive white, rosé, and red wines are available in Greek restaurants.

Greek MENU

OREKTIKA, MEZZEDAKIA, MEZZEDES, or MEZZE (APPETIZERS)

Appetizers play an important role in the Greek dining experience, as most Greeks love to snack on them while drinking their wine or beer, regardless of whether it is lunchtime, early evening, prior to dinner, or late at night at a club. From hot puffs made with phyllo to charcoal-broiled octopus or squid, to zesty cucumber yogurt dip, to spicy marinated olives, a diner can make a complete meal of them if desired.

HOT APPETIZERS

Oktapodi Skaras
Octopus strips marinated in red wine, seasoned with olive oil and oregano, and broiled; served with lemon wedges

Saganaki
Melted cheese, such as *Kasseri*, *Kefalotiri*, or *Kefalograviera*, sprinkled with lemon juice

In some restaurants, the melted cheese is sprinkled with brandy and then ignited when presented to the table. Not purely theatrical, the brandy adds flavor to the cheese. To eat, spread the cheese on bread with a knife.

Sikotaki Marinato
Tiny pieces of lamb liver marinated in lemon juice, garlic, olive oil, oregano, and vinegar, then sautéed in olive oil; served with lemon wedges

Kalamarakia Tyganita
Small pieces of batter-dipped fried **squid**; served with lemon wedges

Keftedes
Small deep-fried meatballs (usually made with beef chuck) seasoned with minced onion, mint, and garlic

Spanakopita
Phyllo puffs filled with a mixture of spinach and feta (see page 121)

Spanakopita may also be served as an entrée.

INGREDIENT NOTES

• **Squid** and calamari are two names for the same ten-armed sea creature that is valued by connoisseurs for its chewy, mildly sweet flesh and its black ink, which can be used to color and flavor other foods.

• **Phyllo**, or filo, is paper-thin dough that is rolled out into sheets and can be filled with cheese, meat, fish, or nuts. Many Greek appetizers, entrées, and desserts are made with phyllo.

Souzoukakia
Oblong-shaped meatballs flavored with cumin and either fried or broiled, then seasoned with fresh lemon juice

Souzoukakia *may also be offered as an entrée, in which case they are baked in a tomato sauce and presented on a bed of rice.*

Tiropeta
Triangular **phyllo** puffs filled with feta cheese mixture

Pikilia Orektika
Assortment of hot and/or cold appetizers

In most cases a platter of assorted Greek appetizers serves more than one person. Check with the waiter and order accordingly.

TYRIA (GREEK CHEESES)
In Greece, cheese, usually made from sheep's or goat's milk, is included with practically every meal—from breakfast, when Greeks may eat a chunk of *Manouri* with some honey and freshly baked bread, to dinner, when they may finish the meal with a little piece of *Kasseri* or other cheese. Following are the most popular varieties:

Feta: a crumbly white cheese; made from sheep's and goat's milk curd

Haloumi: a semisoft cheese, not very salty; usually made from sheep's milk

Kasseri: a creamy yellow farm cheese with a mild flavor; made from sheep's or goat's milk

Kefalotiri: a hard salty cheese (the Greek Parmesan); made from sheep's or goat's milk; used for grating and melted to make *Saganaki*

Kefalograviera: a mild Gruyère-type cheese; made from either sheep's or cow's milk

Manouri: a soft unsalted cheese; made from sheep's or goat's milk whey; served with fruit

Mizithra: soft and hard varieties; made from sheep's or goat's milk whey

COLD APPETIZERS

Melintzanosalata
Puréed baked eggplant combined with olive oil, chopped olives, tomatoes, and fresh lemon juice to make a creamy spread

Skordalia
Crushed garlic and potato purée
Skordalia is also served as an accompaniment to fried fish.

Dolmadakia or Dolmades
Grape leaves filled with a mixture of rice, onions, and scallions, flavored with dill and parsley

Meat-filled dolmades are served as a hot entrée.

Unless the restaurant has a grapevine in its backyard, its grape leaves are probably from a can or a jar. The taste of these leaves is fine but their sodium content may be high because most are packed in brine.

Taramosalata
A creamy spread made with bread, olive oil, fish roe, lemon juice, and sometimes onion and garlic

Tzatziki
A blend of plain **yogurt**, cucumbers, olive oil, and garlic
Tzatziki is also used as a sauce on various meat preparations, including gyro sandwiches

GREEK OLIVES
According to Ancient Greek lore, the goddess Athena gave the Athenians the olive tree, a truly wonderful gift because it prospered throughout Greece's hilly, difficult terrain. Today olives are a mainstay of Greek cuisine, used in appetizers, salads, and some main dishes. Following are the olive varieties you are most likely to come across in the U.S.:

Kalamata: dark purple, small, and almond-shaped, with a pungent flavor; from the southern part of Peloponnese

Amfissa: black and round with a nutty-sweet taste; from the central mainland of Greece

Green: large and crunchy with a mild flavor; from various Ionian islands

Cracked green: made by cracking unripe green olives, placing them in water for several weeks to remove their bitterness, then storing them in brine

Black: small, wrinkled, dry-cured olives with a very strong flavor; from the island of Thassos

SALATA (SALADS) The Greek word for salad, *salata*, encompasses both sliced vegetable mixtures and puréed mixtures, such as *melintzanosalata* (eggplant spread) or *taramosalata* (fish roe spread). Most often salad is served prior to the main course but is left on the table to be enjoyed throughout the entire meal. Many salads in Greek restaurants can serve as meals in themselves or can be shared by two or more people. Check with the waiter when you order.

Domatosalata
Sliced tomato and onion topped with a generous sprinkling of oregano, olive oil, and vinegar

Horiatiki Salata (Greek Salad)
Lettuce, tomatoes, olives, feta cheese, scallions, anchovies, oregano, and sometimes rice-filled grape leaves, with an olive oil and vinegar dressing

The Horiatiki salata, *or what in the U.S. has come to be known as Greek salad, is usually served in a large bowl and is meant to be shared among all the diners at the table. Although the key ingredients remain feta, olives, oregano, and an oil and vinegar dressing, all of the other ingredients may vary based on availability and the chef's preferences.*

SOUPES (SOUPS) Soups are served as a separate course in Greece. Some soups, such as *faki, giovarlakia,* and *kakavia*, can take the place of a main course.

Avgolemono Soup
Chicken and rice soup flavored with an egg-lemon mixture before serving

Avgolemono *means egg-lemon, and this mixture is also used as a sauce with various meat dishes and vegetables.*

INGREDIENT NOTES

• Greek **yogurt**, made from whole sheep's milk or sometimes goat's milk, is thicker and creamier than the commercial cow's milk yogurt commonly available in the U.S. To compensate, Greek chefs in the U.S. either find a source for goat's milk yogurt or drain cow's milk yogurt to remove the water.

Faki
Thick and spicy lentil soup

Faki, *made spicy with vinegar, is a favorite during the Lenten fast, when meat consumption is forbidden.*

Fassoulada
A zesty soup made with navy beans, olive oil, carrots, garlic, and celery

Giovarlakia
Meatballs in an egg-lemon (*avgolemono*) chicken broth

Giovarlakia *is sometimes listed as an entrée, in which case the meatballs are served in a deep dish with the sauce/soup around them.*

Kakavia
A hearty fish soup made with pieces of firm fish (and sometimes shrimp, clams, mussels, and wine) in a vegetable broth

Food historians hypothesize *that* kakavia *was the precursor to the French bouillabaisse, which is a creditable theory considering that Greece was a strong power in the Mediterranean from 900 to 158 B.C.*

PSARI KAI THALASINA (FISH and SHELLFISH)
Seafood is a mainstay of Greek cuisine. On North American menus and in Greece the most popular seafood offerings include porgy, red mullet, striped bass, codfish, shrimp, squid, and mussels. Lobster, although not plentiful in Greece, is well liked, too.

Psari tis Skaras
Fish basted with a mixture of olive oil, lemon juice, and oregano, and cooked either on charcoal or in the oven; served with the remaining basting mixture

Firm-fleshed white fish, such as porgy, red snapper, striped bass, and swordfish, are the most popular types of fish used to make psari tis skaras.

Garides me Saltsa
Shrimp baked in a tomato and onion sauce and topped with feta cheese (see page 121)

Garides me Saltsa *is often listed on menus as shrimp with feta, shrimp with tomato sauce, or shrimp scorpio, a reference to its supposed creation on the island of Scorpios.*

Media Krassata

Mussels cooked in a wine sauce and served on a bed of rice

During elections in Ancient Greece voters cast their ballots by inscribing the names of their candidates inside mussel and oyster shells.

Psari Plaki

Fish fillets, such as striped bass, sea bass, bluefish, or tilefish, baked in wine with a mixture of celery, scallions, and garlic, and topped with tomatoes, lemon slices, and wine

The word plaki *in the dish name refers to the technique of cooking the fish with assorted vegetables and baking it in the oven with other seasonings.*

KOTA (CHICKEN)

Kota Kapama

Chicken pieces braised with vegetables in a tomato-onion sauce flavored with cinnamon; served on a bed of macaroni or orzo

The word kapama *in the name of this dish refers to the technique of braising chicken or beef with vegetables, such as green beans or artichokes, in a tomato-onion sauce and serving the mixture with pasta.*

Kotopoulo Riganato tis Skaras

Chicken marinated in olive oil, wine, and oregano, then broiled, basted with marinade

Kritharaki me Kota

Braised chicken pieces baked in a casserole with orzo; served with grated cheese and yogurt to be spooned over top

Kota Souvlaki

Boneless chicken marinated in olive oil, wine, and oregano, then broiled on a skewer with vegetables, such as mushrooms, bell peppers, and tomatoes

Souvlaki may be served either on the skewer on a bed of rice, in which case the diner slides the chicken and vegetables off the skewer to eat, or removed from the skewer on a bed of rice, or inside a pita. When *souvlaki* is presented inside a pita, it is usually topped with chopped lettuce and a cucumber-yogurt-garlic sauce.

Kota me Spanaki Avgolemono

Browned chicken pieces simmered with scallions and spinach (and possibly leeks or peas); topped with an *avgolemono* (egg-lemon) sauce

VOTHINO (BEEF) Until a few years ago, when Greece joined the Common Market and beef started to become readily available and affordable, Greeks ate very little of this kind of meat. Historically, however, Greek restaurants in the U.S. have adapted lamb recipes for beef to satisfy their American clientele.

Pastitsio

A hearty layered tubular pasta casserole made with either ground beef or lamb and two types of white sauce (one thin to bind the pasta, the other thick and spooned over the top); sprinkled with cinnamon

Yemista Lahanika

Vegetables, such as tomatoes and bell peppers, stuffed with seasoned chopped beef sautéed with rice

Stifado

Stew made with small pieces of boneless beef chuck or lamb chunks combined with small white onions, flavored with cinnamon, oregano, and bay leaf, and baked in a casserole

Moussaka

A hearty layered casserole made with either chopped beef or lamb and eggplant, potato, and/or zucchini slices; topped with a heavy cream sauce

The vegetable layers in moussaka may vary depending on the chef's preference. Some chefs incorporate all three vegetables; others depend on only eggplant or potato.

Beefteki

A Greek version of a hamburger, seasoned with oregano, mint, and crushed garlic; served in a pita or bun or on top of a bed of rice

Feta or Kasseri *cheese (see page 121) may be added to* beefteki *to create a Greek cheeseburger.*

Gyro

Cylinder of compressed pieces of beef slow-roasted on a rotating spit and thinly sliced from the outside as it cooks; served with yogurt sauce inside a folded pita

The gyro (correctly pronounced "yeero," though many people, both Greeks and Americans, say "jiro") is a relatively new addition to the Greek food assortment. It is usually eaten by hand, although a knife and fork make it much easier—and much less messy. Gyros are not usually found on menus at formal Greek restaurants. Inexpensive, casual places, such as diners, may offer an industrial version made with ground beef, ground lamb mixed with beef, or even ground chicken.

Keftedes

Broiled or deep-fried meatballs flavored with oregano, mint, and onions

ARNI (LAMB)
Lamb—roasted, baked, stuffed, and ground for casseroles—is a mainstay of Greek cuisine. Greeks prefer their lamb cooked to the well-done stage, but in some restaurants you may be able to convince the chef to prepare lamb chops or steaks to a lesser degree of doneness; roast leg of lamb and most lamb casseroles are not adaptable.

Arni Exohiko
Chunks of lamb combined with vegetables (such as potatoes, artichoke hearts, beans, peas, or green beans) and baked in **phyllo** (•120)

Arni me Avgolemono
Small lamb pieces browned with onions and simmered with various vegetables, such as artichokes, escarole, leeks, or spinach, then covered with an *avgolemono* (egg-lemon) sauce

Arni Kleftiko
Chunks of lamb combined with potatoes, celery, and onions, and baked in a foil packet

The work kleftiko *means "stolen" in English, a reference to the Greek bandits who at one time roamed the countryside, sneaking down into the villages to steal their provisions, then cooking their meals in paper in order to hide the aroma and keep their presence hidden from the authorities.*

Arni Psito me Patates
Lamb marinated in olive oil, oregano, and garlic, then roasted with potatoes

Arni tis Souvlas
Leg of lamb marinated in olive oil, wine, and oregano, with slivers of garlic inserted into the meat, and barbecued

Paidakia
Broiled lamb chops seasoned with garlic and oregano

Kritharaki me to Kreas
Boneless lamb chunks braised in a casserole, then combined with orzo (rice-shaped pasta) to finish cooking; served with grated *Kefalotiri* cheese (see page 121) to be sprinkled on by diner

Papoutsakia
Eggplant slices stuffed with chopped lamb and baked

The word papoutsakia *means "little shoes," a reference to the resemblance between little shoes and eggplant slices.*

HIRINO (PORK)

Ghouronaki Psito

Roasted piglet marinated in olive oil, lemon juice, and thyme, and cooked on a skewer

A pig roasting on a spit is a common sight at psistaries, *Greek restaurants that specialize in barbecued foods.*

Hirino me Prasines Elles

A casserole of pork tenderloin pieces and cracked green olives

Kondosouvla

Pork and vegetables broiled on a skewer; served on the skewer on a bed of rice

LAHANIKA (VEGETABLES) Greeks

like their vegetables cooked for a long time, well beyond the *al dente* stage, until they are rather soft. Favorites include artichokes, green beans, dandelion greens, and peas. Some Greek restaurants in the U.S. accompany each entrée with the "vegetable of the day." More formal establishments usually offer a selection of vegetables from which to choose.

Anginares à la Politika

Artichoke hearts slow-simmered with olive oil, lemon juice, and spices; served either at room temperature or cold

Fava

A purée of yellow split peas blended with onions and garlic; served with a drizzling of olive oil over the top

Fava is a good choice for a vegetarian entrée. It is also a popular choice

among Greeks during Lent, the 40 days prior to Holy Easter.

Gigantes

Large white beans simmered until soft in a mixture of chopped onions, garlic, and parsley; often served with olive oil to be drizzled on at the diner's discretion

Horta Vrasta me Ladolemono

Boiled green vegetables, such as chickory, dandelion greens, endive, or escarole; served with an olive oil and lemon dressing

Tiganites Patates

Thick slices of potatoes deep-fried, generally in olive oil, then topped with oregano and grated cheese

Horta Yahni

Braised vegetables, such as cauliflower, fava beans, okra, tomatoes, or green beans, cooked with onions

The term yahni *in this dish name refers to a technique in which onions are cooked until wilted, then combined with tomatoes, vegetables, and seasonings and slowly cooked until quite soft.*

Spanakorizo

A combination of spinach and rice flavored with mint

Greek Pizza

Pita topped with cooked vegetables, such as spinach and tomatoes, and feta cheese, then baked

Greek pizza is a recent addition to Greek menus at informal restaurants in both the U.S. and Greece.

GLYKISMATA (DESSERTS)

Many casual Greek restaurants do not serve desserts but, instead, send their customers to local shops that specialize in Greek sweets and coffee. Desserts play an important role in the Greek dining tradition and should not be missed—even if it means a short walk or car trip to another location.

Karidopeta

Single-layer, dark, moist nut cake (made with coarsely chopped walnuts or almonds) topped with a light honey/sugar syrup

Like most Greek cakes, karidopeta *is made in one layer, without icing, in a rectangular pan and is cut into diamond-shaped servings.*

Pasta Flora

A lattice-topped tart filled with apricot purée

The name pasta flora *means "flower tart," a reference to this dessert's flower-like appearance.*

Ravani

Golden yellow cake made with farina or semolina and topped with a light sugar/honey or orange-flavored syrup

Fenikia or Melomakarouna

Oblong, honey-dipped cookies covered with chopped nuts

Diples

Thin strips of dough tied, folded, or twisted into bows or loops and deep-fried, then dipped in a honey syrup and topped with chopped nuts

Rizogalo
Creamy rice pudding with a sprinkling of cinnamon on top

Loukoumades
Made-to-order deep-fried honey balls topped with honey; served warm

Kourabiedes
Butter cookies shaped by hand and covered with powdered sugar

Kourabiedes *are sometimes enriched with chopped almonds and adorned with a clove; the clove is not meant to be eaten. They are traditionally baked at Christmas and to celebrate a child's birth or baptism.*

Baklava
Alternating layers of chopped nuts and **phyllo** (●120) topped with a light honey/sugar syrup

Galatoboureko

A custard-filled dessert made with **phyllo** (●120) topped with a light honey/sugar syrup

Kadaife
Shredded dough filled with chopped nuts and cinnamon and topped with a honey/sugar syrup

Koulourakia
Crisp, golden-colored, subtly sweet cookies shaped by hand; sometimes covered with sesame seeds

Koulourakia *may be flavored with wine, vanilla, orange, or ouzo (anise-flavored liqueur, see page 131), depending on the preference of the cook.*

PIOTA (BEVERAGES) Most Greeks consider wine the natural choice with meals, especially dinner; beer is also consumed but not nearly as often. Many conclude their meal with Greek coffee, and a few drink herbal tea. A sweet dessert wine, such as Muscat or Mavrodaphne, or brandy may also be sipped at the end of an evening in lieu of coffee.

Greek Beer
Imported beers from Greece, such as Sparta and Olympia, are far superior to the early brands that were first brought to the U.S.

Ouzo

Strong anise-flavored liqueur,
offered as an apéritif

*Ouzo, distilled from the
residue of pressed grapes, is considered the national alcoholic
beverage of Greece. Natives
drink it straight (with a glass of
water on the side) at different
times of day but not usually with
dinner. When combined with
water, it turns cloudy. It should
be served at room temperature.*

Greek Coffee

*Greek coffee is made in a spe-
cially designed long-handled
cylindrical pot called a* briki,
*and is served in small demitasse
cups with foam, called* kaimaki,
*on top. It is very strong and is
sweetened according to the
instructions of the diner, namely*
sketos, *without sugar;* metrios
vrastos, *medium-strong with
minimal sugar; or* varys glyko,
*strong and sweet. Note that nei-
ther milk nor cream are served
with it, and that the thick coffee
grinds settle on the bottom of the
cup, making it inadvisable to
swallow every last drop.*

GREEK WINE

Recent improvements in Greek wine production
have made the selection of wines at Greek restaurants
more appealing. Outstanding Greek vineyards have developed
on both the mainland, such as in the regions of the
Peloponnese, the Attica plain, and Macedonia, and the islands,
including Crete, Cephalonia, and Samos. In recent years the
government of Greece has also classified the wines into 28
"controlled appellation" regions, and, as a result, more high-
quality Greek wines—ranging from full-bodied reds to fruity
whites to mellow rosés—are being exported to the States today
than at any time in the past. Key producers of high-quality
wines include Boutari, Carras, and Koutakis.

A sweet dessert wine frequently found on Greek wine lists
is Mavrodaphne. It is meant to be sipped after dinner, prefer-
ably with fruit, such as apple slices. Another excellent dessert
wine that is becoming more common is Muscat from Samos,
which is also sweet and a good accompaniment to fruit.

INDIAN
cuisine

★

Cheers–No translation in Hindi or any
other language spoken in India

Bon appétit–No translation in Hindi or any
other language spoken in India

Thank you–*Dhanya vad* (**don**-ya vad)

INDIAN CUISINE IS ONE OF THE MOST DIVERSE AND complex in the world—attributable to a variety of factors, including the many invasions of India by outside powers, its numerous religious divisions, its caste system, and its varied terrain. Most Indian restaurants in the U.S. feature the cuisine of north India with just a smattering of classic south Indian fare thrown in. North Indian cooking is famous for its elaborate meat preparations and rice pilafs as well as its velvety sauces and delicate use of flavorings. It is also known as Moghulai food, in reference to the Moghuls who invaded India in the 16th century and left an indelible mark on the Indian diet—as well as its art, architecture, painting, and landscaping. In contrast, in south India (where much of the population follows a vegetarian regime), the emphasis is on rice, lentils, pancakes, seafood, vegetables, and coconut, and flavorings tend to be very spicy—sometimes fiery. Because much of the food of south India is steamed, it is, in general, healthier than the food of the north, which tends to be cooked in oil.

Principles of Flavor

What makes Indian cuisine stand apart from all others is the expertise with which aromatics—that is herbs, spices, and seasonings like garlic and onions—are prepared and combined. Indian cooks know that the properties of each one change depending on how it is handled (for example, whether a spice is used whole or ground; sautéed in butter or oil; roasted whole, then crushed; roasted whole, then soaked in warm milk; or added at the beginning or the end of the recipe). It is a science that has been developed over centuries, one that takes into consideration not only taste but aroma; color; preservative properties; thickening, tenderizing, and souring capabilities; and even medicinal attributes. It is through the use of aromatics that an Indian cook demonstrates skill, creativity, and individuality.

Following are some of the most common aromatics used in Indian cooking:

Dry Spices: bay leaves, black mustard seeds, black peppercorns, cardamom, cayenne pepper, cinnamon, cloves, coriander, cumin, nutmeg, red chilies, turmeric

Fresh Seasonings: basil, cilantro (also known as coriander), garlic, ginger, green chilies, kari leaves, mint, onion, scallion, and shallot

---

JUDGING THE SPICING OF INDIAN FOOD

- Spices should blend into the sauce and meat.

- Spices should not stand out as separate ingredients.

- Spices should never taste raw or, as an Indian would say, "catch the throat."

- Spices should never be so strong that they overpower the essential character of the dish.

Foreign Influence

The history of India is full of periods of rule by outside forces and each one left its mark on the country's cuisine. For example, the Moghuls brought meat and rice dishes from Persia in the 16th century. (From the nearby Middle East, India also inherited the fried triangular pastries called *samosas* as well as *kababs*.) The Portuguese, who ruled the southern state of Goa during the 16th century, introduced the chili pepper, and the British, who ruled throughout the 18th and 19th centuries, spurred on the development of soups and sweet chutneys.

Ordering

A complete non-vegetarian Indian meal should include a meat dish, vegetable dish, bread and/or rice, lentils *(dal)*, yogurt dish *(raita)*, chutney and/or pickles. To compose a vegetarian meal, replace the meat with additional vegetables and lentils. Some Indian restaurants automatically assemble a complete meal to accompany each entrée. Others require that diners order each component separately. In India meals are served family-style, with each person helping him- or herself from communal bowls. In Indian restaurants in the U.S. this is rarely the case unless diners make a specific request to be served this way. When choosing individual components of a meal, try to balance taste and texture. For example, if the meat has a lot of sauce, pick a vegetable that doesn't have a sauce. If the vegetable is soft, like spinach, choose a crunchy chutney. If a curry is very spicy, be sure to order a refreshing *raita* to cool off your palate.

Service and Dining

Often in India and sometimes in Indian restaurants in the U.S., the components of a meal are served together on a *thali*, a circular metal tray. The bread or rice is usually placed in the center and all the other foods, typically curries, are served in small bowls, called *katoris*, around the perimeter. Each diner may get his or her own *thali* and eat directly from it, pouring or spooning the food from the bowls onto the rice or eating directly from the bowls. Or, the food for a group may be brought out together on one *thali*, in which case diners transfer portions of food from the *thali* to their own plates.

Condiments

In India most meals include at least one chutney and/or pickle. Some restaurants in the U.S. automatically include them with each meal while others require that you order them specifically (they are well worth the extra expense as they add another dimension to the eating experience). Eat them separately or mix them into your main dish,

 CHUTNEYS
In India at least one fresh or cooked chutney (or relish) accompanies most meals. Cooked chutneys, such as mango or lemon, are made ahead of time (if they are pre- served, they can be made months in advance). Fresh chutneys are made daily with fresh vegetables, fruits, and herbs: for example, mango and green chili, tamarind, coriander, or mint. Chutneys can be liquid or jam-like and range from mildly nippy or sweet to fiery hot. They are served either on the edge of the plate or in separate, small dishes.

according to your own taste. If you have been given an indi- vidual portion of a condiment, it is acceptable to dip the spoon with which you are eating or a piece of bread, *samosa*, or other "finger" food directly into the condiment bowl; if you are sharing condiments with a group, using a serving spoon, transfer a portion onto your own plate before eating it straight or dipping food into it.

Garnishes

Some Indian pilafs and desserts are garnished with decora- tive flecks or ultra-thin sheets of a silver foil called *varak*. It is odorless, tasteless, and edible. Pilafs may also be served with whole spices—for example, cloves, bay leaves, kari leaves (which look like small bay leaves and have a strong,

PICKLES
Though many different kinds of pickle are enjoyed in India, including lemon, green mango, carrot, gooseberry, hot chili, and turnip, the most popular and the most commonly available pickles in Indian restaurants in the U.S. are chopped lemon and mango pickles that have been marinated in oil and spices. Depending on the cook, Indian pickles can range from salty to fiery hot to sour and hot to sweet and hot.

sweet aroma and a somewhat bitter taste), or cardamom pods. These whole spices are meant to enhance the appearance of the dish but are not meant to be eaten. Most other Indian garnishes and flavorings are edible.

Rice and Bread

Rice and/or bread are eaten with every Indian meal. In the South, where more liquid dishes are prepared, rice is more common because it is needed to soak up the sauce. In the North, where many dishes are prepared without sauces, bread is eaten more often. (Not surprisingly, rice is cultivated in the South and wheat is grown in the North.) It is not uncommon to eat both bread and rice with the same meal; although, if both were served, an Indian would always eat the bread first.

Often in Indian restaurants in North America rice is included in the price of the entrée but bread is not. Always inquire because an Indian meal is not complete without at least one or the other. Brown rice, which is most commonly eaten in the poorer rural areas of India (because it is less expensive), is hard to come by in Indian restaurants in North America.

Indian lore tells us that grains of rice should be like two brothers: close but not stuck together.

AN INDIAN DIGESTIVE
Many Indian restaurants set a bowl of fennel seeds, which boast a licorice-like flavor, and sometimes cardamom seeds (which have a warm flavor with a hint of eucalyptus) on a table by the door. Before leaving, take a few (using the spoon provided), as they are said to aid digestion and refresh the palate.

Utensils

Although most—if not all—Indian restaurants will automatically give you utensils with which to eat, it is perfectly
acceptable to eat in the traditional Indian fashion, with
your hands. Though in the past it was only acceptable to
pick up food from a plate with one's right hand, modern
Indians accept that some people are naturally left-handed.

TIPS FOR EATING WITH YOUR HANDS

• To eat with your hands, you must have either rice or
bread with your meal. Most Indian restaurants will serve
one or the other automatically.

• Eat with one hand only.

• Use serving utensils to transfer food from a communal
plate to your individual plate, holding the serving utensils
with a clean hand.

• Place foods next to each other on the plate; only very wet
dishes should be spooned on top of rice and then not on all
the rice because you will need rice for picking up other
foods. If a very wet dish is going to be eaten with bread (not
rice), it will be served in its own individual bowl.

• When eating food with rice, using the fingers of one
hand, gather rice and whatever other food you would like
to eat into a neat bundle, then raise your hand to your
mouth (palm facing you) and use your thumb to push the
food into your mouth.

• When eating food with bread, break off a piece of bread
and use it as a scoop with which to carry food to your
mouth.

• Try not to dirty your fingers beyond the second knuckle (counting from the fingertips).

• Do not gesture with your dirty fingers.

Signature Dishes

Curries; Tandoori Chicken (barbecued chicken); assorted breads

Common Misconceptions

Curry is a powdered spice. Neither a powdered spice nor a specific dish, the word "curry" (a Western invention) simply implies a dish made with a richly spiced sauce or gravy, one that can be thick, thin, or anywhere in between and can be part of a meat or vegetable preparation. Many a diverse dish within the Indian repertoire—nearly any one that includes a seasoned sauce—can be called a curry.

All dishes labeled "curry" taste the same. In India no cook worth his or her salt would consider using the same combination of spices when making curries with different ingredients. The flavoring in a meat curry would never be the same as in a chicken curry nor the flavoring in a vegetable curry similar to that of a seafood curry. One way to judge the authenticity of the cooking in an Indian restaurant in the West is by sampling several different curries and comparing their flavors. If each one does not stand on its own, try another restaurant the next time you dine Indian.

Indian MENU

SHURUAAT (APPETIZERS) Appetizers
are not part of the traditional Indian meal, though they
have become more popular in recent years as a result
of Western influence. The items listed as appetizers
on many Indian menus are actually the foods that
in India would be eaten as mid-morning snacks or
with tea at five in the afternoon. Very often one
serving of an appetizer in an Indian restaurant is
enough to serve two people.

Papadum
Lentil wafers

Papadums, *also known as*
papads, *are crisp, crunchy
wafers, usually made with finely
ground lentils. They come flavored in various ways, such as
with peppercorns, garlic, or
cumin seeds. In India they are
often served as a snack with tea
as well as with the main meals
of the day. They are not meant
to be used to scoop up food (as are
the soft breads, such as* chapati
or poori), *but are eaten on their
own like chips.*

Meat or Vegetable Samosas
Deep-fried triangular turnovers

*These savory pastries, accom-
panied by a chutney, are common
street food throughout India.
They are often very spicy.*

Aloo Chat
Cold potato appetizer

Chat *is an Indian salad often
made with seasoned potatoes
and/or chick-peas plus tomatoes
or cucumber and onion. It can
also be made with chicken,
seafood, and fruits. Its main*

*flavoring can come from mint or
spices, such as cumin, pepper,
asafetida (the product of a fen-
nel-like plant that grows in the
Middle East and north India;
used for its onion-like aroma and
as an enhancer to other tastes),
and black salt (which has a tangy
taste and a smokey aroma). It is
often topped with a sweet
tamarind chutney and accompanied by yogurt.* Chat *should be
served cool but not chilled.*

Vegetable Pakoras
Deep-fried diced vegetables, usually coated in batter

The batter for pakoras, *also
known as* bhajias, *is made with
chick-pea flour or a combination
of chick-pea and rice flours.*
Pakoras *are commonly served
with a spicy chutney, such as one
made with green chilies. The
most common vegetables used for
pakoras are potato, onion, cauliflower, cabbage, and whole
chilies.* Pakoras *can also be made
with cheese, chicken, or fish,
though this is more common in
America than in India.*

Sadha Dosa

Large, thin southern Indian rice and lentil pancake

The sadha dosa *is the same as the* masala dosa *but without a filling. Also available is the* sadha paper dosa, *which is a very thin, nearly transparent, version of the* sadha dosa.

Chana Bhaji

Chick-peas dry-cooked with spices and herbs

Masala Dosa

Large, thin southern Indian rice and lentil pancake wrapped around a potato, onion, and nut filling

DOSAS ARE USUALLY served with a coconut chutney. To eat, break off a piece of the *dosa* and dip it in the condiment.

SHORBA (SOUPS) Soups are not part of a traditional Indian meal. Indian cooks created them during British occupation to accommodate the palates of their rulers.

Mulligatawny Soup

Spicy soup made with lentils, tomatoes, and spices

The word mulligatawny *is derived from* molagu *(pepper) and* tunni *(water), and the humble pepper water once provided sustenance for many an Indian. Over time, however, creative cooks began adding different ingredients, and what developed were innumerable varieties of this now famous soup. Most Indian restaurants in America make their mulligatawny with lentils, chicken, tomatoes, and spices in a meat-stock base, but don't be surprised if every now and then you come across a restaurant that serves a* mulligatawny *made in another fashion, such as with pieces of meat, in* dal *or rice water or a vegetable broth instead of meat broth, or without lentils and with such thickening agents as coconut milk or yogurt.*

Nariyali Soup

Creamy shredded coconut soup with yogurt, almonds, and pistachios

Subzi Ka Shorba

Mixed vegetable soup mildly flavored with herbs and spices

ROTIS (BREADS)
Bread is one benchmark by which to judge an Indian restaurant. Indian breads should always be light and fluffy, and all of them, except for *naan*, should be very thin. Most are cooked to order.

Note that Indian restaurants often use confusingly similar terms to describe different kinds of bread. There are no definitive recipes, so what follows can only serve as a guide. To be sure about what you are ordering, ask your waiter such questions as whether the bread is made with white or whole-wheat flour, if it is cooked on a griddle or in a tandoor oven, and if it is cooked with a fat, such as oil or butter.

Naan
Slightly leavened white-flour bread baked in a tandoor oven without fat or oil; served with or without butter

At about ¹/₂ to ³/₄ inch thick, naan are significantly thicker—and, therefore, heavier—than the other unleavened breads. Some chefs add yogurt to the dough.

Peshawari Naan
Lightly leavened white-flour bread stuffed with potatoes, nuts, and spices, and baked in a tandoor oven

Chicken Naan
Lightly leavened white flour bread stuffed with chicken and herbs and baked in a tandoor oven

Keema Naan
Lightly leavened white-flour bread stuffed with spices and minced lamb and baked in a tandoor oven

The word keema *means ground meat.* Keema *is also the term used for any dish made with ground meat.*

Onion Kulcha
Unleavened white bread stuffed with onions, flavored with cumin seeds, and baked in a tandoor oven

BAKING BREAD IN A TANDOOR OVEN
It takes skill and practice to bake bread in a tandoor oven (see page 150). The flat, round piece of dough is set on a piece of cloth, dampened, and then smacked onto the oven wall. After about one minute, the slightly blistered bread, infused with a mild smokey flavor, is speared and removed with a long skewer designed especially for this task.

"STUFFED" INDIAN BREADS

Although stuffed is the word often used in descriptions of Indian breads that include such ingredients as potatoes and meat, these breads are not stuffed in the way an American diner might expect. Rather, the layer of "stuffing" is chopped or mashed quite fine, then rolled in between two layers of raw dough so that all three layers are integrated. The result is still a thin piece of bread. These "stuffed" breads are considered side dishes; they are not meant to be used as scoops for eating other foods. (The exception to this rule are *kulcha*, which are sometimes used for scooping.) In a well-prepared stuffed bread the flavor of the stuffing, not the bread, predominates.

Poori
Puffy whole-wheat bread deep-fried in oil

Chapati or Roti
Light, soft, thin, unleavened whole-wheat bread cooked on a griddle *(chapati)* or in a tandoor oven *(roti)* without fat or oil; served with or without butter

The skill of the cook is revealed in the roundness and thinness of his or her chapati *and* roti. *These breads may also be listed on a menu as* rotli *or* phulka.

Paratha
Multi-layered whole-wheat bread, cooked with butter on a griddle

Keema Paratha
Paratha stuffed with chopped meat and peas

Aloo Paratha
Paratha stuffed with mashed and spiced potatoes

Among the standard flavorings used to make stuffings for parathas *are onions, jalapeño peppers, ginger, and cilantro.*

Mughali Paratha
Paratha stuffed with chopped meat, peas, eggs, onion, and green bell pepper

GHOSH, MURGHI, aur SAMUNDER SE (MEAT, POULTRY, and SEAFOOD DISHES)

Fish Masala
Fish cooked in a hot and spicy sauce

Do-Piaz Curry
Choice of lamb, chicken, or ground meat cooked with onions and tomatoes in a spice-flavored sauce

Shaag Curry
Choice of lamb, beef, chicken, or ground meat cooked with spinach and potatoes in a spice-flavored sauce

Dansak Curry
Choice of lamb, beef, chicken, or ground meat, cooked with lentils and hot spices

This thick, filling, porridge-like dish, is one of the most famous of all Parsi dishes. (The Parsis fled from Persia 1,200 years ago because of religious persecution and settled in India in the state of Gujarat and in Bombay.) This dish is traditionally made with lamb and three kinds of lentils. Though it appears among the curry offerings on many Indian menus in the West, it is considered a dal *not a curry in India because it boasts an abundance of lentils and almost no gravy.*

Shrimp, Crabmeat, or Lobster Curry
Shrimp, crabmeat, or lobster cooked in a spice-flavored sauce

Vindaloo Curry
Choice of spicy vinegar-marinated lamb, beef, or chicken cooked in a very hot and spicy curry sauce

The vindaloos, *which originated in the state of Goa on the southwestern coast of India, are the hottest of the curry dishes. They are almost always made with red chilies. The marinated meat in a* vindaloo *lends a subtle, sour flavor to the finished dish.*

Mutter or Chana Curry
Choice of lamb, beef, chicken, or ground meat cooked with green peas (*mutter*) or chick-peas (*chana*) in a spice-flavored sauce

Rogan Josh
Lamb cooked in a rich, creamy yogurt sauce with almonds and spices

Dishes like rogan josh *that include creamy sauces are often accompanied by* pullaus, *or pilafs.*

CHAVAL (RICE DISHES)

Most good Indian restaurants serve Basmati rice, the fragrant, long-grained rice that is cultivated in the foothills of the Himalayas. It is creamy white to pale yellow in color and slightly sweet and nutty in flavor.

Peas Pullao
Basmati rice cooked with mild spices and peas

A pullao, *or pilaf, is a dry rice dish (made without any kind of curry, or gravy). It is much subtler in taste than a* biryani *and is made by mixing together the ingredients rather than layering them. A* pullao *is usually made with peas and served as a side dish in Indian restaurants in North America, although it can be made with all sorts of other ingredients in addition to the rice—for example, fruits and nuts, chicken, or beef.*

Shahjahani (Chicken) Biryani
Long-grained rice flavored with saffron and layered with a mixture of boneless chicken, nuts, and spices

Shahjahan was the Moghul emperor responsible for the building of the Taj Mahal. When an Indian dish is given a name derived from his name, it is an indication that the dish is prepared in north Indian style.

Lamb, Beef, or Vegetable Biryani
Long-grained rice flavored with saffron and layered with a mixture of lamb, beef, or vegetables, nuts, and spices

A biryani *is a layered casserole that originated in north India. The rice is partially cooked, layered with a rich curry made with meat and/or vegetables, and then cooked again until all of the flavors are intermingled. A vegetable* biryani *is likely to include potatoes, peas, cauliflower, and carrots.*

SABZI (VEGETARIAN DISHES)

Given that over half the population of India abstains from eating at least some meat due to religious beliefs (for example, Hindus and Sikhs refrain from eating beef; Muslims do not eat pork; and Jains do not eat red meat, poultry, fish, shellfish, or eggs, and their products) or, in some cases, poverty, it is not surprising that the vegetarian cuisine of India is vast and diverse. Unfortunately, however, the vegetarian dishes served in Indian restaurants in the West are not usually among the best prepared. When judging a vegetable dish remember that the vegetables should be cooked through but not mushy and definitely not watery, and the flavor of both the vegetables and the sauce (if there is one) should be distinct. If you find a restaurant that excels in this area, tell your friends about it.

Aloo Bainghan
Eggplant and potatoes cooked with spices and cilantro

Aloo Palak
Potatoes and spinach cooked with tomatoes and ginger in a tomato sauce

Aloo Gobbi Masala
Cauliflower and potatoes cooked with freshly ground spices

Aloo Mutter
Peas and potatoes cooked in a delicately spiced creamy, often buttery sauce, or in a tomato sauce

Paneer
Cubes of **paneer** cooked with fresh spinach and spices

This dish may be listed on a menu as sag paneer *or* palak paneer. Sag *means leafy greens;* palak *means spinach.*

Paneer Makhanee
Chunks of **paneer** flavored with fresh tomatoes and spices in a creamy, often buttery sauce

INGREDIENT NOTES

• **Paneer** is similar to cottage cheese but has more body. Indians make it at home by adding a sour substance, such as lemon juice, to boiling milk, then pouring off the watery whey to yield a soft, crumbly cheese reminiscent of bean curd (called *chenna*). Next the curds are compressed into a cake and cut into small cubes called *paneer*.

MASALA DEFINED

A *masala* is a blend of aromatic spices. Though a *masala* can include a wide range of spices, the most classic *masala*, a north Indian blend called *garam masala*, usually counts cardamom, cinnamon, cloves, peppercorns, nutmeg, cumin, and coriander among its ingredients. The south Indian equivalent to *garam masala* is *sambaar podi*, which is likely to include turmeric, coriander, red and black pepper, fenugreek, cumin, and several kinds of legumes (such as yellow mung beans and yellow split peas). Very often foods served in Indian restaurants are given names that include the word *masala*, which tells the diner that the dish is seasoned with aromatic spices, nothing more. Since Indian cooks pride themselves on their secret recipes for *masalas*, dishes with the same name can vary widely from restaurant to restaurant—or from Indian home to Indian home.

Matar Paneer
Cubes of **paneer** cooked with green peas and mild spices

This popular vegetarian dish is sometimes prepared in a tomato sauce.

Malai Kofta
Soft cheese and vegetable croquettes simmered in a creamy sauce

A dish with the word kofta *in its name is made by combining finely ground meat or vegetables with onion and spices, shaping the mixture into balls, broiling or frying the balls, then simmering them in a sauce (usually a spicy one) to imbue them with additional flavor.*

Vegetable Jalfrazi
Fresh vegetables cooked with onion, peppers, and tomatoes in a spicy sauce

Chana Masala
Chick-peas and potatoes cooked with onions, tomatoes, and spices

Bhindi Masala
Okra cooked with tomatoes, onions, and spices
Assorted vegetables and home-made cheese in a creamy sauce

You will find the word korma *throughout Indian menus. It refers to meat, vegetables, or cheese braised in a mildly flavored marinade (which usually includes yogurt, cream, or nut butter); the marinade becomes a velvety sauce and is served with the* korma. *Some cooks add poppy seeds or dried coconut to the sauce in order to thicken it.*

TANDOORI DISHES (CLAY OVEN DISHES)

Boti Kabab

Cubes of lamb marinated in yogurt and mild spices and cooked on a skewer in a tandoor oven

Boti kababs *are often sold during the winter at roadside stands in the north of India.*

Tandoori Chicken

Whole or half chicken marinated in yogurt and mild spices and cooked on a skewer in a tandoor oven

Tandoori chicken is the most popular tandoor-style dish. It is properly made with two marinades: salt and lime juice, then yogurt, onion, garlic, ginger, green chilies, and a garam masala *(a spice mixture that may contain cardamom seeds, cinnamon, nutmeg, cloves, peppercorns, and black cumin seeds). The two marinations are often combined in one step in restaurant kitchens.*

Murgh Tikka

Boneless pieces of chicken marinated in yogurt and mild spices and cooked on a skewer in a tandoor oven

The word tikka *means cutlet in Hindi.*

Seekh Kabab

Minced lamb combined with onions, herbs, and mild spices, and cooked on a skewer in a tandoor oven

A kabab *can be made with chunks of marinated meat threaded on a skewer or with ground meat (sometimes combined with lentils, nuts, or dried fruit) shaped into sausages, patties, or croquettes.*

IN INDIA, tandoori dishes are always served with a raw onion relish and fresh lime. The onion relish made with red chili oil that is sometimes served in the U.S. is a purely American phenomenon of obscure origin.

THE TANDOOR OVEN

A tandoor is a large earthenware pot, about three feet deep and half as wide, in which meat is cooked over charcoal on long vertical skewers, and bread is cooked stuck to the sides. The pot, which is believed to have originated in the northeastern part of Persia (today Iran), is traditionally buried in the ground, though today more portable above-ground tandoors are popular. Meat cooked by the slow, steady heat of a tandoor is moist and tender and imbued with the earthy aroma of the oven.

The most distinguishing feature of tandoor-style dishes is their red-gold color. Originally achieved through the use of saffron, today economical cooks use food coloring.

SATH MAIU (SIDE DISHES)

Chana or Massor Dal
Split legumes cooked in water with seasonings

Aloo Mint Raita
Yogurt, sour cream, mint, and potato

Plain Raita
Yogurt, sour cream, and chopped cucumber

DALS

Dal is the Hindi word for legumes (beans, peas, or lentils) and is also the word used to refer to seasoned, hulled (or skinned) and split legumes that are cooked in water. In India *dals* are served with nearly every meal, but, unfortunately, this side dish is barely represented in U.S. restaurants. While there are many different kinds of beans, peas, and lentils that can be used to make *dal*, Indian restaurants don't usually specify which they use on their menus nor do they give much indication as to how the *dal* is prepared. An informed diner might ask the following questions:

What kind of legume is used to make the *dal*?
The most common answer will be *chana dal* (yellow split peas) or *masoor dal* (orange lentils).

Raitas *are cooling, yogurt-based side dishes commonly served with Indian meals. Among the ingredients that can be included in a* raita, *aside from yogurt, are raw or cooked vegetables, fruits, nuts, and seasonings, such as cilantro, mint, or chilies. Most* raitas *are also flavored with* rai *(mustard seeds). Since yogurt in India is traditionally made with buffalo's milk, which is richer than cow's milk, sour cream is often added to the yogurt used for* raitas *in the U.S.*

Is the *dal* wet or dry?
Dal can be creamy and soup-like (considered wet), if the legume with which it is made is allowed to fall apart while cooking, or dry and somewhat lumpy. Wet *dals*, the more common of the two in American restaurants, are usually eaten with rice (pour a little bit of dal over the rice and mix together), whereas dry *dals* are eaten with either bread (use the bread as a scoop) or rice. Of course, *dal* can also be eaten on its own, if desired.

Is the *dal* spicy or mild?
Most often *dals* are mild because they are meant to counteract the spiciness of meat and vegetable dishes.

MITHAI (DESSERTS)

In India a meal most commonly ends with fresh fruit or sweetened yogurt rather than the richer desserts presented at Indian restaurants in the U.S. Sweets, such as ice creams or rice puddings, are reserved for weddings or other special occasions, when the dessert is traditionally served at the same time as the main meal.

Mango Ice Cream

Ice cream made with mangoes; often flavored with nuts and **rosewater**

Rasmalai

Cottage cheese-like dumplings in thickened milk flavored with such ingredients as sugar and cardamom; served with pistachio nuts

Barfi

Fudge-like confection flavored with such ingredients as coconut, almonds, pistachios, cocoa, or **rosewater**

Gulab Jamun

Deep-fried cake-like milk balls flavored with **rosewater** and soaked in syrup

Kulfi

Indian ice cream

Indian ice cream, which is much thicker than American ice cream, is made by boiling milk until only a third of it remains, flavoring the boiled-down liquid with such ingredients as saffron, cardamom, almonds, pistachios, dried fruit, or rose essence, and freezing the mixture, often in conical containers designed specifically for this purpose. Before ordering kulfi *at a restaurant, ask if it is home-made; some of the mass-produced* kulfi *available in this country is less than wonderful.*

Kheer

Rice pudding studded with raisins and nuts, such as almonds or pistachios, and lightly flavored with **rosewater** and cardamom

---

INGREDIENT NOTES

• **Rosewater** is a mixture of water and rose essence, which is extracted from small, fragrant red roses that are grown in India specifically for this purpose. For good luck rosewater is often sprinkled on guests at weddings and other religious gatherings in India.

THANDA-GARAM (BEVERAGES) Most

Indians drink ice-cold water, unsweetened lemon water (water into which fresh lemon juice has been squeezed), or *jeera* water (water that has been flavored with cumin seeds) after they have finished their meal; during the meal, they may drink water or *lassi*—or refrain from drinking at all.

Aam Lassi
Cold yogurt drink made with mango purée

Sag Lassi
Cold yogurt drink, available plain, salty, or sweet

Lassi *is the milk shake of India. Plain or salty* lassi *is usually made with yogurt, ice water, a pinch of cumin, and salt, if desired. For sweet* lassi, *the cumin and salt are omitted and sugar and rosewater are added.*

Chas
Cold yogurt drink with fresh ginger juice and mint

Madras Coffee
Freshly brewed coffee with milk

This south Indian-style coffee is made by brewing coffee, then combining it with sweetened boiling milk and shaking to create a froth on top. South Indian coffee is usually about one-third milk. In the north of India, coffee is commonly drunk in the morning only. In the south of India, where a large percentage of the world's coffee beans are harvested, coffee is consumed with passion throughout the day.

Chai (Indian Tea)
Darjeeling and Assam, both strong in flavor, are two of the most commonly served Indian teas. Traditionally, Indian tea is made by steeping tea leaves in a combination of hot water and milk; it is often sweetened before it is brought to the table. Unsweetened tea, served with milk and sugar on the side, is known as English tea or tray tea. If the menu says "chai," the restaurant probably prepares tea the Indian way. Ask your waiter to be sure.

Masala Chai
Indian tea flavored with spices

Indians drink a lot of masala chai *during the warm summer months when the spices with which it is flavored induce perspiration and help them to cool off.*

Indian Beer
Kingfisher (finely carbonated, creamy, hoppy, bitter lager), or Taj Mahal (malty, sweet, floral, European-style pilsner lager)

Indians who do not abstain from consuming alcohol because of religious restrictions tend to drink beer with snacks before a meal during the summer. They do not drink it with their meals.

ITALIAN
cuisine

★

Cheers–*Cin cin* (cheen-**cheen**) or *Salute* (sah **loo**-tay)
Bon appétit–*Buon Appetito* (bwon a-pa-**tee**-to)
Thank you–*Grazie* (**grat**-zee-eh)

THE INHABITANTS OF THE ITALIAN PENINSULA elevated dining to an art in the banquet halls of Rome more than 2,000 years ago, and from this tradition has evolved an elegant, straightforward cuisine treasured throughout the world for its use of fresh ingredients and its wonderful bounty of flavors. For generations of Americans, a pizza or a bowl of macaroni and cheese has represented the first foray into Italian cooking, or any foreign cuisine for that matter. Even this rudimentary introduction has often led to an unwavering affection for Italian food. The Italian love of a good meal is contagious, and the cuisine, in all its variety and richness, invites a lifetime of exploration.

Principles of Flavor

Italian cooking is flavored with capers, eggplant, olives, rosemary, parsley, sage, and other ingredients that thrive in the Mediterranean sun. Olive oil is key to Italian cooking. It is the base of many sauces, is often used instead of butter for cooking, and is drizzled over greens and vegetables as a simple, flavorful dressing. Tomatoes are the base for hundreds of pasta sauces. Garlic is ubiquitous, flavoring sauces, soups, and meat dishes. Basil is the national herb of Italy, making its most dramatic appearance on American menus in pesto sauce; in the summer months when basil is fresh, it is an earthy addition to salads.

ITALIAN REGIONAL CUISINE

Traditionally there are a great many regional differences as well as differences between the cuisines of northern and southern Italy; for example, the more prosperous north uses cream and butter instead of olive oil and favors beef over pork. Few Italian restaurants specialize in the cuisine of one region, however, and even though many Italian restaurants in the U.S. bill themselves as "northern Italian" (perhaps to distinguish themselves as more elegant than the spaghetti and meatball joints down the street), you are likely to encounter dishes from many regions on a menu. Following are the regions most commonly represented:

Lombardy: Beef, veal, and risottos dominate the cuisine of this prosperous northern region.

Piedmont: Steaming bowls of polenta, local cheeses, such as Fonduta, and rich red Barolo wines are trademarks of this region in the foothills of the Alps.

Liguria: Lemons, oranges, olives, and green vegetables flourish in the mild climate of Italy's northernmost area on the Mediterranean coast, best known gastronomically for its pesto (basil) sauces.

Veneto: Game birds, Adriatic creatures like inkfish, octopus, and their kin, and calf's liver are typical of Venice and the rich lands that sweep westward from the Adriatic.

Emilia-Romagna: The bounty of this vast stretch of north-central Italy includes pasta dishes, such as lasagne and tortellini, Parmesan cheese, balsamic vinegar, and prosciutto.

Tuscany: Beef cattle graze in the valleys, while vineyards (especially those yielding rich Chianti) and olive groves flourish on the hillsides of central Italy.

Rome: Italy's capital, in the Lazio region, has taken food from all over the country to create a cosmopolitan cuisine that ranges from *porchetta* (spit-roasted suckling pig) to spaghetti *alla carbonara*, with an earthy sauce of cream, eggs, cheese, and bacon. Food prepared *alla romana* is often stuffed or cooked with mozzarella cheese and tomatoes.

Naples and the Campania: The tomato reigns in this southern region, appearing in spicy sauces and pizza.

Sicily: Seafood, most notably swordfish, abounds in the waters surrounding this southern island where chefs also specialize in sweet desserts, including *tiramisù* (see page 181) and other pastries.

Foreign Influence

Italy has been the crossroads of Western civilization for thousands of years, and little wonder that it has adapted ingredients from all over the world. The ancient Greek settlers brought such diverse foods as capers and carrots with them from Asia Minor and planted wheat in Sicily that later provided the Roman Empire with bread and pasta. Olives probably originated in the eastern Mediterranean and made their way to Italy by the 6th century B.C.

The biggest foreign influx came in the 16th century, when explorers returned from the New World with many ingredients that we now consider Italian staples, including corn, bell and hot peppers, beans, even tomatoes.

Ordering

A traditional Italian meal consists of a series of small courses. It begins with soup, pasta, or risotto and is followed by a fish or meat course, often accompanied by vegetables, and a palate-cleansing salad course. Italians often forgo a sweet dessert in favor of fruit or cheese, accompanied by bread, or simply coffee. The appetizer course is traditionally served only on special occasions. While many Italian restaurants in the U.S. serve courses in this traditional manner, in others an appetizer or salad will be followed by one main course, either a pasta dish or meat or fish. In Italy pizza is reserved for casual meals or snacks, though in the U.S. it appears on many menus as an appetizer and/or a main course.

When ordering, make sure that each course complements the next and that flavors do not conflict or overwhelm each other. For example, pasta with a rich, meaty sauce is better followed by fish or chicken than by a heavy meat dish.

Service and Dining

Informal, attentive, and friendly—these are the hallmarks of service in Italy, and you should expect the same from an Italian restaurant here. Unless the meal is being served family-style, courses should come out of the kitchen one at a time, with enough time in between for digestion and conversation, all the while sipping a glass or two of wine.

Condiments

Well-prepared Italian food requires few or no condiments. A waitperson should offer to grate fresh Parmesan or grind fresh black pepper over the appropriate dishes. Oil and vinegar, with a dash of salt, is the tried and true Italian way to dress a salad.

Often you'll find a bowl of olive oil on the table. It should be extra-virgin or virgin, and the idea is to dip your bread, a small chunk at a time, into the oil, maybe adding a dash of salt or sprinkle of vinegar.

Garnishes

Many regions of Italy have been impoverished for centuries and, therefore, anything that shows up on a plate is meant to be eaten. A sprig of rosemary or parsley is there to impart flavor, not beauty.

Bread

Bread is ever-present on the Italian table, often from the moment diners sit down until the last bit of sauce or dressing has been wiped from their plates. In Italy bread is traditionally eaten without butter, though some Italian restaurants in the U.S. provide a few pats for their American clientele.

There are hundreds of varieties of Italian bread and just as many variations on what might turn up in your bread basket at an Italian restaurant—everything from a round crusty loaf that in the U.S. is often called peasant bread, to garlic bread, to a thick, doughy baguette, to raisin rolls, to long, thin bread sticks called *grissini*.

Utensils

A knife, fork, and spoon are used, of course, though some basic Italian etiquette dictating how best to use these tools comes into play when the pasta arrives. It is de rigueur to twist several noodles around the tines of your fork, pressing the tines into the plate or even your spoon for leverage. If this is too difficult, go ahead and cut the pasta into bite-size pieces. Informal as Italian dining is, though, it is not acceptable to bend over your plate and simply inhale the pasta with each intake of breath.

It is quite acceptable to eat pizza and focaccia, which is often cut into squares or wedges, with your hands, and to use bread to sop up sauces and salad dressings.

ITALIAN

Signature Dishes

A*ntipasto* (assorted appetizers that might include fresh
grilled vegetables, salami, mozzarella, and squid);
Insalata Caprese (mozzarella with basil and tomatoes);
Minestrone (vegetable soup); *Fettuccine alla Panna* (fettuccine
with cream, butter, and nutmeg; also known as fettuccine
Alfredo); *Spaghetti alla Carbonara* (spaghetti with cream,
cheese, and bacon); *Frito Misto di Mare* (assorted fried fish,
often including squid); *Ossobuco* (braised veal shank);
Saltimbocca (thinly sliced veal wrapped in a wafer-thin layer
of ham and sautéed in butter); *Vitello* or *Pollo Piccata al
Marsala* (veal or chicken pounded thin and fried in butter
with Marsala wine); *Biscotti* (twice-baked cookies, usually
dipped in *vin santo*)

Common Misconceptions

Italian food is heavy. Well-made Italian food is light and
easily digestible, despite the myth that it is heavy and heavily
studded with garlic and onions. In a good restaurant, even a
rich tomato or cream sauce is used sparingly and deftly, and
garlic and onions are essential though unobtrusive ingredients.

Italians stole pasta from the Chinese. Marco Polo did dine
on some form of Chinese pasta at the court of Kubla Kahn
during his 13th-century travels to the Orient and he did,
indeed, bring dried pasta back with him, but this was a bit like
bringing coals to Newcastle. Etruscans were dining on pasta
even before the Romans inhabited the Italian peninsula.

Italian MENU

ANTIPASTI (APPETIZERS)

An appetizer course is not an essential component of an Italian meal, and many Italians will order appetizers only on special occasions. On the other hand, an order of several appetizers can serve as a satisfying lunch or light supper.

Bruschetta
Slices of bread grilled or run under a broiler, then rubbed with garlic and topped with a drizzle of **olive oil**

Crostini
Slices of toasted bread lightly buttered and topped with any of a wide variety of ingredients, often anchovies, liver spread, or tomato paste

Mozzarella in carrozza
Mozzarella sandwiched between two slices of bread, dipped in a mixture of flour and egg, then deep-fried

The literal translation of mozzarella in carrozza *is "mozzarella in a carriage."*

Coppa di gamberetti
Shrimp cocktail

Carciofini in umido
Warm artichoke hearts sautéed in tomato and garlic

Cocktail di Vongole
Clam cocktail, usually made with baby clams dressed with lemon juice and a little **olive oil**

Bresaola
Finely sliced, salt-cured, air-dried beef

This raw fillet of beef, cured in salt and air-dried for several months, is a specialty from the northern region of Lombardy. When properly prepared, it is both delicate and a bit sharp. It should be dressed at the table with a few drops of olive oil or fresh lemon juice and ground pepper.

INGREDIENT NOTES

• **Olive oil** has been a staple of the peninsula's food scene since the days of the Roman Empire. It is a key ingredient in salad dressings and sauces, and is often used instead of butter for cooking. Olives are collected by hand in the fall and crushed under millstones. The pulp is then pressed, and the resulting oil is categorized by its quality. Extra-virgin, made only from the first pressing, is the highest grade and is followed by five other categories, including virgin and pure. Extra-virgin olive oil is usually reserved for uncooked dishes because its treasured flavor and aroma break down when subjected to high heat.

• **Mozzarella**, a rich but relatively low-fat white cheese, makes frequent appearances on

Polenta con Gorgonzola
Cooked cornmeal with strips of **Gorgonzola**

Polenta, *a sort of cornmeal mush, was the basic food of the Roman legions and is still a staple in the northern Italian diet. Today it is often topped with butter or cheese and offered as an antipasto or is served as an accompaniment to a main course. Polenta is traditionally simmered in a copper pot called a* paiolo, *stirred constantly for about thirty minutes with a wooden spoon made from chestnut, and poured, piping hot, onto a white napkin spread over a wooden board for serving.*

Antipasto Misto
Mixed appetizers

You will know you are in a restaurant that takes cooking seriously if you see a tabletop laden with a good selection of these appetizers. Antipasto misto *usually includes tuna fish, beans, hard-boiled eggs, anchovy fillets, grilled red peppers, salami, prosciutto (Italian ham), seafood salad, raw anchovies, squid, and an assortment of other items, the variety of which depends only upon the imagination of the chef.*

Carpaccio
Very thinly sliced (nearly transparent) beef fillet; served raw with a dressing of **olive oil**, mustard, brandy, Tabasco, cream, and possibly tomato sauce

Now a staple on Italian menus, carpaccio only came on the food scene in 1961, created in the kitchen of Harry's Bar in Venice. It is named for the Italian Renaissance painter Vittore Carpaccio, and if you are a carpaccio purist, you will insist that the red of the beef be exactly the same hue as the reds the artist used in his palette.

menus as an antipasto and as an ingredient in other dishes. It can be made with either cow's milk or buffalo's milk, the latter being richer and highly coveted, but much harder to find and only used in its uncooked form. Good restaurants serve fresh mozzarella, which is delicate and fragrant and distinctly different than the processed version of this cheese. Some restaurants offer smoked mozzarella, which should boast a lovely golden color that resembles the hay over which it is properly smoked.

• **Gorgonzola**, considered one of the best blue cheeses in the world, is named after what was once a small village outside of Milan but is now considered an eastern suburb of that cosmopolitan city. It is rich, creamy, and piquant, its degree of piquancy dependent upon its age.

Polenta con Fungi Porcini
Cornmeal topped with **porcini** mushrooms

Spiedino
Mozzarella, roasted pepper, and **prosciutto**, skewered, then broiled and often topped with an anchovy or tomato sauce

Generally, the term spiedino *refers to any dish that is skewered when cooked, as in* spiedino di pollo *(chicken on a skewer). However, when the word appears by itself on the antipasto portion of a menu, it usually refers to a cheese preparation like this one.*

Suppli
Rice croquettes filled with mozzarella and **prosciutto** or other ingredients, such as chicken livers, wild mushrooms, and sweetbreads, then deep-fried until golden brown

Cozze
Mussels, often stuffed with bread crumbs, garlic, and tomatoes, or any variety of other ingredients

Cozze al Vino Bianco
Mussels steamed in white wine

Cozze Posillipo
Mussels in a spicy tomato sauce seasoned with garlic and parsley

Posillipo is a coastal town just above Naples.

Prosciutto e Melone
Wedges of melon, usually cantaloupe, wrapped in or topped with very thin slices of **prosciutto**

Zucchini Fritti
Zucchini cut into strips and deep-fried

Calamari Fritti
Squid, usually the tentacles, cut into rings and deep-fried

INGREDIENT NOTES

• Each spring and fall Italians head for the forested mountainsides in search of delectable wild mushrooms. Most **porcini** make the trip across the Atlantic in dried form and are then reconstituted in warm water before contributing their musky, earthy flavor to such foods as pasta sauces, stuffings, risotto, and lasagne.

• **Prosciutto** translates generally as "ham," though it is more specifically the cured, air-dried ham from one of several Italian locales that specializes in its production. Some of the most highly regarded prosciuttos are *prosciutto di Parma*, from the same city that lays claim to the famous Parmigiano-Reggiano cheese; *prosciutto di Carpegna*, named for a town in central Italy; and *prosciutto di San Daniele*, named for a town in the Friuli region of northern Italy. Wherever it originates, the pork used to make prosciutto is cut from the hind thigh of a young pig, salted for

TOMATOES

Tomatoes (*pomodori* in Italian) are the basis of a litany of Italian dishes. Interestingly, even though these "apples of gold" were among the New World crops introduced in Italy in the 16th century, they only took their prominent place in the Italian kitchen in the 18th century, when a strain was cultivated that would flourish in the Italian soil.

Plum tomatoes are commonly used in Italian sauces, and when fresh tomatoes are out of season, commercially canned Italian plum tomatoes are considered acceptable, even in the kitchens of the finest restaurants. Beefsteak tomatoes are sliced for salads. Sun-dried tomatoes (fresh tomatoes that have been dried, not necessarily in the sun, and are sometimes packed in olive oil) are increasingly popular in the U.S. and are often eaten as part of an antipasto and in pasta sauces.

Insalata Caprese
Fresh mozzarella with tomato and basil

Caprese *in a dish title indicates that the dish is a specialty of the Isle of Capri.*

Insalata del Pescatore
Seafood salad made with such ingredients as shrimp, squid, and baby octopus, dressed simply with high-quality olive oil

Vongole Oreganate
Clams topped with bread crumbs, *pancetta*, and oregano, and baked

Many different foods are baked or broiled with oregano (chicken and fish filet are most common, besides clams) and are thus called oreganato *or* oreganata.

15 to 25 days, and cured (hung to dry) for about nine months to a year.

In restaurants in the U.S., prosciutto comes to the table in a variety of dishes; for example, with melon or figs as an antipasto, wrapped around swordfish or a breast of chicken, or as a pungent ingredient in pasta sauces.

• *Pancetta*, a common ingredient in many popular pasta sauces, is the Italian equivalent of bacon. Like bacon, *pancetta* comes from the belly of the pig. Usually it is salted and spiced with pepper and other seasonings, such as cloves, nutmeg, cinnamon, or crushed juniper berries.

Panzanella

Country bread plus vegetables, such as tomatoes, cucumber, and bell pepper, tossed with a mixture of olive oil, vinegar, and such flavorings as finely chopped artichoke, capers, and garlic

Panzanella was developed by Italians as a way to put stale bread to use. The literal translation of panzanella *is "little swamp."*

Caponata

Fried eggplant mixed with onions, zucchini, celery, and black olives, often enlivened with such extras as artichokes or baby octopus; served cold, as a type of relish

Funghi Ripieni

Mushrooms stuffed with bread crumbs, **pancetta** (•165), and garlic

Carciofi alla Giudea

Fried artichokes; the tough outer leaves are removed and only the tender core (the inner leaves and heart) is fried

Bocconcini

Golf ball-size nuggets of **mozzarella** (•162) in olive oil, often sprinkled with red pepper flakes

Bocconcini is also the name of a dish made with small pieces of veal cooked in a tomato and white wine sauce.

MINESTRE e ZUPPE (SOUPS) Both

minestre and *zuppe* translate roughly as soup, though to an Italian cook they are vastly different. *Minestre* are gentle broths to which pasta, vegetables, or other ingredients are added so that each ingredient stands out; *zuppe* are thicker soups in which the ingredients blend together thoroughly. Italians do not tend to order both soup and pasta at the same meal, especially since many soups contain pasta, beans, or rice.

Minestrone

Vegetable soup

There are as many different recipes for this classic as there are cooks. Rice, pasta, dried beans, or olive oil may or may not be added, and the vegetables may either be sautéed in butter or added to the stock raw.

However, all minestroni should be simmered for at least two hours and should be accompanied by freshly grated Parmesan cheese. Vegetables in a well-made, slowly cooked minestrone retain their shape and are not mushy.

Minestre Pasta i Fagiole
Chicken or beef broth with pasta and beans

Stracciatella
Egg drop soup, in which egg and **Parmesan** are beaten together and added to a boiling chicken or beef stock

Stracciatella Romana
Stracciatella (see above) with spinach

Zuppa de Pesce
Fish soup

There are hundreds of different recipes for this soup, depending on the part of Italy where the chef comes from. Many versions are flavored with tomatoes and garlic. The trick for the chef is to let the flavor of each fish retain its character.

Ribollita
Tuscan bean soup

Made with the freshest vegetables of the season and dried beans, this soup is made in advance, then ribollita, *"reboiled," and ladled over thick slices of crusty bread. Don't complain if it comes to the table at room temperature—this is a common way to serve this thick, delicious soup. In Tuscany, where it originated,* ribollita *is never served with Parmesan cheese, though it may be elsewhere.*

Tortellini in Brodo
Tortellini in beef or chicken broth

PASTA e RISOTTO (PASTA and RISOTTO)

In Italy pasta or risotto is usually served as a first course, followed by a meat or fish course. In America, however, pasta and risotto are often offered as so-called main courses.

Contrary to the belief of some non-Italians, fresh pasta (*pasta fresca*) is not superior to dried pasta (*pasta secca*). Each has a particular texture and consistency, thereby making it suitable to different shaping and saucing. Regardless of whether a dish is made with fresh or dried pasta, however, it should be cooked "*al dente*," literally "to the tooth," that is, cooked through but still retaining a little resistance.

On some Italian menus pasta and risotto are listed under the heading *Farinacei*, which translates to grain products.

Gnocchi al Pesto
Gnocchi with **pesto** sauce

Cannelloni alla Piedmontese
Squares of pasta dough wrapped around a filling of veal, **prosciutto** (•164), and **Parmesan** (•167), covered with *balsamella* (*béchamel*, or white) sauce, and baked

Risotto di Mare
Rice with seafood

Risotto con Funghi
Rice with wild mushrooms

Cannelloni alla Napoletana
Squares of pasta dough wrapped around a filling of tomato sauce and mozzarella, covered with tomato sauce and **Parmesan** (•167), and baked

Spaghetti Puttanesca
Spaghetti with a hearty sauce featuring tomatoes, anchovies, galic, olives, and **capers**

The literal translation of puttanesca *is "in the manner of the prostitute." This hearty sauce originated in the slums of Naples but is served all over Italy.*

INGREDIENT NOTES

• The classic ingredients of the uncooked Genoese sauce called **pesto** are basil, olive oil, and grated cheese, often Parmigiano-Reggiano and Pecorino. Additional ingredients, such as pine nuts or walnuts, are dictated by local preferences.

• **Capers** are the sun-dried, cured buds of a bush that thrives in the Mediterranean region. They are a pungent addition to many Italian dishes, especially those from southern Italy.

PASTA SHAPES

Following are pasta shapes that appear often on Italian menus in the U.S.

Cannelloni: large, stuffed tubes or squares of pasta

Capellini or ***Capelli d'angelo:*** thread-like strands

Farfalle: butterfly-shaped (farfalline are a small version of farfalle)

Fettuccine: long, flat, about ⅜ inch wide, and ribbon-like (a slightly narrower and thicker version of tagliatelle)

Fusilli: spiral-shaped

Gnocchi: small dumplings made with flour or potatoes

Lasagne: long, wide, and flat rectangles

Linguine: (also known as bavette): long, flat, and about ⅛ inch wide

Maccheroni: short, hollow tubes

Orecchiette: small, ear-shaped

Orzo: rice-shaped

Pappardelle: long, flat, and about 1 inch wide

Penne: short, hollow, tubes with diagonally cut ends (pennette is the shorter, narrower version)

Perciatelli: hollow spaghetti (also known as bucatini)

Radiatori: short tubes with ridges that make them look like car radiators

Ravioli: stuffed pasta squares

Rotelle: wheels with hubs and spokes

Spaghetti: long, narrow, solid strands

Tagliatelle: long, flat, about ¼ inch wide, and ribbon-like

Tortellini: small, stuffed rings (also known as cappelletti)

Ziti: narrow, hollow tubes

Risotto alla Milanese
Rice with saffron

Risotto alla milanese, *the most typical dish of Lombardy, is the traditional accompaniment to* ossobuco *(braised veal shanks). It is the only risotto served as an accompaniment; in all other cases risotto is considered a course of its own.*

Well-made risotto is both creamy and firm. This magic is achieved by using varieties of rice that are sheathed in both a soft starch that dissolves in cooking to create a creamy texture and a harder starch that maintains its firmness when cooked, and by cooking the rice following a very specific, labor-intensive process: The rice is first sautéed in butter or butter and oil; it is then slowly simmered—while being stirred constantly—in liquid that is added gradually.

When ordering risotto, expect a longer than usual wait because of the slow cooking process. Once it arrives, do as many Italians, and spread the risotto around your plate to release some of the steam and cool it off.

Spaghetti alla Carbonara
Spaghetti with a sauce made of cream, eggs, cheese, and bacon

Carbonara *sauce, which originated in Rome, is made by tossing pasta with bacon sautéed in olive oil; then raw egg and Parmesan cheese are added.*

Spaghetti Pomodoro
Spaghetti with a simple, fresh tomato sauce

Italian sauces made with fresh tomatoes tend to be seasoned very lightly in order to allow the flavor of the tomatoes to shine.

Penne con le Sarde
Penne with sardines, **fennel**, raisins, and pine nuts

Fresh sardines are the key ingredient in this Sicilian specialty. Unlike their less tasty canned relatives, fresh sardines are firm and sweet.

Penne alla Norma
Penne with fried eggplant, tomatoes, and **ricotta** cheese

This dish originates in the Sicilian city of Catania, birthplace of the composer Vincenzo Bellini. It is named for Norma, the heroine in his most famous opera.

Spaghetti all'Amatriciana
Spaghetti with a spicy sauce that counts among its ingredients tomatoes, pork, and chili peppers

The town of Amatrice in southern Italy celebrates its namesake sauce with a fair on the first Sunday after August 15.

Penne alla Vodka
Penne with a sauce of tomatoes, vodka, and cream

Penne alla Marinara
Penne with tomatoes, garlic, and anchovies

Alla marinara *means "sailor's style" but is indicative of no particular cooking method or mixture of ingredients, at least officially, though in North America it has come to signify a light, fresh tomato sauce. It is often used with seafood dishes or may contain seafood itself (anchovies and clams are typical). Pizza alla marinara is a classic from Naples, featuring tomatoes, garlic, and anchovies.*

Penne con Tartufi
Penne tossed with olive oil and **truffle** shavings

Fettuccine alla Panna
Fettuccine with a sauce of cream, butter, and nutmeg

Linguine Pescatore
Linguine with lobster, scallops, shrimp, clams, mussels, or other seafood

Linguine Primavera
Linguine with seasonal vegetables sautéed in olive oil and garlic

Ravioli Verdi
Spinach ravioli stuffed with ricotta and spinach

Lasagne al Forno
Layers of wide pasta noodles and meat, cheese, and/or vegetable fillings, baked in an oven

• The literal translation of **ricotta** is recooked, an apt description of this soft cheese, which is produced by recooking the whey (watery residue) that remains after another cheese, such as provolone, is made.

• **Truffles**, the extremely rare, delectable, and expensive funghi that grow underground close to tree roots, are treasured by Italian chefs—and gourmets throughout the world. The shavings of a truffle can make regal repasts of such humble staples as polenta, risotto, and pasta.

Tagliatelle Bolognese

Tagliatelle in a light sauce of butter and **prosciutto** (●164)

In many restaurants in the United States, the word Bolognese *in a dish title has come to mean "meat sauce." However, in Bologna,* ragù *is the term for meat sauce.*

Tagliatelle con Salsa di Noci

Tagliatelle with walnut sauce

This sauce, which traditionally features walnuts, bread, garlic, Parmesan cheese, olive oil, and heavy cream, hails from Liguria, in northwestern Italy.

Farfallini con Salmone

Farfallini with smoked salmon and cream

Linguine con Vongole

Linguine with clams

Ravioli al Ragù

Ravioli baked with a meat sauce

A ragù *is a hearty meat sauce that is simmered for two hours or more, traditionally in an earthenware pot. The word* ragù *can also refer to fish sauces made by combining more than one species of fish and stewing them with tomatoes and wine.*

Bucatini con Melanzane e Ricotta

Bucatini with eggplant, ricotta cheese, tomato, and basil

Pappardelle al Sugo di Coniglio

Pappardelle in a rabbit sauce

Crespelle di Formaggio

Crepes stuffed with melted cheese and **prosciutto** (●164)

Italians commonly roll up their crespelle, *or* crepes, *with meat, cheese, and vegetable fillings and bake them in the oven with a sauce. In some parts of Italy* crespelle *are referred to as* cannelloni.

Tortellini alla Nonna

Tortellini with **prosciutto** (●164), peas, and cream sauce

Nonna *means "grandmother," and any dish served* alla nonna *usually includes a homey combination of cream and simple ingredients. Other terms that sometimes appear on Italian menus and connote homestyle cooking are* casalinga, *roughly translated, "in the style of the home," and* paesana, *"in the peasant way."*

PESCE e FRUTTI DI MARE
(FISH and SHELLFISH)

Pesce (fish) and *frutti di mare* (shellfish) practically leap out of the seas that surround all but the northern border of Italy and into the pans of chefs, so it is little wonder that Italian seafood dishes are so deliciously prepared. Shellfish may appear *fra diavolo* style, which means that the sauce (usually tomato) is moderately spiced.

Fritto Misto di Mare
Small whole fish, usually dredged in flour and dipped in oil; served with **lemon** wedges

Gamberi
Boiled jumbo shrimp; served with olive oil and **lemon** wedges

Pesce Spada alla Griglia
Swordfish marinated in olive oil and **lemon** juice and grilled

Shrimp Scampi
Broiled shrimp flavored with garlic, butter or oil, and white wine

Though common on Italian menus here, this dish is virtually unknown in Italy. There the word scampi *refers to the lobster-like crustaceans known as prawns or langoustines in the U.S.*

Rane alla Provenzale
Frog legs country-style, sautéed in oil with garlic and oregano

Baccalà alla Fiorentina
Salted codfish, fried and stewed in tomato sauce

Baccalà is an Italian favorite and is prepared differently in various regions. The Florentines like it as described above. In Rome it is dredged in a light batter and deep-fried; in Liguria it may be cooked with spinach or fried and matched with a sauce featuring bread crumbs and garlic.

Involitini di Pesce Spada
Thin slices of swordfish rolled with **prosciutto** (•164), mozzarella, and herbs, then grilled

INGREDIENT NOTES

• **Lemons** grow in profusion in many parts of Italy and are a common ingredient in Italian dishes. They are used in pasta sauces, as a dressing for meat, as a key component in *gelato* (Italian ice cream) and *granitas* (granular ices), or are simply squeezed over plates of fried fish.

Pesce del Giorno
Fish of the day

Salmone alla Griglia
Grilled salmon

Salmon is not indigenous to Italian waters, but makes frequent appearances on menus in the U.S. It is best prepared in simple Italian fashion— marinated briefly in olive oil, garlic, and lemon, then grilled.

Calamari Ripieni
Squid stuffed with herbs and anchovy paste, then sautéed with onion, wine, and tomatoes

Sogliole al Basilico
Sole marinated with basil and olive oil, then baked

Calamari Affogati
Strips of squid sautéed with wine and garlic in tomato sauce

Cacciucco di Pesce
Seafood simmered in a tomato, garlic, and basil sauce

Cacciucco is one of numerous names for fish stew along Italy's coastline. Others include zuppa di pesce, brodetto, *and* cioppino.

Grigliata di Pesce
Assorted grilled fish and shrimp; served with lemon wedges

CARNE e POLLO
(MEAT and POULTRY)
Beef and other red meat offerings tend to be more limited on Italian menus than they are on typical American menus, mostly because meat is expensive in Italy and only the well-to-do can afford to eat it frequently. There are, however, a multitude of Italian poultry recipes, probably more than for any other kind of meat.

Polpette
Meatballs

Meatball recipes vary from town to town (if not family to family) in Italy. For example, they can be made with beef or veal, bound with egg or bread, flavored with varying herbs and spices, grated cheese, pine nuts, or raisins, cooked in oil or butter, and finished with a tomato or mushroom sauce or with lemon juice.

Lombatine di Vitello
Grilled veal chop

Ossobuco
Braised veal shanks sprinkled with *gremolada*, a mixture of lemon zest (the colored part of lemon skin), parsley, and garlic, at the end of the long, slow cooking process; served with *risotto alla milanese* (see page 170)

Costoletta
Veal chop coated in egg and bread crumbs, then fried in butter

According to some food historians, the origin of the preparation of costoletta *dates back to the Renaissance, when it was believed that gold was good for the heart. While only a few could afford to cover their food in gold leaf, the next best thing was to eat food, such as this fried veal chop, that was golden in color. This dish is so closely associated with Milan, where it is believed to have originated, that it is also known as* una milanese.

Costata di Vitello Parmigiana
Veal chops fried in butter, then simmered briefly in stock with grated **Parmesan** (•167)

Involitini di Vitello
Thinly sliced veal topped with bread crumbs, onions, parsley, salami, and cheese, then rolled up

Vitello or Pollo al Limone
Veal or chicken sautéed with white wine and lemon

Vitello Tonnato
Veal scaloppine sautéed in oil and served cold with a sauce of cream, mashed tuna, anchovies, capers, and lemon juice

Parmigiana di Vitello
Veal chop sautéed with tomato and mozzarella

Scaloppine alla Bolognese
Thin slices of veal cooked with alternating layers of **prosciutto** (•164), boiled potatoes, and **Parmesan** (•167) cheese

A dish prepared alla Bolognese, *in the manner of the university city in central Italy, is usually rich, often cooked with butter, eggs, ham, and cheese.*

Saltimbocca
Thinly sliced veal covered with a layer of **prosciutto** (•164) and a sage leaf, usually rolled up and secured lengthwise with a toothpick, then quickly browned in butter

Saltimbocca *translates to "leaps into your mouth," a reference to this traditional Roman dish's exquisite flavor. It is sometimes called* saltimbocca alla Romana.

Vitello or Pollo Piccata al Marsala
Slices of veal or chicken pounded thin, then fried in butter with **Marsala** wine

Piccata is the Milanese word for scaloppini *(or thin, often flattened pieces of meat).*

Petto di Pollo
Boned chicken breast, often sautéed in wine with tomatoes, artichokes, or other vegetables

Petto di Pollo alla Griglia con Arugula
Boned chicken breast pounded flat, grilled, and topped with tomatoes and **arugula**

Pollastrello Arrosto
Roasted baby chicken, often seasoned with sage, garlic, and rosemary

Petto del Pollo alla Paesana
Boned chicken breast sautéed with sweet Italian sausage

Pollo Scarpariello
Boneless chicken sautéed with garlic, lemon, and parsley

Pollo con Carciofi
Chicken sautéed with artichokes, garlic, onions, and white wine

Pollo alla Diavola
Chicken cooked "in the devil's way"

In this classic Tuscan dish, whole chicken is marinated in lemon, cut in half and flattened with a mallet, brushed with olive oil, and cooked over an open flame.

Pollo alla Marengo
Chicken sautéed in butter, white wine, and mushrooms

Napoleon's chef created pollo alla Marengo *on June 14, 1800, to celebrate his victory over the Austrians at Marengo.*

Pollo alla Cacciatora
Chicken prepared "in the hunter's style," first sautéed, then cooked slowly with such ingredients as mushrooms, onions, carrots, tomatoes, and wine

Meat and game, in addition to poultry, can be prepared alla cacciatora. *Recipes vary from region to region.*

INGREDIENT NOTES

• **Marsala** is a fortified wine to which grape must and brandy have been added. It is produced in and around Marsala, a port city in western Sicily. It is used in cooking and is also a popular apéritif.

• **Arugula** (also known as rocket) boasts small flat leaves on long stems and a peppery aroma and flavor.

Scottadito

Grilled baby lamb chops

The literal translation of scottadito is finger-burning, and this dish, which originated in Rome, is grilled quickly and served, true to its name, very hot.

Costoletta d'Agnello

Grilled lamb chops

Bistecca al Ferri

The Italianization of "beefsteak"; a thick cut, often a T-bone, that is broiled

Lombata di Maiale al Forno

Pork roast coated with herbs and roasted *al forno* (in the oven), then simmered with tomatoes

Fegato

Liver, usually from a calf (though pork liver is popular with cooks from southern Italy), often fried with simmered onions

Trippa alla Fiorentina

Tripe cooked in tomato sauce; often served with cannellini (white kidney) beans

Tripe is the name of the stomach lining of several different mammals, including the pig, cow, and sheep. In general, the tripe offered in restaurants comes from cows.

Grigliata Mista

A grilled assortment of meats, often steak, kidney, **pancetta** (•165) sausage, and liver

The word grigliata *can also refer to a mixed grill of at least three different kinds of fish.*

Fritto Misto

Mixed fried foods, such as slices of liver, mozzarella, zucchini, and eggplant

Bollito Misto

A northern Italian feast of boiled meats, including beef, veal, chicken, and *cotechino* (pork sausage); served with a selection of sauces, such as a parsley sauce and a tomato sauce

Bollito misto is not usually part of the regular menu at Italian restaurants in the U.S. However, this elaborate dish may be offered on special occasions. The meat should be carved hot at the table.

VERDURE (VEGETABLES) Vegetables
grow in profusion in Italy's climate and are an important
part of any meal. They may either accompany the main
course or be served afterward.

Peperoni alle Brace
Peppers roasted over an open
flame, then marinated in olive oil
with garlic and capers

Fagioli
Beans, dried or fresh, often
sautéed in olive oil, with onions,
garlic, and other herbs

Cavolfiore
Cauliflower, often prepared by
sautéing the florets in butter and
sprinkling them with **Parmesan**
(•167)

Parmigiana di Melanzane
Slices of eggplants layered with
mozzarella, tomato, **Parmesan**
(•167), and basil, then baked

Grigliata di Verdure
Mixed grilled vegetables

Fagiolini Verdi
Green beans, prepared any number of traditional ways: sautéed in
oil and garlic, stewed in a tomato
sauce, or sautéed with cream and
Parmesan (•167)

INSALATE (SALADS) In Italy, the salad is
traditionally served as a palate cleanser before dessert,
although many restaurants in the U.S. cater to the American
custom of serving it as a first course. It is generally made
with greens and/or raw or cooked vegetables and is dressed
simply with extra-virgin olive oil, vinegar, and salt. While
more elaborate salads, made with such ingredients as rice,
bread, beans, meat, and fish, are plentiful in the Italian
repertoire, they are more commonly offered as an appetizer
or first course or as the featured dish in a light meal.

Insalata Tricolore
Salad of **arugula** (•176), Belgian
endive, and **radicchio**

Insalata Siciliana
A salad of **fennel** (•171),
oranges, and black olives,
dressed lightly with olive oil

INGREDIENT NOTES

• **Radicchio**, a member of the
chicory family, is a slightly bitter
lettuce that grows in shades of
red, green, and white. The radicchio found in the U.S. is usually
reddish purple and white.

BALSAMIC VINEGAR

Balsamic vinegar (*aceto balsamico*) is a welcome newcomer to the Italian dining scene in America. The best is made according to traditional recipes that require the vinegar to be aged for at least 10 years, transferred periodically through a series of 12 kegs made of aromatic woods. You will most likely encounter *aceto balsamico* in salad dressings (a few drops are added to embellish the olive oil and red wine vinegar), though on some sophisticated menus it may also be offered as a topping for fresh fruit and even ice cream. Authentic balsamic vinegar is expensive and used sparingly. Inexpensive impostors are, unfortunately, fairly common and disappointing in taste.

Insalata della Casa
House salad

The house salad at an Italian restaurant is often an elaborate preparation of mixed greens, such as arugula (•167) and Belgian endive, and/or raw or boiled vegetables, such as fennel, asparagus, tomatoes, or cucumber; it may be topped with thin slices of young Parmesan.

PIZZA e FOCACCIA (PIZZA and FOCACCIA)

Pizza and *focaccia* have an ambiguous role on American menus. In Italy, these items would appear on the menu only as a snack or as a light meal in a casual restaurant, such as a trattoria or a pizzeria. In the U.S., however, these items sometimes appear on menus in restaurants, even in formal ones, where they can be eaten as a first course or as a light lunch or early supper.

Calzone
A half moon-shaped savory stuffed turnover made with pizza dough and a variety of fillings

Focaccia
Flat bread

Focaccia is akin to thick pizza crust, though it has the texture of bread. Topped with one or more ingredients, such as olive oil, rosemary, tomatoes, cheese, onions, or anchovies, it is the ubiquitous snack food of Italy and is becoming increasingly popular in the U.S.

ITALIAN PIZZA

True Italian pizzas, which have begun to show up on menus in the U.S., are smaller than their American cousins (often small enough to be comfortably eaten by one person) and are less elaborately topped. They have thin, crunchy crusts and are meant to be baked in wood-burning brick ovens. Tomatoes and cheese are not a requisite ingredient on all authentic Italian pizzas, though most varieties featured on menus in the U.S. include at least one of them. Following are some of the Italian pizza varieties you are likely to find in restaurants in the U.S.:

Margherita: with tomatoes, mozzarella, and basil

Quattro Stagioni: "four seasons," each quadrant topped with a different ingredient, usually artichoke hearts, mushrooms, olives, and prosciutto

Napoletana: with tomatoes, garlic, and oregano

Marinara: with tomatoes and garlic

Additional toppings: seafood *(frutti di mare)*, onions *(cipolle)*, and sausage *(calsiccia)*.

DOLCI (DESSERTS) Italian desserts vary according to the ambitions of the chef. They may be rich and elaborate, such as *tiramisù* or *cassata* (a Sicilian cake), or as simple as a dish of *gelato* (ice cream). Italians often forgo the sweets and finish a meal with fruit or cheese or move right on to the coffee.

Macedonia di Frutta
Not as exotic as one might imagine—fruit salad

Pan di Spagna
Sponge cake, often topped with fresh fruit

Tiramisù
Pan di spagna (see previous page) soaked in brandy and espresso, then layered with Mascarpone cheese (see page 182) and dusted with cocoa powder

Zuppa Inglese
The Italian version of trifle, made with pound cake and egg custard and heavily flavored with brandy and other spirits

Spumone
Molded frozen dessert that may be as simple as several layers of different-flavored ice creams or as elaborate as two or more flavors of ice cream, possibly lightened with whipped cream, sandwiched around sweetened whipped cream flavored with rum, studded with toasted nuts and candied fruit, then frozen in a mold and served in slices with complementary sauce

Biscotti con Vin Santo
Biscuits and sweet wine

Biscotti is the Italian word for all cookies as well as the specific name for the twice-baked, dry biscuits that are traditionally dipped in vin santo, *the sweet dessert wine produced in the vineyards of Tuscany and the Trentino.*

Tartufo
A scoop of vanilla ice cream covered with a coating of chocolate

Fragole Fresche
Fresh strawberries; served with cream or Mascarpone cheese (see page 182)

Panettone
Light buttered yeast bread/cake studded with raisins and lemon and orange peel

According to some food historians, the name of this cake, served at Christmas but a popular treat year-round, is derived from pan di Toni, *or the "bread of Toni," for the Milanese baker who invented it in the 15th century and became a wealthy man for doing so.*

Gelato
Ice cream made with a mixture of egg custard and sugar; available in many flavors

Egg custard renders gelato richer and, to many palates, tastier than American ice cream.

Cannoli
Ricotta-filled fried pastry tubes

This high-cholesterol pastry is made with melted pork fat and fried in oil. It is stuffed with such indulgences as sweetened ricotta cheese, chocolate cream, nuts, or pieces of chocolate.

Crema Inglese
Egg custard often served with stewed fruit or cake

Crostata
Tarts filled with jam, marzipan, ricotta, or a wide array of other fillings

As a general rule of thumb, French restaurants serve better tarts than Italian restaurants, but, of course, there are always exceptions.

Cassata
Sicilian cake in which a layer of pound cake, iced with almond paste and often decorated with marzipan fruits, surrounds a core of ricotta cheese flavored with chocolate

Granita
A refreshing granular ice made by freezing fruit juices or coffee; suitable for dessert or as a mid-day refreshment

---

ITALIAN DESSERT CHEESES

Formaggi (cheeses) are plentiful in Italy, and a good Italian restaurant in the U.S. will often offer a selection, along with crusty bread, from a cart or tray, to close a meal.

Asiago Presato: tangy cow's milk cheese; a good accompaniment to fruit

Bel Paese: mild, soft, creamy cow's milk cheese similar to the French Port Salut

Gorgonzola: rich, creamy, pungent cow's milk cheese exposed to air during the aging process, resulting in blue-veining; aged for at least 50 days

Mascarpone: very soft cow's milk cheese, sinfully high in fat and delicious; can be topped with sugar and served with fruit

Taleggio: soft and creamy cow's milk cheese; mild but rich, excellent with fruit

Parmigiano: young Parmesan, aged less than a year; provides a gentle but solid end to a meal

BEVANDE (BEVERAGES) An Italian meal without wine is indeed like a day without sunshine, and to end a meal without a cup of coffee is like getting dressed but failing to put on your shoes. A bottle or two of sparkling water, such as San Pellegrino, should also accompany a meal. Beer is an acceptable accompaniment for an informal meal of pizza. Aromatic, herbal, or plant-based bitter apéritifs and digestives are also popular.

ITALIAN WINES Italian wines are justly famous, and one of the great pleasures of life is to enjoy one or a selection of them as you partake of an Italian meal. In general, white wine (*vino bianco*) is a good accompaniment to antipasto courses and fish dishes, while red wine (*vino rosso*) complements game, red meat, and poultry. As an overall rule of thumb, the more robust the dish, the more robust the wine should be. When in doubt, the deservedly popular Chiantis are satisfying with just about any dish that calls for a red wine and Pinot Grigio whites are a welcome addition to any fish or other light dish.

Some commonly found wines are noted below. Also keep an eye out for the many new and exciting wines beginning to appear more regularly on menus, mostly varietals such as Pinot Bianco, Tocai, Chardonnay, and Sauvignon Blanc.

RED WINES
Grouped from lightest- to fullest-bodied

Bardolino: subtle, dry, and slightly tart, this DOC wine from around Verona in the Veneto region is excellent with poultry

Valpolicella: dry, light, and flavorful DOC wine from the foothills of the Alps in the Veneto region; excellent with poultry

Chianti: rich wines produced by more than 1,000 growers in Tuscany; the best are the DOCG Chianti Classicos, from the region between Siena and Florence, as well as Ruffina, a small region northeast of Florence. Both are produced as medium- as well as full-bodied wines. Most age well; Chianti becomes *Riserva* afer a minimum of three years of aging. Good with beef or poultry. Plain Chianti is a young, fruity, fresh wine that goes well with pasta or any meat.

ITALIAN WINE CLASSIFICATIONS

Restaurants vary considerably in the way that they list their wines. Most lists are broken down by "red" (*rosso*) and "white" (*bianco*), and sometimes from lightest- to fullest-bodied; some are further categorized by province, not by large geographical wine-growing region, though there is not a taste or quality relationship per se to each province. Provinces likely to be noted include Piedmont, Veneto, Friuli, Tuscano (Tuscany), Liguria, Sicily, Latium (Lazio), and Umbria, even though wine is made throughout Italy. Many Italian wine producers offer proprietary blends that do not reflect any regional characteristics.

The official Italian wine classifications, which were developed only recently, are of limited use in judging the quality of wine because not all wine is officially classified, meaning that some of the finest, most expensive wines are labeled *vino da tavola*, or "table wine," despite their superior quality. Ask your waiter or wine steward for guidance.

Vino da tavola (**table wine**) may be cheap swill or a spectacular, unique wine that just happens to be grown outside of an official region—or is made by a top winemaker who refuses to cooperate with the government and its complex regulations. Labels of this category include only the color, the winery, and its trademark, and no indication of quality.

IGT (Indicazioni Geografiche Tipiche) (**typical geographic indications**) is a new and rarely used designation that implies a decent though not outstanding table wine grown in a particular but large region, equivalent to the French *vin de pays* (see page 87).

DOC (Denominazione di Origine Controllata) (**controlled denomination of origin**) connotes a relatively decent wine grown and processed according to certain standards in a recognized wine-growing region. Similar to the French *Appellation Contrôlée* (see page 87).

DOCG (Denominazione di Origine Controllata e Garantita) (**guaranteed controlled denomination of origin**) is a special recognition for exceptional wines from a specific region. Somewhat equivalent to the French *grands crus* (see page 88).

About 250 wines fall under the last two categories listed above.

Barbaresco: soft, delicate, and one of the DOCG wines from Piedmont; good with lamb

Barolo: velvety, smooth, ruby red, aged for three years in the cask and often as long as seven years in the bottle; one of the great wines of Italy and another DOCG wine from Piedmont; excellent with roasts, red meats, and game

Brunello di Montalcino: a rich and incredibly smooth DOCG Tuscan wine, excellent with game or lamb. Ages well; called *Riserva* after a minimum of five years of aging.

Montepulciano: dry and full-bodied wines from southern Tuscany; Vino Nobile di Montepulciano, one of the finest, has earned the DOCG classification; good with red meat and game

WHITE WINES
Grouped from lightest- to fullest-bodied

Cinqueterre: dry, light, flavorful DOC wine from the seaside region near Genoa in Liguria; excellent with fish

Corvo: dry, flavorful wine from Sicily; good with antipasto and fish

Est! Est!! Est!!!: from Umbria but mostly Latium; a DOC wine that is dry and sweet enough to accompany dessert but is also good with fish

Frascati: light, refreshing DOC wine from Latium; traditionally served with pork but also good with fish and antipasto

Orvieto: dry, crisp DOC wine from Umbria; excellent with fish as well as light pasta sauces

Asti Spumante: a lightly sparkling, sweet DOC dessert wine from Piedmont

Prosecco: sharp, crisp, acidic DOC wine from Veneto that is slightly to fully sparkling *(spumante)* depending on the producer; best suited for antipasto or cheese

Soave: dry, light, and fresh DOC wine from Veneto; excellent with antipasto and fish

Pinot Grigio: dry, very flavorful, and smooth; excellent with fish; grown in several provinces of northern Italy, especially Veneto

OTHER NOTABLE WINES AND SPIRITS

Vin Santo: literally, sacred wine, made from grapes that are spread out to dry for three to four weeks before they are pressed; full-bodied, sweet, and generally served for dipping *biscotti* (see page 181). The best is made in Tuscany, but good wines come from several provinces.

Marsala: a port-like fortified wine from the town of the same name in Sicily; served as an apéritif

Grappa: made by distilling the skins that remain after the juice has been extracted from the grapes during winemaking; a strong and memorable way to end a meal

Amaretto di Saronno: a sweet, almond-flavored liqueur that is gaining popularity as an after-dinner drink in America. It was created in the 16th century by an innkeeper's wife who, when the great painter Bernardino Luni asked her to model for a painting of the Madonna, returned the honor by macerating ground apricot pits in aquavit, creating this amber-colored drink.

Espresso

A small (usually 1½-ounce) serving of strong coffee, made in a special pot or machine that forces pressurized hot water through finely ground coffee; often served with a lemon peel on the side that you may or may not want to put in the coffee

Espresso Doppio

A double serving of espresso (officially 3 ounces)

Cappuccino

Espresso topped with a generous, foamy layer of steamed milk; often dusted with cocoa powder or cinnamon

Italians, and American purists, consider cappuccino and caffè latte (see next page) breakfast drinks that should never be drunk after 11 A.M., though both are quite commonly served at all hours, even after dinner, in Italian restaurants in the U.S.

Caffè Americano
Espresso diluted with hot water to the strength of American coffee

Caffè Latte
Espresso with steamed milk, usually served in proportions of two-thirds coffee to one-third milk

Espresso Macchiato
Espresso with just a touch of foamy milk on top

Latte Macchiato
Steamed milk with just a touch of espresso

JAPANESE
cuisine

★

Cheers–*Kanpai* (cahn-pie)
Bon appétit–*Gochiso ni* (go-she-zo nee)
Thank you–*Domo arigato* (dome-oh ar-ee-gah-tow)

IN JAPANESE COOKING CLOSE ATTENTION IS PAID TO THE quality and seasonality of the food as well as its beauty, and each dish that is served is evidence of the Japanese belief that we eat with our eyes as well as our mouths. Most foods are served in small portions artfully arranged to showcase their natural beauty, and Japanese restaurants themselves are quite often wondrous showcases of woodworking and traditional design.

A country that is made up of four main islands and a hundred or so small ones could not help but develop a cuisine that celebrates seafood, especially when much of the terrain is mountainous and inarable. The result is also a generally healthful cuisine.

Principles of Flavor

M any foods are served uncooked or briefly cooked and are mildly but deftly seasoned in order to preserve the natural flavor of the ingredients. No cream, cheese, milk, or oily sauces are used in Japanese cooking. Most added flavors come from combinations of soy sauce, rice wine (sake), and sugar, as well as from a fish-flavored stock called *dashi*.

Foreign Influence

From China, Japan inherited soybeans and tea, probably around the 7th or 8th centuries, as well as noodles. The Portuguese, who were active in Japan from the mid-1500s until 1638 when they were expelled, left behind recipes for deep-fried foods, which the Japanese adapted to their own diets by using a lighter batter and oil; today these deep-fried foods are known as tempura. Meat became popular for the first time in Japan after 1850 when the Japanese reopened their doors to foreign trade, and the Western population started to grow.

Ordering

A Japanese meal usually has a marked beginning, middle, and end, the formula for which is based on the Japanese banquet meal:

Beginning: Appetizer, clear soup, fresh, uncooked fish

Middle: One-pot dish and vinegared or dressed salad or a grilled food, steamed food, fried food, and simmered food

End: Boiled rice, miso soup, pickles, followed by green tea and fresh fruit

Whereas a banquet meal might include foods from all of the categories in this formula, an informal meal might consist of only uncooked fish followed by a grilled food and then rice, miso soup, and pickles. Alternatively, a casual meal or snack might consist of one dish, such as a noodle soup, a *donburi* (a large bowl of rice topped with meat, fish, vegetables, or eggs), or a couple of selections from the sushi bar.

In some Japanese restaurants the task of formulating the meal will be taken care of for you. For example, if you order a dish from the middle category, the restaurant will automatically accompany it with the appropriate foods from the beginning and end categories.

Japanese servings are traditionally smaller than American servings, though some Japanese restaurants in the U.S. accommodate their American clientele with very generous portions. If you don't think that what you ordered will fill you up, don't hesitate to request an extra appetizer or bowl of rice. Otherwise, note that noodle soups as well as *donburi* can be quite filling.

Service and Dining

The components of a meal may be brought out separately in courses or they may be served at the same time in a tray with many compartments.

Condiments

Most tables are set with a bottle of Japanese soy sauce for use with sushi and sashimi.

Garnishes

Almost all Japanese garnishes are edible. One exception is a decorative green plastic garnish, reminiscent of a picket fence, that is sometimes presented with sushi. Originally this type of garnish was made out of tea leaves and it still is at the best Japanese restaurants.

Utensils

The better restaurants supply narrow, pointed, sometimes lacquered chopsticks and a tiny bar on which they can be rested. (Chinese chopsticks have blunt ends.) The average restaurant uses disposable, plain wooden chopsticks that the diner must break apart; many people rub them together before use to eliminate the small splinters that are typical. If you don't know how to use chopsticks and don't want to eat with them, ask for a fork and a spoon.

USING CHOPSTICKS

If you are eating food off your own plate, pick it up with the pointed end of the chopsticks. If you are picking up food from a communal plate, use the back end of the chopsticks to transfer the food to your own plate, then reverse the chopsticks and use the pointed ends for eating. When you are not using your chopsticks, place them on the chopstick rest (a very small bar that can be made out of pottery, porcelain, or bamboo) or, if there is no chopstick rest, place them across the lowest saucer or plate at your place setting.

EATING RICE WITH CHOPSTICKS

It isn't really difficult to eat rice with chopsticks because the rice used in Japanese cooking is much stickier than the longer-grained rice more commonly known in the U.S. Also, it is perfectly acceptable—and expected—that you will lift the bowl close to your mouth so that you do not have to carry the rice a long way with chopsticks.

CHOPSTICK NO-NOS

- **Don't hold** chopsticks too low or you will not have any leverage.
- **Don't hold** chopsticks too tightly.
- **Don't point** or gesture with chopsticks.
- **Don't stick** chopsticks upright in a bowl.
- **Don't take** anything from someone else's chopsticks.

Rice

In most cases a small bowl of rice will come automatically with your meal, though it will not be served with a *donburi* (rice in a large bowl with various toppings) or a meal consisting of sushi only since both count rice as one of their main ingredients already. Rice, called *gohan* in Japanese, has been a staple crop in Japan since antiquity. The word *gohan* also translates to "honorable food."

Signature Dishes

Sushi and *sashimi* (sliced raw fish, with or without rice); *Fish or Meat Teriyaki* (broiled fish or meat with sweet soy sauce-based glaze); *Sukiyaki* (sliced meat, seafood, or vegetables cooked in simmering broth at the table)

The MSG Question

Some Japanese restaurants may use MSG but in very small quantities. The quantities are so small, in fact, that it is unlikely that anyone would have a reaction to it. Still, if you are concerned about MSG, ask the waiter about it before you order.

Common Misconceptions

Japanese cuisine is all raw fish. While the Japanese savor their sushi and sashimi, raw fish is only one aspect of their complex cuisine.

In Japanese restaurants, you must eat sitting on your knees, on the floor. It is actually difficult to find an informal restaurant where this is the case. However, some of the better Japanese restaurants maintain traditional straw-matted tatami rooms, usually containing one table each. Many of these tables are suspended over pits, a setup that allows you to dangle your legs in comfort. If you would like to sit in a tatami room (you will be requested to remove your shoes to protect the mats), call the restaurant in advance to reserve one.

COOKING CATEGORIES

Japanese cooking is broken down into categories according to how dishes are prepared rather than by the foods themselves. The organization of Japanese menus in the U.S. often reflects these categories.

Zensai: appetizers

Suimono: clear soups

Misoshiru: soup made with miso

Sunomono and Aemono: salads and dressed foods

Sushi and Sashimi : sliced raw fish, with or without rice

Gohanmono: rice dishes

Yakimono: broiled or grilled foods

Agemono: deep-fried foods

Nabemono: foods cooked in one pot at the table

Nimono: boiled foods

Mushimono: steamed foods

Menrui: noodles

Tsukemono: pickles

Kudamono: fruit

Nomimono: beverages

Japanese MENU

ZENSAI (APPETIZERS) Appetizers in a
Japanese restaurant might consist of an assortment of very
small vegetable or fish dishes, such as pickled mushrooms
or cooked shrimp, a salad, or a small portion of a hot dish
featured elsewhere on the menu as a main course, such as
yakitori or *negimaki*.

Hijiki
Mild, black seaweed often cooked
with *dashi* (fish stock), soy sauce,
and **mirin**

*This dish may also include
carrots and fried tofu. Some
Japanese believe that eating*
hijiki *promotes healthy hair
growth.*

Tatsuta-age
Fried chicken wings

Kara-age
Deep-fried chicken in
ginger sauce

Kyo-age
Deep-fried bean curd in
tempura sauce

Yakko-tofu
Cold bean curd with grated
ginger, dried fish (bonito) flakes,
scallions, and soy sauce

Oshinko
Pickled daikon

*Daikon is a large, white
radish. Although in Japan
pickles are most commonly
eaten with rice at the end of
the meal, they often appear on
the appetizer list in American
restaurants. Other vegetables
that are commonly pickled and
served in Japanese restaurants
in the U.S. are cucumber, a tiny
plum that is good for digestion,
and Chinese cabbage.*

Nasu Shigiyaki
Broiled eggplant with sweet miso
(fermented soybean paste) sauce

Fried Oysters
Lightly pan-fried oysters

Ganmodoki
A mixture of crumbled bean curd,
sesame seeds, and vegetables,
often bound with grated mountain
yam (a white root vegetable), that
is formed into patties or balls and
deep-fried

INGREDIENT NOTES

• **Mirin** is a very sweet golden-
colored rice wine. It is used in
cooking to imbue foods with a
light sweetness and to create a
glaze on grilled foods. It is not a
drinking wine.

Age-dofu
Fried bean curd

Oshitashi
Steamed spinach served cold
with dried fish (bonito) flakes

Gyoza
Large, sealed, fried or steamed
dumplings filled with either meat
or seafood

Shumai or Siu Mai
Small, delicate steamed
dumplings filled with either meat
(usually pork) or seafood (usually
shrimp or crab) that are open on
the top so the filling is visible

Shumai *are a Chinese food
that often turn up on Japanese
menus.*

MISOSHIRU and SUIMONO (SOUPS)

Soups are often served in covered lacquered bowls. The
cover holds the heat as well as the flavor and aroma of the
soup in the bowl until you are ready to start eating. Unlike
Western cooks, who often rely on a variety of different
stocks to make soups, the Japanese use only one: It is called
dashi and it is made with kelp and bonito fish shavings.
From this stock two basic kinds of soup are made: *misoshiru*
and *suimono*.

Misoshiru (Miso Soup)
Dashi (fish stock) with miso
(fermented soybean paste) plus
various amounts of solids, such
as tofu, seaweed, sliced or
chopped scallions, daikon,
or other vegetables,
and sometimes
meat, fish, or
poultry

*This is the most
popular breakfast
food in Japan, but
it is also served at
other times of the
day.*

Suimono
Clear soup embellished with
artfully cut vegetables and bite-
size pieces of tofu, fish, chicken,
or egg, then garnished with fresh
herbs

TO EAT SOUP in a Japanese restaurant, pick out the solids with your chopsticks, then sip the liquid. If desired, hold
the bowl with both hands with fingers
below the rim, and drink directly from it.
The wood underneath the lacquer of the
bowl acts as an insulator so that
you will not burn your hands.
Japanese soups are meant to be
eaten very hot.

SUNOMONO and AEMONO (SALADS)

Salads are broken down into two categories: *sunomono* (vinegared foods) and *aemono* (foods mixed with dressings). They are customarily served in small bowls and are meant to complement the main dish in taste, color, and texture.

Kaiso Salad
One or more kinds of raw or blanched seaweed, often with a sesame dressing

Moyashi Salad
Raw bean sprout salad, often with dressing of oil, vinegar, ginger, and soy sauce

Green Salad
Lettuce and cucumber, often with dressing of oil, vinegar, ginger, and soy sauce

SASHIMI (SLICED RAW FISH) and SUSHI (SLICED RAW FISH with RICE)

Raw fish is the main attraction at the sushi bar. The methods for preparing the fish can be broken down into three categories: *sashimi*, *nigirizushi*, and *makizushi*. Often restaurants list sashimi under its own heading and then list *nigirizushi* and *makizushi* under the heading "sushi."

The rice used to make sushi is steamed, then tossed in a dressing of rice vinegar, sugar, and salt, while a chef's assistant fans the rice so that it will cool off quickly. This gives it a glossy sheen and a slightly sticky chewiness.

Sashimi Combination
Assorted pieces of sliced raw fish presented on a platter, sometimes with rice on the side

Tekka Donburi
Tuna and seaweed in large rice bowl

Chirashi
Assortment of sliced raw fish in a box, with rice

In Japanese chirashi *means "scattered." In this dish,* sashimi *is either scattered on top of sushi rice or mixed into the sushi rice.* Chirashi *is commonly eaten for lunch or as a snack in Japan.*

SUSHI BAR TERMINOLOGY

Sashimi is sliced raw fish. For the Japanese it is the slicing that is considered the cooking of the fish, as the flavor of the same fish varies depending on how it is sliced. For example, a fish can be cut into thick slices (about 3/8 inch); it can be cut into long thin strips that are artistically arranged on top of each other; it can be cubed; or it can be cut so thin that it is transparent. In Japan the slicing of raw fish is considered an art form.

Nigirizushi is sliced raw fish that is pressed over a pad of rice. It can also be made with fish roe in which case a band of *nori* (seaweed) is wrapped around the rice and the roe to hold it together. Often the sushi chef puts a little *wasabi* (horseradish-like condiment) between the rice and the fish. Pick up the *nigirizushi* with either chopsticks or your hands and eat in one or two bites.

Makizushi (also known as *norimaki*) is rolls of raw fish and rice wrapped in seaweed and cut into bite-size rounds. It is made by spreading sushi rice over a sheet of seaweed *(nori)*, laying thin strips of fish and/or vegetables down the center, then rolling everything up together. When the mixture is rolled up into a thin roll with the help of a flexible, bamboo mat, it is called *hosomaki* and is meant to be eaten with chopsticks. A similar, thick roll is called *futomaki*. When it is rolled by hand into a loose cone, it is called a hand roll, or *temaki*. To eat hand rolls, pick up the narrow end with your fingers and bite from the wide end down, as you would an ice cream cone. When *hosomaki* is made inside out (with the rice on the outside and the seaweed on the inside) it is called *uramaki*. *Uramaki* is sometimes coated on the outside with sesame seeds. It is usually more expensive than regular *makizushi* because it takes the sushi chef more time to make.

ORDERING SUSHI AND SASHIMI

Ordering sushi and sashimi can usually be done à la carte (by the piece) or in predetermined combinations. While beginning sushi and sashimi eaters sometimes prefer to order a combination, which gives them a chance to try a variety of fish, connoisseurs almost always order à la carte, basing their choices on what they like best and what looks most appetizing on a particular day. Some chefs reserve the best pieces of fish for the clients who order à la carte. Unfortunately, it is generally more expensive this way.

Following are the fish most commonly offered at sushi bars. Most of the fish listed here can be prepared as *sashimi*, *makizushi*, or *nigirizushi*. Newcomers to the world of sushi would do best to start with salmon, tuna, and yellowtail, all of which are quite mild and tender.

Awabi: abalone

Chutoro: pinkish tuna meat

Ebi: shrimp (cooked)

Hamachi: yellowtail

Hirame: flounder

Ika: squid (cooked)

Ikura: salmon roe

Kani: crab

Maguro: tuna

Mirugai: geoduck

Namauni: sea urchin

Saba: mackerel

Sake: salmon

Suzuki: sea bass

Tamago: slices of omelet sweetened with sugar and mirin (Japanese rice wine)

Tobiko: flying fish roe

Tako: octopus (cooked)

Toro: fatty tuna belly (considered the best part of the tuna for sushi)

Unagi: freshwater eel (never served raw; instead, glazed with a sweet, smokey sauce and grilled)

Uni: sea urchin roe

SUSHI BAR ETIQUETTE:
If there is a waitperson, it is not considered appropriate to ask the sushi chef for drinks or any food aside from sashimi or sushi. When you are finished eating, ask the waitperson—not the chef—for the check. Sometimes the sushi chef will hand you a small dish of pickles, cooked shellfish in a vinegar sauce, or other accompaniment that is not on the menu and you did not order. Sushi chefs make these *tsukidashi* when the mood strikes, and it is unlikely that a charge for them will appear on your bill.

Sushi Combination
Assorted raw fish with rice, usually a combination of *makizushi* and *nigirizushi*

Tekkamaki
Tuna roll

Unakeyu
Grilled freshwater eel and cucumber roll

Oshinkomake
Pickled daikon roll

Uramaki and Tobiko
Inside-out roll with flying fish eggs

California Roll
Cooked crab, avocado, and cucumber roll

To please their American clientele, many Japanese restaurants make sushi rolls with vegetables and cooked instead of raw fish. Interestingly, the California roll, the most famous of these rolls and an American creation, has now made its way to Japan.

Kappamaki
Cucumber roll, made with small slivers of cucumber

This refreshing sushi roll is named after Kappa, a water goblin in Japanese mythology.

Futomaki
Large roll about two inches thick, available with a variety of usually cooked fillings, such as **crab cake**, carrot, spinach, egg, and pickled daikon (see page 202)

EATING *FUTOMAKI* can be difficult because it is so large. Pick it up with your chopsticks and do the best you can. Some people find it helpful to remove bits of the filling first.

INGREDIENT NOTES

• **Crab cake** is not actually crab at all; it is pressed cod made to look like king crab legs or crab claw meat.

SUSHI BAR CONDIMENTS

Daikon: This mild white radish can be grated, diced, or shredded. It is said to help with digestion, especially of fats. It is used most often as a garnish for sashimi. Other garnishes for sashimi include purple or green seaweed and cucumber, all of which are edible.

Wasabi: When eating sashimi, mix a little bit of this green horseradish-like condiment into the soy sauce. Do not do this if you are eating *nigirizushi* because the chef has probably already added it. Though a popular habit among many American diners, using too much strong *wasabi* blocks out the delicate taste of the raw fish. Freshly grated *wasabi* is best, but, unfortunately, rarely served.

Soy sauce: Pour a small amount from the bottle on the table into the saucer at your place setting—keep it shallow, so you can still see the bottom of the dish. Very lightly dip the sushi into the saucer before eating. When eating *nigirizushi*, dip the fish side, not the rice side, into the saucer. When eating *makizushi*, dip the side, not the bottom or top, into the saucer.

Ponzu sauce: Citrus-flavored soy sauce, often made with lime juice, soy sauce, and rice vinegar; served with certain kinds of sashimi, such as octopus, crab, and red snapper.

Pickled ginger: A small mound of thin, pickled ginger slices is usually served with sushi. The slices are meant to be eaten between bites of fish in order to refresh the palate.

GOHANMONO (RICE DISHES)

A dish name that ends with *don* is a *donburi,* thus all the rice dishes that follow fall into this category. The word *donbur* refers both to a specific type of bowl —a deep, lidded bowl that is about six inches in diameter across the top (about

twice as large as a standard rice bowl) and is often made out of beautiful porcelain—and the food that goes into it. In Japan, *donburi* is a popular lunch or snack, and *donburi* "fast-food" restaurants are common, especially in big cities.

Katsudon
Pork cutlet with egg and onion on rice

Oyakodon
Chicken, egg, and vegetables on rice

Tendon
Shrimp and vegetable tempura (see page 204) on rice

Unadon
Broiled eel on rice

YAKIMONO (BROILED or GRILLED FOODS)
Restaurants that specialize in grilled food prepared tableside, generally known as steak houses, have been developed both in the U.S. and in Japan. Each table is usually constructed with a grill in the center, and the chefs verge on the acrobatic as they slice and flip the sizzling food under the diners' noses.

Yakitori
Grilled chicken on skewer

This is one of the most popular foods in Japan. The chicken is basted with a thick, sweet soy-based sauce and grilled or broiled. In Japan it is eaten at home, as a street food, and in restaurants specializing in yakitori. When grilled with salt only, it is called shioyaki.

> YAKITORI: Dip the skewered meat into the sauce, then eat the meat directly from the skewer.

Una-ju
Broiled eel on rice; served in a box

Beef, Pork, or Chicken Teriyaki
Broiled meat with **teriyaki** sauce

Beef Negimaki
Rolled broiled beef stuffed with scallion and cut into bite-size pieces; served with **teriyaki** sauce

Butaniku Shogayaki
Thinly sliced pork sautéed in ginger sauce

Salmon, Bluefish, or Lobster Tail Teriyaki
Broiled seafood with **teriyaki** sauce

INGREDIENT NOTES

• **Teriyaki** is a sweet sauce (often made with soy sauce, sugar, and sweet rice wine) that is applied to food in the last stages of grilling or pan-frying and is sometimes served as a condiment. The literal translation of *teri* is luster or gloss and describes how the sauce looks on the grilled or broiled (*yaki*) foods.

AGEMONO (DEEP-FRIED FOODS)

Deep-fried Japanese foods are made with light batters and are cooked in clean oil that is hot enough to seal the exterior of the food the moment it is immersed; this ensures that no oil penetrates the food and the natural juices are retained.

Tonkatsu

Deep-fried pork cutlet over shredded raw cabbage; served with a Worcestershire-based sauce that is thinner than **teriyaki** sauce (•203)

Inspired by the European breaded cutlet, this is one of the most popular meat dishes in Japan. It is also a very filling one.

Kushi-age

Deep-fried shrimp, scallops, **crab cake** (•201), and fish on skewer

Nishiki-age

Deep-fried chicken stuffed with carrot and spinach

Tempura

Deep-fried shrimp or other seafood and vegetables; served with ginger-flavored dipping sauce

NABEMONO (ONE-POT FOODS)

Sukiyaki

Thinly sliced beef, pork, chicken, seafood, or vegetables (or a combination) cooked in a pot of simmering broth at the table

Though usually sukiyaki is cooked by the diners, who pluck the chosen food off a platter and cook it themselves, it is sometimes prepared by a chef. In Japan the meat is often dipped into raw egg right after it is cooked, but this practice is uncommon in the U.S., where eating eggs that are not fully cooked is considered a health hazard.

Shabu Shabu

Thinly sliced beef and vegetables, including Chinese cabbage and mushrooms, cooked in a simmering chicken or fish stock by diners at the table; served with soy-based dipping sauce flavored with sesame, lemon, or lime

Hamanabe

Crab, shrimp, fish, and vegetables in soybean broth

Hamanabe is the Japanese equivalent of the hearty French seafood soup bouillabaisse.

MENRUI (NOODLES) Noodles of two kinds
are commonly served in Japanese restaurants: *soba* (thin,
light brown noodles made with buckwheat flour) and *udon*
(round or flat, chewy noodles made with white flour). In
Japan noodle shops specializing in noodles in hot broth
and cold noodle dishes abound, while they have only
recently begun to take hold in the U.S., mostly in the form
of inexpensive, informal eateries.

Noodle soups are sometimes listed under the heading
"Udon and Soba" and may be offered with a variety of
ingredients in the broth, including curry powder, omelets,
or grated yam.

Ten Zaru
Cold *udon* (flour) or *soba* (buckwheat) noodles with a sauce

*Cold noodles are commonly
served on a plate or flat basket
accompanied by a cold dipping
sauce. The dipping sauce is usually made with a combination of
dashi (fish stock), soy sauce,
mirin (•196), and possibly grated ginger and red pepper. The
noodles may be garnished with
thin strips of seaweed.*

Yaki Udon
Sautéed *udon* (flour) noodles with
beef and vegetables

Yaki Soba
Sautéed *soba* (buckwheat)
noodles with vegetables

*Yaki soba is the Japanese
version of the Chinese noodle
dish known as lo mein.*

Ten Zaru Udon or Soba
Cold noodles with dipping sauce

Niku Udon or Soba
Noodles in broth with beef

Nabeyaki Udon or Soba
Noodles, vegetables, and meat
cooked together in the casserole
in which they are served

Tempura Udon or Soba
Noodles in broth with
deep-fried prawns

Kitsune Udon or Soba
Noodles in broth with fried
tofu on top

Kake Udon or Soba
Noodles in broth garnished
with finely chopped scallion

NOODLE SOUPS are
customarily served in piping
hot broth and are meant to be
consumed fast along with a bit
of air to cool them off, which
means that diners are expected
to make a loud, sucking
sound—the so-called
"slurp" that American
parents scold their
children for making.

OKASHI (DESSERTS)

Desserts in Japan are usually limited to fruit. Sweets are more commonly served with tea at other times during the day. However, many Japanese restaurants in the U.S. choose to offer desserts, especially ice creams, on their menus.

Green Tea Ice Cream
Vanilla ice cream with powdered green tea leaves mixed in

Some people describe the flavor of green tea ice cream as mildly spinach-like.

Red Bean Ice Cream
Vanilla ice cream with a sugared paste of red **azuki beans** mixed in

Ginger Ice Cream
Vanilla ice cream flavored with powdered ginger

Tempura Ice Cream
Scoops of deep-frozen ice cream rolled in batter, then deep-fried

Yokan
Dense red bean jelly made from sugared **azuki beans**

NOMIMONO (BEVERAGES)

Green tea, Japanese beer, and sake are all appropriate accompaniments to a Japanese meal. It is also not uncommon for the Japanese to drink mild whiskey (with water and ice) with their food; straight, strong whiskey would obliterate the delicate flavors of Japanese food.

Green Tea
Light, pale, delicately flavored tea

Green tea (made from unfermented tea leaves) is as much a part of Japanese cuisine as fish and rice. It is meant to be drunk very hot, without cream or sugar.

JAPANESE TEAPOT lids do not have tongues that hold them on securely. It is, therefore, important to hold the lid while serving.

INGREDIENT NOTES

• **Azuki beans** are small, reddish beans. To divert evil spirits, azuki beans are spread around Japanese homes on New Year's Day.

Sake

Wine made from fermented rice with approximately the same alcohol content as table wine

Sake is often served heated in a small porcelain bottle or cup and is meant to refresh the palate and to increase the appreciation of the temperature differences between hot and cold foods. Sake is not drunk with soups, which are meant to be drunk while still very hot, nor with rice because rice and sake are considered too similar to complement one another. Sake is also used in cooking to tenderize and flavor foods and to flavor broths.

IN JAPAN, SAKE is poured at the beginning of the meal but no one begins drinking until the host initiates. It is considered bad manners to pour one's own sake; instead, all guests wait for another guest or the host to pour sake for them. When a guest has had his or her fill of sake, he or she turns the cup upside down.

Beer

Kirin, Sapporo, and Asahi beer—all strong, flavorful lagers that are generally dry and smooth

Japanese beer is world renowned and often served in very large bottles that are easily shared.

MEXICAN
cuisine

★

Cheers–*Salud* (sah-**lood**)
Bon appétit–*Buen Apetito* (bwain ah-pay-**tee**-tow)
Thank you–*Gracias* (**grah**-see-us)

MEXICAN RESTAURANTS UNDENIABLY FORM ONE of the fastest growing sectors in the restaurant industry in the U.S. Until about 10 years ago most Mexican eateries focused on Americanized (heavily sauced and cheese-covered) versions of corn-based dishes typical of northern Mexico, such as tamales, enchiladas, and tacos. Today these restaurants, while still prevalent, are being eclipsed by California-inspired burrito joints *(taquerías)*; inexpensive cafés featuring Mexican regional home cooking; and pricey *alta cocina* establishments where ambitious chefs improvise on hundreds of classic and sophisticated regional Mexican dishes (there are eight major culinary regions), thus introducing a whole new aspect of this complex cuisine to an increasingly knowledgeable audience. Meanwhile, Cal-Mex, Tex-Mex, and Southwestern styles of cooking, American interpretations of Mexican cuisine, continue to flourish.

What all these restaurants have in common is the use of the chili pepper in all its permutations—fresh, stuffed, dried, smoked, powdered—and myriad sauces of complex taste. These sauces, including the well-known and numerous *moles* (pronounced "mo-lehs"), remain the heart of Mexican cooking.

MOLES

Moles are complex cooked sauces, as opposed to simpler sauces that are used only as toppings. They contain chilies and aromatic herbs and a host of other ingredients that may include chocolate, tomatillos (green tomato-like berries), ground nuts, ground pumpkin seeds, tomatoes, and onions. There are hundreds of recipes for *moles*.

Principles of Flavor

The flavors that define Mexican cooking are chilies, garlic, white onions, scallions, cumin, oregano, epazote (a pungent herb with a woody flavor), cinnamon, cilantro, and chocolate. One distinctive ingredient, a dark corn fungus called *huitlacoche*, is found more and more often on the menus of better restaurants.

Foreign Influences

Many of the staples of the Mexican diet—beans, chilies, tomatoes, chocolate, vanilla, and foods made with a corn dough called *masa*, such as tamales and tortillas—were derived from the cooking of the Indians who inhabited Mexico before the arrival of the Spanish in the 16th century. The Aztecs were the predominant tribe, and they prepared their food by stewing, roasting, or steaming, techniques that are still common in Mexico today. The Spanish introduced lard and frying, which was most noticeably applied to the preparation of beans. Whereas Aztecs traditionally cooked beans by boiling them in an earthenware pot, the Spanish-influenced technique involved mashing the boiled beans and

CHILIES

It is said that the cooking of Peru and Mexico are the hottest in Latin America. This is achieved in both cases by a deft manipulation of chilies not found in other Latin American cuisines. Though Mexico boasts well over 60 varieties—ranging from mild to spicy-hot—the following six are the most commonly used in restaurants in the U.S.

Chile habanero, close cousin of the Scotch Bonnet pepper, is considered the hottest of the chilies grown in Mexico. Its distinctive, lingering flavor is as highly valued as its piquancy.

Chile jalapeño, used either fresh or pickled, is among the most widely known chilies outside of Mexico. *Chile chipotle*, a smoked and dried jalapeño chili, is used to impart a smokey flavor.

Chile poblano, ranging in piquacy from mild to hot, is among the most popular fresh chilies. Dark, green, and large, it is commonly used to make *chiles rellenos* (stuffed chilies). When a poblano is dried when ripe, it is called an *ancho*.

Chile serrano, a small, slender hot chili often used in guacamole and salsa.

Chile tepín is a very small, very hot chili that is generally used dried.

Chile verde is a medium-hot chili often used in gua-camole and ceviche (see page 220).

frying them until a stiff paste formed, creating what we know as *frijoles refritos*, or refried beans (despite this dish's name the beans are only fried once, but really well). With the arrival of the Spanish also came many new raw materials with which Mexican cooks could work, including pork, rice, cheese, onions, garlic, and spices and herbs, such as cumin, cinnamon, and oregano.

In the 19th century, German immigrants came to Mexico and introduced beer. A more recent influence on Mexican cooking has been the health consciousness movement that began in the U.S. For example, lard is being replaced by light vegetable oils for frying, and there is an increased emphasis on the use of fresh over canned ingredients, improving the quality and appeal of many Mexican dishes in an ironic return to the pre-Columbian style.

Ordering

The Mexican meal follows the familiar pattern of appetizer, soup, main course, and dessert. Note that some soups, *caldos* (see pages 224-225) in particular, are large enough to serve as an entire meal, and often popular dishes, such as *antojitos* (*masa*-based dishes like enchiladas and tacos) are automati-

---

MEXICAN-AMERICAN CUISINE

Due to the great number of Mexican immigrants as well as the popularity of the cuisine, Mexican food has always been easy to find in the U.S. However, some of the most popular and familiar dishes are not truly Mexican (they are identified on the menu found later in this chapter). For example, neither cheddar cheese nor sour cream are common in Mexico, flour tortillas are a rarity, and guacamole is generally served as a side dish rather than a topping. American versions of Mexican food can be roughly categorized as follows:

Cal-Mex: emphasis on big burritos and healthier versions of many dishes

Tex-Mex: oriented toward such meaty basics as *fajitas* and chile con carne (see pages 224 and 226), as well as rice and beans

Southwestern: lighter, innovative style, with greater use of fresh chilies

---

cally served with rice and refried beans, making it unlikely that you will need an appetizer or dessert to fill you up.

Condiments

Condiments found on the Mexican table include chili sauces, pickled jalapeño peppers and other vegetables, and *salsa cruda* (sometimes called *salsa fresca*, just plain *salsa*, or *pico de gallo*, which is the northern Mexican term and translates as "rooster's beak"), an uncooked, fresh relish made with chopped tomatoes, onions, scallions, cilantro, oregano, sometimes jicama (a root vegetable similar to a potato), and a modest dose of hot chilies.

The pickled jalapeño peppers are often combined with carrot and onion slices, and, while the peppers retain their intense hotness, the carrot and onion slices (and other vegetables) remain relatively mild.

The chili sauces, which are intensely flavorful, can be red or green. The red (sometimes called *salsa ranchero*) is based on roasted tomatoes (when made with smoked chilies the sauce takes on a brown tinge) and the green *(salsa verde)* is based on boiled tomatillos. The hotness depends on the chef and in some cases may not exist at all.

Garnishes

Garnishes that appear on Mexican foods often include radishes (frequently carved into decorative shapes), chopped scallions, white onions, and fresh chilies.

Bread

A stack of warm tortillas on a serving plate, wrapped in a warm towel or other heat-preserving cover, is a feature of nearly every dining table in Mexico. These tortillas are used to sop up extra sauce, to wrap up bites of meat, beans, or rice, to push food onto the fork, and to act as a mild backdrop for spicy and/or rich food. The tortilla also protects the hands from sauces or fillings. In good Mexican restaurants in the U.S. fresh tortillas are brought to the table automatically. If they are not, don't hesitate to request them.

CORN vs. FLOUR TORTILLAS

A tortilla is a small, round, flat, unleavened bread cooked on a griddle. Corn tortillas, which are made from a corn dough called *masa*, were a staple of the Indian diet long before the arrival of Europeans in Mexico and are still by far the most common form of tortilla there. Flour tortillas, which are typical of northern Mexico (especially the northwesern state of Sonora), contain lard, are rolled as opposed to pressed like corn tortillas, and are larger and more delicate than corn tortillas. Flour tortillas have flourished in California, where an immigrant Mexican population cut off from a ready supply of the corn used to make *masa* and thus corn tortillas, has turned to white flour to make their tortillas.

The most commonly available corn tortillas are yellow, but different colored tortillas, such as red and blue ones, have become available to consumers in recent years. These colored tortillas are made from "heirloom" or antique varieties of corn that have been continually cultivated by Indian tribes, mainly in Peru and New Mexico.

Other forms of bread encountered on the Mexican table are *bolillos*, crusty rolls, tapered at both ends, that are used to make *tortas* (sandwiches); and *sopapillas*, golden brown, deep-fried puffs that are often served with honey and are much favored in Tex-Mex and northern Mexican cooking, where they are a sweet antidote for fiery hot foods.

Utensils

Warm tortillas and tortilla chips (used as scoops) supplement the knife, fork, and spoon commonly employed when eating Mexican food.

Signature Dishes

Tacos (soft or crisp tortillas with a savory filling, such as chopped pork or beef tongue, topped with onion, tomato, and cilantro); *Enchiladas* (tortilla rolled around fillings of cheese, chicken, or beef and drenched in sauce); *Frijoles refritos* (refried beans); *Pescado a la Veracruzana* (whole fish, often red snapper, cooked in a briny tomato sauce containing green olives, garlic, onions, and chilies); *Pollo con Mole Poblano* (chicken in a rich chocolate sauce that features chilies)

Common Misconceptions

Mexican food is always spicy-hot. While it's true that Mexicans like their food well seasoned, in most Mexican restaurants in the U.S. the dishes are relatively mild, and diners are expected to either request extra spiciness when they order or add as much extra heat as they want with bottled sauces, pickled jalapeños, and/or *salsa cruda*, all of which have been formulated to blend with the other flavors of the dish.

Mexican food is always fried in lard. While it's true that lard was a major component of Mexican food many years ago, today most frying is done in light vegetable oil. When in doubt, ask the waiter what kind of cooking fat is being used.

Mexican **MENU**

ENTREMESAS (APPETIZERS)

Tortilla chips (called *totopos* in Spanish and sometimes *tostaditas*) and *salsa cruda* (see page 213) are brought to the table automatically in many Mexican restaurants, and these fried munchies can easily serve as your appetizer, especially if the chips are freshly made and the salsa tasty. Keep in mind, however, that with this approach you miss the chance to try some of the most interesting traditional (read non-American) items on a Mexican menu, such as ceviche, *nopales*, and guacamole.

Run out of tortilla chips and salsa before your food arrives? Don't hesitate to ask for more of either since most restaurants will gladly replenish your supply without charge. Then, when the main course arrives, keep the remaining chips on the table to use as dippers for sauces and soups.

Guacamole

A cold, uncooked dip made by chopping and often mashing **avocados** and blending them with chopped white onion, tomato, chilies, **cilantro**, and fresh lime or lemon juice; served with tortilla chips or as a sauce for tacos or other *antojitos* (see page 221)

Guacamole is a pre-Columbian dish, believe it or not. Try it with small, warm, soft tortillas instead of chips.

Aguacate Relleno

A halved **avocado** filled with shrimp or another filling, such as chicken, cheese, vegetables, lobster, or crab

INGREDIENT NOTES

• **Avocado** is a fruit with a dark green skin, buttery, light green flesh, and a big seed. Avocado is used in guacamole, in salads, or sometimes as a garnish for soups.

• **Cilantro**, also known as coriander and Chinese parsley, is an herb native to Mediterranean Europe that in its fresh form is used extensively in Mexican cooking. Although it looks like flat-leaf parsley, it has a completely different and curious odor that has been likened to chemicals, rubber, bedbugs (the word coriander comes from the Greek *koris*, meaning bedbug), and, in a more appetizing vein, a mixture of cumin and caraway. For some it is an acquired taste but, once acquired, this herb makes an appealing addition to many dishes, including soups, guacamole, and *salsa cruda*.

Gordita
(Tex-Mex and northern and central Mexican)
A cornmeal dough, or *masa,* pocket stuffed with meat, beans, or cheese, and fried on a griddle

Jalapeño Relleno
Fresh or canned chili stuffed with tuna, cheese, or peanut butter (it's really true!)

Ensalada de Nopalitos
A salad of fresh or canned **nopales** with a vinegar dressing

Quesadilla
Flour or corn tortilla filled with cheese, folded in half, and heated on a griddle; bean, meat, and vegetable fillings available upon request

Restaurants differ considerably in their interpretations of the quesadilla. Many make them with two flat, unfolded tortillas, one soft and one crispy. Others layer them, and call them quesadillas sincronizadas. *Some restaurants drop the tortilla altogether and make their quesadillas with pastry dough.*

Mexican Pizza
A giant quesadilla made by heating one or two large flour tortillas and topping or filling them with cheese and an abundance of other ingredients, such as **Mexican chorizo** or chopped vegetables

MEXICAN CHEESES
There are not a lot of different kinds of cheese made in Mexico, but what is available is used to very good effect. Two of the most common are *queso fresco*, a crumbly white cheese similar to a mild feta, and *queso asadero*, a firm cheese that strings when melted. Many restaurants in the U.S. rely on two cheeses rarely used in Mexico: mild, unaged Monterey Jack, which originated in Monterey, California, and mild cheddar.

• *Nopales* are sliced cactus pads. They are pale to dark green in color, have a mildly tart flavor that is reminiscent of green beans, and, when cooked properly, are simultaneously tender and a little crunchy, with an okra-like slipperiness.

• **Mexican chorizo** is a sausage made with fresh pork, ground dried chilies, and vinegar. Some Mexican restaurants in the U.S. substitute Spanish-style chorizo, which differs from the Mexican variety in that it is cured.

Taco Salad (Cal-Mex)

Lettuce, beans, cheese, tomatoes, and seasoned ground beef; served either in an edible bowl made from a deep-fried flour or corn tortilla (literally a *tostada)* or piled on top of tortilla chips

Ceviche (or Seviche)

A salad of raw seafood, often including squid, shrimp, red snapper, and conch, that has been marinated in lemon or lime juice until firm and opaque, then tossed with chilies, onions, tomatoes, and **cilantro** (•218)

Chimichanga (Southwestern)

A flour tortilla wrapped tightly around a filling of chicken or beef and deep-fried; often served with guacamole, salsa, sour cream, and/or shredded cheese (sort of a deep-fried burrito)

Chile con Queso (Tex-Mex)

Fresh or canned jalapeño or serrano chilies in a smooth, yellow cheese sauce; served with tortilla chips for dipping

Nachos (Cal-Mex)

Tortilla chips topped with melted cheese, chilies, and sometimes sour cream, guacamole, and/or **chorizo** (•219) and chicken

Empanadas

Meat-filled pastries
The word empanar *means "to bake in pastry."*

Queso Fundido

Baked cheese dip (for tortilla chips or fresh tortillas), sometimes flavored with **chorizo** (•219) and chilies or **chili powder**

INGREDIENT NOTES

• **Chili powder** is a spice mixture made with dried red chilies, often ground with such spices as oregano, toasted cumin, garlic, coriander, and cloves.

ANTOJITOS

Antojitos, which can be translated as "little things that you crave," have come to mean foods based on *masa*, a dough made from field corn. The corn is soaked and boiled in lime water (a process that breaks down the hulls), then ground into a paste, traditionally on a flat stone known as a *metate*. This dough is used to make tortillas, tamales, enchiladas, and tacos. *Antojitos* can be eaten as snacks, appetizers, or as main courses—the custom in many Mexican restaurants in the U.S., where they are often accompanied by rice and refried beans; in Mexico, *antojitos* are most commonly eaten as a light supper or as a snack. Unfortunately, most Americans have been exposed only to a few basic selections from this small part of the Mexican menu and think that they represent the whole of Mexican cuisine. Such a shame!

Tamale

Masa (corn tortilla dough) pocket stuffed with pork, chicken, seafood, or vegetables, wrapped in a corn husk or banana leaf, and steamed; served without sauce

TAMALES usually arrive at the table still wrapped in corn husks and steaming hot. Sometimes they are also tied around the middle with a small strip of corn husk, a sign that great care was taken to make them. To unwrap, grab one end of the bow and pull. Next, grasp the corn husk where it protrudes beyond the end of the tamale, hold it a few inches above the plate, and shake gingerly. The tamale should slide out, and you should be left holding the husk. Alternatively, in casual surroundings, tamales can be eaten with the hands by gently squeezing out a bite-full of filling at a time.

Burrito (Cal-Mex)

A large flour tortilla stuffed with any combination of ingredients such as rice, beans, cheese, meat, poultry, mixed stewed or sautéed vegetables, *salsa cruda*, guacamole, or sour cream

Although the word burrito means "little burro" in Spanish (and indeed these snacks are small in northern Mexico, where they originated), most burritos made in North America are anything but little. The centerpiece of Cal-Mex cooking, they are often so overstuffed that one could feed two people. East LA-style restaurants pride themselves on their enormous burritos, filled with rice and beans in addition to other fillings.

IN MEXICO A TACO is made by wrapping two soft corn tortillas around a filling of meat or chicken. In Mexican restaurants in the U.S., tacos are often made with mass-manufactured tortillas deep-fried in a "U" shape. Tacos made with these shells, which are not nearly as tasty as fresh tortillas, are hard to eat, since the shell breaks in two and the filling starts to fall out with the first bite. To counteract this problem, try biting with your teeth without letting your lips touch or squeeze the taco.

Taco

One or two soft corn tortillas wrapped around one or more fillings, or those fillings inside a single tortilla deep-fried in a "U" shape

VIVA LA DIFERENCIA!

Though it may seem obvious to connoisseurs, Americans often forget the difference between a burrito and an enchilada: Burritos are neat packages made by stuffing *flour* tortillas with rice and sometimes everything but the kitchen sink, and are served *without* sauce. Enchiladas are made by stuffing *corn* tortillas, usually with just one filling, then absolutely *drenching* them with sauce.

Enchilada

Corn tortilla rolled around filling of cheese, chicken, or beef, and drenched with a sauce, such as **mole poblano**, **mole verde** (•227), or tomato sauce, and grated cheese

Don't confuse enchilada *with* enchilado. *The former is described above. The latter is any filling for* antojitos, *including* enchiladas, *that may also be served as a separate dish, and is usually very spicy.* Enchilado *served on its own is meant to be wrapped in fresh tortillas by the diner.*

Enchilada Suiza

A casserole of corn tortillas stuffed with chicken, beef, or cheese, and topped with green **tomatillo** sauce and sour cream

Flautas (or Taquitos)

Corn tortillas filled with cheese, beef, or chicken, and deep-fried; served drenched in a red or green sauce

Flauta is the Spanish word for "flute." Notice the resemblance between these deep-fried tortilla tubes and the musical instrument.

TACO AND OTHER *ANTOJITO* FILLINGS

Taco and other *antojito* fillings vary immensely. Following is a list of possible choices. Most of the meats are shredded (pulled off the bone):

al carbón: char-grilled filling of any kind
al pastor: roasted pork
carne asada: grilled or roasted beef
carnitas: braised pork nuggets
chorizo: pork sausage
lengua: beef tongue
longaniza: pork sausage, similar to chorizo, without the skin
mariscos: seafood
mixto: combination of meats
picadillo: ground seasoned beef with vegetables (hash)
pollo: chicken

Chalupa
A deep-fried corn tortilla with the edges turned up to form a *chalupa* (boat), filled with beans, meat, or other ingredients; similar to a tostada but with more filling

Sope
Two corn tortillas sandwiched around ground meat or cheese, sealed on the edges, and fried

Chile Relleno
Fresh, fairly mild poblano or Anaheim chili stuffed with cheese, coated with a light egg batter (sometimes spiked with beer), then fried and smothered with tomato sauce

Tostada
A flat, deep-fried corn tortilla topped with such ingredients as beans, cheese, chicken, chopped tomato, onions, shredded cheese, sour cream, or guacamole

Tostaditas *are small* tostadas; tostaditas *is also the word used by some people to refer to tortilla chips.*

Mole Enchilada
A corn tortilla filled with chicken, cheese, or beef, and topped with *mole poblano* and grated cheese

INGREDIENT NOTES

• The **tomatillo** is a green fruit covered by a thin papery husk. Its flavor is mild, with notes of lemon, apple, and herbs. It is also known as the Mexican green tomato, but it is actually a berry related to the Cape gooseberry and the American ground cherry.

• *Mole poblano* is a rich, dense, earthy sauce that counts among its ingredients turkey broth, plantains, raisins, toasted tortillas, chocolate, several kinds of chilies, ground nuts and seeds, anise, and cinnamon. Because of its popularity, it is often referred to as just plain *mole*, even though it is only one of hundreds of different kinds of *moles*, or sauces.

Chilaquiles
Fried or plain tortilla pieces, chili sauce, and meat, baked or stir-fried

The good taste of this popular dish belies its origin as a way to use up stale tortillas and leftover sauce. It is served all over Mexico, often for brunch. Subject to much improvisation, it can also be made with scrambled eggs, bell peppers, and **tomatillos** *(•223).*

Tamale Pie (Tex-Mex)
Chile con carne baked in a corn-bread crust

Fajitas (Tex-Mex)
Grilled strips of marinated beef or chicken, or whole shrimp, with onions, tomatoes, bell peppers, chilies, guacamole, and sour cream; often presented on a sizzling platter; served with flour tortillas meant to be wrapped around the fillings by the diner

Fajita *means "skirt steak," but this dish has been popularized to the extent that it is made with almost anything.*

SOPAS (SOUPS) Mexican soups fall into one of two categories—*caldos* (broths with many solid ingredients, often served as a main course) and *sopas* (more like the thicker soups in European cuisines). Soup plays a central role in the Mexican diet, especially at the main meal of the day, the *comida*, which is traditionally eaten after 2 P.M.

Sopa de Frijoles Negros
Spanish black bean soup, flavored with onion, garlic, *epazote* (a pungent herb with a woody flavor), and green bell peppers

Sopa de Mariscos
A tomato-based seafood chowder

Sopa de Tortilla
Chicken, fried tortilla strips, and chilies in a broth; often served with a dollop of sour cream and sliced avocado

Caldo de Res
A hearty soup made with beef stock and vegetables, such as carrots, zucchini, green beans, or corn

Sopa del Día
Soup of the day

Pozole
Hearty soup/stew made with chicken or pork meat, broth, and hominy (specially treated corn); garnished with onion, **cilantro** (•218), and radish

POZOLE AND OTHER SOUPS are often served with bowls of chopped vegetables and herbs, such as radishes, green onions, and cilantro, on the side. These should be mixed with the soup prior to eating according to your own taste. Sometimes the radishes are served whole, in which case you have a choice of cutting them up yourself or eating them whole.

Menudo
A thick soup featuring **tripe**, with or without *pozole*

Menudo *can be spicy or mildly flavored depending on the chef's hand. In Tex-Mex as well as Mexican cooking, menudo is thought to have curative powers and is often recommended for hangovers. It may be served with garnishes, such as chopped onions, cilantro, and peppers.*

Consome de Chivo
Goat soup made with pieces of roasted goat and vegetables, such as chick-peas, carrots, potatoes, and *chipotle* chilies (see page 211)

INGREDIENT NOTES

• **Tripe** is the lining of an animal's stomach. Tripe from a cow is by far the most commonly used, but you will also see dishes made from pig or sheep tripe.

• *Pozole* (or *posole*) is a hearty soup/stew as well as the name for what in the southern U.S. is known as hominy: corn that has been treated with slaked lime (calcium hydroxide, a salt). The large, white, *pozole* kernels have an agreeably starchy taste and smooth, dense texture. They are also found in some tripe soups and occasionally burritos.

CARNE (BEEF)

Carne Asada
Grilled marinated skirt steak

If the steak is garnished with other foods, such as sautéed poblano chilies, the garnish is represented in the dish name; i.e. carne asada con rajas.

Carne Alambres
Marinated beef or other meat on a skewer

In simple, small restaurants, this dish, which translates as "meat on a skewer," is usually made with beef, but in more upscale restaurants, it can be made with chicken (pollo).

Bisteck Encebollado
A thin steak fried with onions

Milanesa Res
A breaded and deep-fried steak, with or without sauce

Cecina
Strongly flavored steak made with a beef cutlet that has been preserved by salting and drying

Lengua
Beef or veal tongue stewed in chili sauce

Torta Milanesa
Deep-fried beef (or pork) cutlet on a *bolillo* (crusty roll)

Although it's commonplace to refer to tacos as Mexican sandwiches, they really do make sandwiches in Mexico and they are known as tortas. *Inexpensive and very filling,* tortas *are made with meat, lettuce, onions, and tomatoes on crisp rolls, often slathered with mayonnaise, guacamole, or refried beans.*

Chile con Carne (Tex-Mex and Northern Mexican)
Chopped or ground beef seasoned with chili powder and onions in a thick stew; sometimes served *con frijoles*, with beans

Picadillo
A Spanish-influenced dish of fried, seasoned ground beef, sometimes mixed with almonds and dried fruits such as raisins

Picadillo is also used as a stuffing for antojitos *(corn-based dishes, such as tacos) and vegetables, such as chilies.*

POLLO (CHICKEN)

Pollo con Mole Poblano

Chicken pieces stewed in **mole poblano** (•223), often sprinkled with sesame seeds

Pollo con mole poblano, *which originated in the state of Puebla (hence the name), is one of the most popular dishes in Mexican cuisine, and some variation of it is made in nearly every part of the country.*

Pollo con Mole Ranchero

A stewed, boneless chicken dish from southern Mexico, made with more bitter chocolate and more hot chilies than *pollo con mole poblano* (see above)

Pollo con Mole Verde

Chicken pieces in a mellow **mole verde**

Arroz con Pollo

Chicken pieces cooked with rice, spices, and **saffron**

Mixiotes

Chicken pieces wrapped in parchment and steamed, sometimes in beer; served with a spicy brown sauce the base of which is beer in which the chicken may have been steamed

Adobo

Chicken marinated in a vinegar and chili marinade, then roasted

Since adobo *is a vinegar and chili marinade used on both pork and poultry, the technically correct (but rarely encountered) term for this dish is* pollo adobado.

Pipián con Carne de Pollo

Chicken pieces in a simple sauce of crushed **pumpkin seeds**

Pollo Asado

Grilled or roasted chicken, on the bone

INGREDIENT NOTES

• *Mole verde*, or green sauce, counts among its ingredients chicken broth, tomatillos, ground lettuce and other greens, ground toasted pumpkin seeds, fresh green chilies, epazote (a pungent herb with a woody flavor), and cilantro.

• **Saffron**, one of the most expensive spices, is replaced by less expensive substitutes such as turmeric in all but the finest restaurants.

• **Pumpkin seeds**, called *pepitas* in Spanish, are eaten dried as a snack and are used fresh and dried as a thickener and flavoring agent for stews and *moles* (sauces).

OTRAS CARNES (OTHER MEATS)

Carnitas
Pan-fried or braised pork nuggets; served with tortillas and *salsa cruda* (see page 213)

Al Pastor
A large cut of spit-roasted meat with garlic and herbs

Al pastor means "shepherd style" but usually indicates pork. Ask to be sure. The pork in this dish is often sliced (and sometimes served with roasted pineapple chunks) as a taco filling.

Ternera al Horno
Roasted veal, usually served with a **cilantro** (•218) and **tomatillo** (•223) green sauce

Chicharrones
Crispy deep-fried pork skins stewed in red or green chili sauce, or served by themselves as a snack

Torta de Jamón y Queso
Ham and cheese sandwich on a *bolillo* (crusty roll)

Chuletas de Puerco
Grilled pork chops; often served with **mole verde** (•227)

Cochinita Pibil
Mayan dish made of chopped pork shoulder, marinated **annatto** seed, and **Seville orange** juice, wrapped in a banana leaf, and pit-roasted or barbecued; served with pickled red onions and soft corn tortillas

Barbacoa
Mature goat meat or mutton wrapped in a banana leaf and steamed, roasted, or barbecued

Barbacoa means "barbecue." This dish can be made with other meats.

Cabrito
Baby goat, usually roasted or barbecued

INGREDIENT NOTES

• The **Seville orange** (known as *naranja agria* in Spanish) is a bitter orange that is used often by Mexican cooks as a flavoring and in marinades.

• **Annatto** or annatto seeds (called *achiote* in Spanish-speaking regions) are small, delicately flavored berries that give foods a yellowish orange color. They are used in the U.S. to color cheddar cheese, margarine, and smoked fish, and are sold in supermarkets in a paste or powder form (combined with garlic, cumin, oregano, and food coloring).

PESCADOS Y MARISCOS (FISH and SHELLFISH)

Seafood is abundant along Mexico's Atlantic and Pacific seaboards but not in the country's interior. Veracruz, located on the Gulf Coast, is particularly well known for its seafood cookery with a Spanish influence. Small, simple restaurants in the U.S. tend to limit their seafood offerings to shrimp (some do not offer seafood at all), but more upscale establishments feature both classic and innovative seafood dishes.

Camarones al Ajillo
Shrimp sautéed in oil with lots of garlic

Langosta al Mojo de Ajo
Lobster meat marinated in garlic sauce and fried

Escabeche
A Spanish Caribbean-inspired dish of fried fish, such as red snapper or kingfish, or shellfish, such as scallops; served with a pickling sauce of vinegar or lime juice, chilies, and onions

Caldo de Pescado
A hearty fish stew that includes among its ingredients chilies, garlic, and carrots

Huachinango a la Veracruzana
The fabulous red snapper, Veracruz style—a whole fish in tomato sauce with green olives, garlic, chilies, capers, and a touch of vinegar

Camarones Enchilados
Shrimp in a fragrant tomato sauce flavored with garlic, bell peppers, and cinnamon; sometimes rolled in tortillas

Mojara a la Plancha
Grilled ocean perch

HUEVOS y GUARNICIONES (EGGS and SIDE DISHES)

Eggs are as popular in Mexico as they are on this side of the border. Although most often eaten for breakfast, they can also serve as a luncheon dish or as a light supper. They are often accompanied by rice and beans as are many other Mexican dishes.

Huevos Rancheros
Fried eggs served on tortillas with *salsa cruda* (see page 213) or other fresh or bottled hot tomato sauce

Huevos Mexicanos
An omelet or scrambled eggs cooked with onions, green and red bell peppers, chilies, and tomatoes

Huevos con Jamón
Eggs scrambled with ham

Breakfast Burrito (Cal-Mex)
A flour tortilla stuffed with scrambled eggs, **chorizo** (•219), and hot sauce

Mexican Rice
Rice cooked with onion and chicken stock, sometimes flecked with bits of green bell pepper or tomato, and fried briefly

Frijoles
Pinto, pink, or **black beans** served stewed or mashed and fried (in which case they are called *frijoles refritos,* refried beans)

POSTRES (DESSERTS)

Mexican restaurants are not known for a profusion of desserts, and, in fact, desserts are de-emphasized. Flan is one of the most popular. A *batida* (milk shake made with fruit) is a good, sweet conclusion to a meal, as is a cup of Mexican cocoa.

Flan
Spanish baked custard flavored with cinnamon and coated with caramel sauce

Churros
Rope-shaped, sugar-dusted cakes reminiscent of donuts, often fried in lime-flavored oil

INGREDIENT NOTES

• **Black beans** are a bit earthier than the milder pink or pinto (mottled pink-beige) beans.

Buñuelo

Deep-fried flour tortilla with granulated sugar on top

Buñuelos *can also be rolled around an apple filling before being deep-fried.*

Sopapilla con Helados

Deep-fried pastry puff with ice cream on top

Tamales de Dulce

Tamales stuffed with a mixture of sweetened *masa* (corn dough), raisins, coconut, pineapple, and/or nuts

Tamales de dulce, *which are sometimes dyed red with food coloring, are typically served at Christmas and New Year's celebrations.*

BEBIDAS (BEVERAGES)

Jarritos Soda

Piña (pineapple), *fresa* (strawberry), *tamarindo* (**tamarind**), *limón* (similar to key lime), and *toronja* (grapefruit)

Jarritos is a Mexican brand of fruit-flavored soda.

Batidos

Milk shakes made with fresh or canned fruit, including banana, mango, strawberry, and pineapple

Restaurants are usually happy to mix fruits for milk shakes according to personal preference.

Aguas Frescas

Refreshing, sweet, water-based drinks flavored with **tamarind**, hibiscus buds, strawberries, melon, or other fresh fruits

Jugo de Naranja

Orange juice

Mexican Chocolate

Thick hot chocolate made with **Mexican chocolate**

• **Tamarind** is a fruit. Its seed pod contains a sweet-sour pulp that is used to make a syrup for flavoring sodas. It is also a popular cooking ingredient in many parts of Asia.

• **Mexican chocolate** is very coarsely ground and compressed into blocks. It is flavored with cinnamon and ground nuts, usually almonds, which serve to thicken the hot drink. Rarely used to make candy or pastries, it's used mainly in *moles* (cooking sauces) and hot chocolate, a very popular beverage in Mexico.

Sangría

A refreshing red wine punch sweetened with fruit juice; served over ice

The word sangría *means "bleeding" in Spanish, a reference to this drink's blood-red color.*

Tequila

Distinctive, strong Mexican liquor made from the sweet sap of the agave plant

REAL AFICIONADOS OF tequila drink it as a shot, but only after rubbing a wedge of lime across the outside of the thumb, sprinkling that moist spot with salt, and then licking the salt off. The shot is followed by a bite into the lime wedge. If you mix the tequila with *sangrita* (a spicy drink made of orange and sometimes tomato juice, grenadine, salt, and chili) in your mouth, then you are really doing tequila Mexican style.

Frozen Margarita

Tequila, lime juice, and ice processed in a blender to the consistency of slush and served in a stemmed, salt-rimmed glass (salt omitted on request)

Many Mexican restaurants in the U.S. pride themselves on their frozen margaritas (almost certainly an American invention). If you don't specify "frozen" when ordering, however, you might be served a traditional margarita, which is not made in a blender, is not made with ice, and is generally less sweet than the frozen version.

Beer

Mexican beer is often served with a wedge of lime; in fact, it is customary to rest a wedge of lime on the lip of the long-neck bottles most Mexican breweries use. Squeeze the lime into the bottle, according to taste, before drinking. If the restaurant doesn't serve lime with Mexican beer, ask for it. Or better yet, ask for a salt-rimmed glass filled with ice, squeeze in lots of lime juice, and then pour in your beer. You'll have a michelada, *a traditional coastal Mexican favorite.*

MEXICAN BEER

Mexico is famous for good beer, and any one of the following is recommended as a reliable accompaniment to a meal.

Corona Lite: light and refreshing, similar to popular mass-produced American beers

Corona Extra: even lighter than Corona Lite

Carta Blanca: light beer with a distinctive sharp edge

Chihuahua: another light beer with a pleasing, tangy taste

Superior: there's a light version and a dark version, the dark being more flavorful

Tecate: medium beer with a full flavor, often served in cans (as opposed to bottles like most other Mexican beers)

Dos Equis (XX): amber beer with memorable flavor; highly recommended

Dos Equis Light: lager with little flavor

Negra Modelo: dark, full-flavored beer likely to appeal to ale and stout drinkers

Pacífico Clara: a full-flavored light beer

MIDDLE EASTERN
cuisine

ALTHOUGH THE MIDDLE EAST IS A VAST REGION incorporating many different countries, cultures, and religions, it can be defined by its cuisine. Over the course of thousands of years this region has shared a long history in which ideas and customs have commingled through trade, nomadic migrations, and conquest and unification by various empires. Meat grilled on spits, elaborately stuffed vegetables, salads, yogurt, and the subtle use of spices are just a few of the common denominators.

Vegetarians and people who are health conscious in general will find much to enjoy in Middle Eastern restaurants. Vegetable and salad dishes abound, and the frequent use of high-protein legumes and grains is a custom that goes back to ancient times.

The Middle Eastern dining experience is also enhanced by a tradition of hospitality and generosity toward all guests. In general, the purveyors of this cuisine are anxious to please and to win friends and admirers of their way of eating. If you express a particular interest in Middle Eastern food, you may find yourself the recipient of an unexpected special dish. It is with a mixture of pride and amusement that Middle Eastern cooks watch as the Western world discovers a "new" healthful way of eating that is, in fact, the way people of the Middle East have been eating since the dawn of civilization.

Principles of Flavor

Herbs frequently encountered in Middle Eastern dishes include mint, dill, flat-leaf parsley, and cilantro. Garlic is used in most savory dishes. Spices are frequently used but always subtly, and when incorporated into a dish correctly, no single spice flavor is apparent. Commonly used spices and spice combinations include ground red pepper, paprika, and cinnamon; nutmeg, cinnamon, cloves, and ginger or allspice; and ground coriander and cumin. Saffron is used extensively in Morocco and Iran, where its pale yellow color is thought to bring happiness.

Olive oil is used for its flavor as well as for a cooking fat. It is mixed with vinegar or lemon juice (which adds an important sour note to many dishes) in salad dressings and marinades. The use of nuts is extensive in Middle Eastern cooking and the choice of nuts differs regionally: pine nuts, kernels from the cones of a pine tree, are found in the Mediterannean region and in Syrian and Egyptian cooking, walnuts are used in Turkey, and almonds in Iran.

Foreign Influence

The countries within the Middle East that seem to have contributed the most to the shared cuisine of the region are Iran, Lebanon, Jordan, Syria, Turkey, and Morocco, and they did so in ancient times. From outside the region in Asia came citrus fruits, almonds, rice, and sugar cane. (The Arabs, in turn, carried these items westward to Europe.) The Middle East was part of the "spice route" between the Far East, Central Africa, and Europe and adopted many of the spices it was trafficking. The choice of spices such as saffron and the prevalence of eggplant and rice-based dishes reflect the influence of India. African couscous found its way into Middle Eastern foods by way of Morocco. The more recent culinary acquisitions (during European colonial times) include tomatoes and sweet peppers from the New World.

Ordering

Meals in the Middle East are social occasions to linger over with friends and family, so start off slowly by ordering a wide assortment of appetizers and a round of drinks. The beverage of choice with this course is *arak*, an anise-flavored apéritif. Next, order several entrées to share. A mixed grill dish is a good choice if you want to sample several traditional kebabs at once. Vegetable dishes should not be overlooked as either entrées or side dishes; a stuffed vegetable is a must because it is a classic. Main dishes are usually served with rice and/or bread but it is always worth checking with the waiter to find out if you need to order either separately. Also note that there is no definitive English spelling for most Middle Eastern menu terms, so each restaurant simply interprets the language in its own creative manner.

Service and Dining

Traditionally Middle Easten meals are eaten family-style. The main dish, usually meat, chicken, or fish, is accompanied by rice and a vegetable (unless the main dish contains a lot of vegetables as is often the case with cous-cous, pilafs, and stews), yogurt, and salad. Coffee is served after the meal with or without a sweet dessert. Bread is eaten with every meal. *Mezze* (appetizers and drinks) can serve as a first course or a meal in themselves.

Condiments

Condiments, such as a garlic or tahini sauce, are usually included on the plate with the food they are meant to accompany, either next to the main food or on top of it. It is expected that diners will use their bread and/or rice to sop up any extra sauce.

Garnishes

All the common garnishes used in Middle Eastern restau-rants are edible. These garnishes may include chopped herbs, paprika, pomegranate seeds, chopped nuts, or spices mixed with olive oil and drizzled over the top of a dish.

Rice and Bread

Bread is a very important staple in the Middle Eastern diet and is served with every meal. The Middle Eastern bread most familiar to the Western world is pita, *khoubiz* in Arabic. It is fat-free, only slightly leavened, and is soft and flat. Known also as "pocket bread" because of the way the two sides pull apart, it can be cut open and easily filled to make a sandwich. In a tasty variation, the pita is brushed with olive oil and sprinkled with *za'tar*, a blend of thyme, marjoram, sumac, and salt, before baking. Pita along with other flat breads (such as the pocketless Afghan bread called *lawasch*) can also serve as the base for a dish or can be torn into bite-size pieces and used as an eating utensil.

Rice is as important as bread in some parts of the Middle East, such as in Iran and Afghanistan, and is served either as a side dish for grilled meats and stews or as a main dish when cooked with meat, vegetables, fruits, nuts, and spices. Noodles and pasta are also encountered in Middle Eastern cooking and were so long before Marco Polo found his way back from China.

Utensils

Flatware is set on the table in U.S. restaurants and very often in the Middle East, but it is possible to eat an entire meal in a traditional Middle Eastern fashion, that is, without lifting a fork, using either your fingers or pieces of bread to scoop up food. Eating with one's left hand, which was considered disrespectful and evil in the past, is still frowned upon by some traditionalists. Whichever hand you eat with, do not to lick your fingers until the end of the meal (licking is a sign that you are finished) or put your fingers in your mouth (or touch your mouth at all)—sort of pop the food in.

In most U.S. restaurants each diner is given an individual plate but in some non-Westernized Middle Eastern countries a communal platter from which all diners eat with their right hand is more common. Appropriately enough, handwashing in these areas is an important ritual that everyone takes part in before and after a meal.

Signature Dishes

Kebabs (pieces of marinated meat, poultry, or fish skewered either alone or with vegetables and grilled); *Tabbouleh* (parsley and bulgur salad); *Hummus bi Tahini* (puréed chick-peas, sesame seed paste, and garlic); *Couscous* (a fine-grained semolina served with stew); *Baba Gannoujh* (puréed roasted eggplant, sesame seed paste, and garlic); *Falafel* (spicy fritters of ground chick-peas and fava beans)

Common Misconceptions

Alcoholic beverages are forbidden. Although the religion of Islam, which forbids the consumption of alcohol, has had an important influence on Middle Eastern customs, in practice the use of alcohol is a matter of personal preference.

Meat is eaten uncooked. Raw meat dishes do appear on Middle Eastern menus. However, cooked meats and, in particular, grilled ones, are much more prevalent.

Middle Eastern MENU

Most of the dishes listed on the menu that follows are those that are commonly found on restaurant menus in the U.S. regardless of the country of origin of the restaurant owner or chef. In cases where a dish is specific to a certain country and may only appear on a menu if the restaurant owner or chef has close ties to that country, the country is noted after the dish name.

APPETIZERS Appetizers, or *mezze*, mean drinks, friends, good conversation, and many different little dishes to nibble on. (In some Middle Eastern countries, a host may offer his or her guests 50 or more to choose from.) Sometimes appetizers are small portions of items that appear as entrées, salads, or vegetable dishes on a menu. Or they can be other cooked or uncooked vegetables, salads, or dips, bite-size pieces of fried liver, sausages, spiced olives, cheese, pickles, or meat-, spinach-, or cheese-filled pastries. The selection of appetizers is so extensive and interesting in some Middle Eastern restaurants that you may be tempted to make a complete meal out of an assortment of them.

Mezze are frequently served with a basket of flat bread, such as pita. If it is not already cut up, tear it into small pieces, then wrap a piece around a morsel of food, such as a falafel, mound of tabbouleh, or piece of fried liver, and use the bread to lift it up. Your "package" of food should be small enough to eat in a quick bite. Or fold a piece of bread and use it as a scoop for spreads or other liquidy foods.

Baba Gannoujh

Creamy dip of roasted eggplant puréed and mixed with **tahini**, lemon juice, cumin, and parsley

It is the roasting of the eggplant that gives baba gannoujh *its appealing smokey flavor.*

Mujadarra

A soupy lentil, rice, and onion dish; served at room temperature

Mujadarra *is Middle Eastern "comfort food," humble but satisfying.*

Stuffed Grape Leaves

Tightly wrapped shiny green leaf packets filled with rice, onions, tomatoes, parsley, mint, cinnamon, and allspice

Stuffed grape leaves, which are popular throughout the Middle East, can have either a vegetarian or meat filling. They can be served warm or cold, the meat-filled generally being served warm as a main dish.

Fresh Herbs (Iran)

A plate of assorted fresh herbs, such as parsley, mint, chives, dill, tarragon, and cilantro

No Iranian appetizer table is complete without a plate of fresh herbs, which are eaten with bread, cheese, and a yogurt and cucumber salad at the beginning of the meal, then left on the table to be enjoyed with the main course as well.

DOLMEH: STUFFED FOODS

Dolmeh is a Turkish word that in Turkey refers to any stuffed savory food. Throughout the rest of the Middle East it generally means a stuffed vegetable—either one made by hollowing out a vegetable (such as squash, tomato, bell pepper, or eggplant) and filling it or one that is made by wrapping a grape leaf vine or cabbage leaf around a filling.

Hummus bi Tahini

Creamy purée of chick-peas, **tahini** (sesame paste), lemon juice, and garlic garnished with a drizzle of olive oil and a sprinkling of a red spice, such as paprika, ground red pepper, or **sumac**

The word hummus *refers to chick-peas, the main ingredient in this appetizer dip or spread. It is also the shortened and more common name for* hummus bi tahini.

INGREDIENT NOTES

• **Tahini** is a paste made from roasted sesame seeds.

• **Sumac** is a non-poisonous variety of the plant with which many people are unhappily familiar. It yields hairy brownish red berries—treasured in the Middle East for their sour, fruity flavor—that can be dried and crushed into powder or steeped in hot water and squeezed to yield juice.

Fried Eggplant with Yogurt

Slices of fried eggplant between two layers of **yogurt**; sprinkled with crushed dried mint

Plaki (Turkey)

Cold white bean salad with onions and other vegetables, such as carrots and potatoes, dressed with lemon juice, olive oil, parsley, tomato paste, and fresh mint and dill

Taramasalata (Turkey)

Creamy dip of puréed salted fish roe, bread, olive oil, lemon juice, and, sometimes, garlic and onion

The bread in taramasalata cuts the strong flavor of the roe and adds body to the dip.

Sigara Boregi (Turkey)

"Cigar"-shaped **phyllo** dough pastries filled with meat, cheese, or spinach and deep-fried; also called Moroccan cigars

Leavened doughs that are more bread-like can be used to make sigara boregi as well.

Falafel

Spicy deep-fried balls of ground chick-peas, fava beans, onion, garlic, cilantro, cumin, and pepper

When falafel is served as an appetizer it comes with a green salad and taratour bi tahini, a tahini sauce made with sesame paste, garlic, water, and lemon juice. It is also a popular street food, in which case it is eaten as a sandwich: a split pita is stuffed with salad, tahini sauce, and falafel. The falafel sandwich is so popular in Israel that it is jokingly called the "Israeli hot dog."

Torshi (Iran), Kabis (Lebanon)

Pickled vegetables or fruits, such as a combination of pickled carrots, eggplant, celery, parsley, and garlic, or peach or persimmon

Labneh

A slightly tart ricotta-like cheese made from **yogurt** to use as a spread or dip for bread

INGREDIENT NOTES

• **Yogurt** is an important part of the Middle Eastern diet and is found in myriad forms—in soups, sauces, desserts, and beverages. It can also be used as a cooking liquid. In the Middle East, yogurt is most often made with goat's milk, which is stronger in taste than the cow's milk most commonly used to make yogurt in North America.

• **Phyllo** (or filo) is the paper-thin dough used for both sweet and savory pastries.

Kibbe Nayya (Lebanon and Syria)
Raw ground lamb or beef, **bulgur**, onion, and seasonings worked into a very smooth paste; served with lettuce leaves or bread for scooping

Though prepared in numerous countries in the Middle East, kibbe *is considered the national dish of Lebanon and Syria. There are many variations, some of which require shaping, filling, and cooking the meat, but* kibbe nayya, *in which the meat is served raw, remains one of the most popular.*

Merguez
Moderately spicy Moroccan sausages

Banjan Borawani (Afghanistan)
Fried eggplant combined with tomatoes and spices and baked; served with a **yogurt** and garlic sauce

Aushak (Afghanistan)
"Ravioli"-style pasta stuffed with leeks; served on a **yogurt**-mint sauce and topped with a meaty ground lamb or beef sauce

SOUPS Middle Eastern soups are made with myriad combinations of legumes, meat, poultry, and vegetables and tend to be hearty and filling. One exception is the light and refreshing cold yogurt and cucumber soup called *cacik*, which is also found on appetizer and salad menus in a less liquid form.

Mashawi (Afghanistan)
Yogurt-based soup with beef, **mung beans**, chick-peas, and black-eyed peas

Cacik (Turkey)
Cold yogurt, cucumber, and garlic soup, seasoned with mint

• **Bulgur** (or *burghul* in Arabic), wheat kernels that are processed by steaming, drying, and grinding, has a nutty taste and a tender, chewy texture. It is a popular ingredient in Lebanon and Syria.

• **Mung beans** are small, round beans with yellow flesh, most often green skin (they can also be found with yellow or black skin), and a mildly sweet flavor. They are commonly used to grow bean sprouts.

Hareera (Morocco)
Chicken soup with noodles or rice and chick-peas

Hareera *is traditionally eaten at sundown during Ramadan, the holy period during which Muslims fast throughout the daylight hours.*

Melokhia (Egypt)
A chicken or beef stock-based soup with **melokhia** leaves; seasoned with garlic, cilantro, and ground red pepper

SALADS
Salads are served at most Middle Eastern meals and are infinite in their variety. Creamy dips, such as *hummus* and *baba gannoujh*, listed in the appetizer section on many menus, are considered salads as well.

Israeli Salad
Tomatoes, cucumbers, lettuce, and other fresh vegetables dressed with tahini sauce

Tabbouleh
Parsley, **bulgur** (•245), onions, fresh mint, and chopped tomatoes dressed with olive oil and lemon juice

Tabbouleh *recipes vary from cook to cook, but when authentic always include a very generous amount of parsley.*

Laban (Lebanon), Cacik (Turkey)
Yogurt (•244) with cucumber, garlic, and mint

Brain Salad
Sliced calf brain marinated in lemon juice, olive oil, pepper, and parsley; served cold

Brains are a Middle Eastern delicacy. Some people believe that eating calf brain will enhance intelligence while others believe that because a calf is an ignorant animal, eating its brain will have the reverse effect.

Fattoush
Lettuce, cucumber, tomatoes, scallions, parsley, mint, green pepper, and toasted pita bread with a dressing of olive oil, lemon juice, and garlic

INGREDIENT NOTES

• **Melokhia** is the green leaf of a plant related to okra, though its flavor is closer to that of spinach. Like okra it releases a viscous liquid when cooked, thereby thickening liquids to which it is added. Dried melokhia leaves are much more readily available than fresh in the U.S.

VEGETABLE DISHES

Imam Bayildi (Turkey)
Eggplant stuffed with sautéed onions, garlic, tomatoes, and parsley

Bamia Bezeit
Okra, tomatoes, onions, and garlic sautéed in olive oil and often seasoned with cilantro; customarily served at room temperature

Turlu (Turkey)
Mixed vegetable casserole that can include eggplant, zucchini, peppers, okra, green beans, tomatoes, onions, and garlic
Both bamia bezeit *and* turlu *are sometimes made with meat.*

Ful Medames (Egypt)
Simmered fava beans seasoned with olive oil and lemon juice; garnished with chopped parsley and served with hard-boiled eggs
This ancient Egyptian dish is eaten throughout the day in Egypt, where it is referred to as "the poor man's meat," but it is especially popular for breakfast. Each person squeezes on some lemon juice and adds olive oil and pepper to taste, then crushes and blends the beans and eggs together. It is sometimes spooned on top of hummus *in Israel.*

FISH and SHELLFISH

Kilic Sis (Turkey)
Skewered pieces of swordfish with a sauce of ground hazelnuts, garlic, olive oil, and vinegar

Seafood Kebab
Fish and shrimp, marinated, skewered, and broiled

Samke Harrah (Lebanon)
Baked fish (such as red snapper) with a hot chili pepper sauce

CHICKEN

Chelo Khoresh Fesseonjon (Iran)
Stew of chicken (or duck) with ground walnuts, **pomegranate** juice, and sweet spices, such as cinnamon and nutmeg; served over *chelo* (see right)

Chicken Polau (Iran)
Rice with chicken (or other meat) and fruit, such as raisins and apricots, seasoned with cinnamon

Cerkes Tavugu or Circassian Chicken (Turkey)
Pieces of chicken with a thick sauce of ground walnuts and paprika; served cold

Chicken Tajine (Morocco)
Stew of chicken, prunes, and almonds; served with couscous and sometimes hot sauce

MOROCCAN TAJINES

Morocco is known for its *tajines*, gently simmered stews of various combinations of meat, poultry, fruits, and nuts, as well as its complex spice combinations, and, of course, couscous. The combination of meats with fruit, vegetables, and nuts is inherited from Iran.

CHELO: IRAN'S RICE SPECIALTY

Numerous Middle Eastern countries maintain their own signature rice dishes, but perhaps none is more celebrated than the Iranian specialty known as *chelo*. The rice is partially cooked, then steamed with butter or oil. It is served either with a layer of stew, called a *khoresh*, on top, or plain (often as an accompaniment to kebabs), in which case it is traditionally topped with butter and a raw egg yolk in its shell (the yolk is mixed into each portion). *Polo* (or *polou*), reminiscent of pilaf, is rice plus other ingredients, such as meat, vegetables, fruit, nuts, and spices, that are partially cooked separately, then combined and steamed together.

Shish Tawook
Boneless chicken marinated in lemon and garlic and grilled

INGREDIENT NOTES

• The **pomegranate** is a fruit native to southwestern Asia. Its sour juice is a common ingredient in Iranian cooking, and its colorful seeds are used as a garnish in Lebanon and Syria.

Quail or Cornish Game Hen (Lebanon)

Grilled quail or Cornish hen; served with garlic sauce

Schnitzel (Israel)

Breaded and fried chicken breast fillet

Israel is a nation of immigrants from all over the world, a reality that is reflected in its cuisine. Dishes that originated in such diverse locales as Eastern Europe, South America, and Yemen have supplemented the indigenous—essentially Arab— cuisine. In Israeli restaurants in the U.S. you are just as likely to find European schnitzel and goulash as you are to find Middle Eastern falafel.

MEAT

Lamb is by far the most commonly consumed meat in the Middle East. Beef is expensive and not widely used. The consumption of pork is restricted by Jewish and Muslim dietary laws, and is therefore rarely encountered. Organ meats (such as brain and liver) are highly appreciated, and a great delicacy is sheep's head, which may be available in some U.S. restaurants but probably won't appear on the menu in recognition of Western sensibilities.

Shish Kebab

Marinated cubes of lamb grilled on a skewer with tomato and onion

Doner Kebab (Turkey), Shawarma (Lebanon)

Thin slices of marinated and grilled lamb; served on pita bread topped with lettuce, tomato, and tahini sauce

This dish is the familiar gyro. Slices of lamb are wrapped around a long vertical spit and slowly roasted. As the meat cooks, the outside pieces are sliced off and served, leaving the inner pieces to continue cooking.

Iskender

Doner kebab (see left) in hot **yogurt** (●244) and tomato sauce; served over flat bread, usually pita

Kefta Kebab

Ground lamb or beef combined with onion and spices and grilled on a skewer or baked with tahini sauce

Lamb Chops

Marinated grilled lamb chops

Lahm bi'Ajeen

Thin layer of ground lamb and spices baked on a round crust

Moroccan Couscous

Couscous steamed over a broth or a stew made of such ingredients as lamb, chick-peas, onions, turnips, and other vegetables; sometimes served with broth and **harissa** on the side

The word couscous *refers to both ground durum wheat (called semolina) and a dish composed of the semolina matched with a stew. The dish, of which there are infinite variations, is African in origin but has been adopted by many Middle Eastern countries. It is the national dish of Morocco.*

COUSCOUS: If you are served couscous with broth and harissa on the side (as is the custom in Algerian restaurants, where this dish tends to be particularly hot), dilute the harissa in a ladleful of broth before pouring the broth over the semolina grains and/or stew mixture. This way the harissa will be distributed throughout. Harissa can be added to other soups and stews as well. Always use it sparingly as it is very hot.

AFGHAN COOKING

Afghanistan is known for its *korma*, which is related to an Indian dish of the same name, as well as its noodle dishes, rice dishes, and extensive use of yogurt.

Korma Sabzee with Lamb (Afghanistan)

Thick spicy stew made with chunks of lamb, split peas, onions, and garlic, seasoned with chili pepper, cumin, and cilantro; served over rice

Loubiah

Chunks of lamb with green beans in tomato sauce

Manti (Turkey)

Steamed dumplings filled with beef or lamb; served with a yogurt and garlic sauce

INGREDIENT NOTES

• **Harissa** is a fiery condiment, the principle ingredients of which are dried red chili and garlic, along with ground red pepper, caraway, coriander, cumin, and olive oil.

DESSERTS

DESSERTS Middle Eastern sweets are numerous and varied and include pastries, puddings, and cakes. They are enjoyed as a snack with coffee and sometimes after a meal.

Baklava
Rich, flaky **phyllo** (•244) pastries filled with ground nuts, such as pistachios, almonds, walnuts, or cashews, and steeped in honey or a sugar syrup

Konafa or Kadaif (Turkey)
Buttery pastry filled with a nut or creamy cheese filling, topped with long, ultra-thin strips of dough that become crispy when baked, and steeped in a sugar syrup

Asure (Turkey)
Thin pudding studded with such ingredients as chick-peas, navy beans, rice, nuts, or assorted dried fruits; flavored with **rosewater**

Semolina Cake (Egypt)
Sheet cake made with **semolina**; cut into squares or diamonds and garnished with blanched almonds before baking and moistened with a sugar syrup after baking

Klaicha
Hard, dry cookie with date filling

Firnee (Afghanistan)
Pudding flavored with almonds and **cardamom**

Couscous bi Sikkar (Egypt)
Couscous tossed with butter, then sprinkled with sugar and toasted almonds

Rahat Lokum (Turkish Delight)
A taffy-like candy that comes in different colors and flavors (such as pink and flavored with **rosewater**, or orange and flavored with orange blossom water)

Each cube of rahat lokum *is dusted with powdered sugar and cornstarch so the candies won't stick to one another and to provide a smooth surface for the fingers (with which this candy is eaten).*

• **Rosewater** is distilled from rose petals and is used as a flavoring in both desserts and main dishes in the Middle East.

• **Semolina** is coarsely ground durum wheat.

• **Cardamom**, a relative of ginger, has a sweet flavor hinting of eucalyptus. It is widely used in Middle Eastern cooking.

BEVERAGES People of the Middle East who do not adhere to the Islamic restriction on the consumption of alcohol often enjoy alcoholic beverages with their food. Other popular choices include yogurt drinks as well as water, which may be served in a traditional vessel called a *breek*, a squat pitcher with a spout in the middle. The diner is meant to hold up the *breek*, tilt his or her head back, and pour the water directly into his or her mouth. Rest assured that when a *breek* is placed on the table in restaurants in the U.S., it is accompanied by glasses.

The drinking of coffee in much of the Middle East is imbued with ceremony and ritual. All business transactions commence with it; no visitor arrives without being served some and must drink at least three of the tiny cups to be gracious; long summer evenings are wiled away in cafés on account of it; and grounds are "read" to tell fortunes.

Arak

A potent, anise-flavored apéritif that can be made with either grapes or dates

Arak *is usually served chilled in small glasses with water (either added for the diner or in a separate glass to be added by the diner). When the water is added, the liqueur turns cloudy.*

Turkish Coffee

Dark, rich, sweetened coffee with creamy foam on top; served in small cups without milk

Turkish coffee *is made in a specially designed long-handled pot. Coffee grounds, sugar, and water are heated until foaming, then the foam is spooned into small coffee cups, the liquid is boiled again, and the process is repeated one or two more times. Finally, the coffee in the pot is poured into the cup and the beverage is served. Because the grounds are still floating in the coffee when it is served it is best to wait a few minutes to allow them to settle before taking a sip.*

Tea

Tea could be called the national drink of Iran, where it is served in glasses, with sugar cubes on the side. Diners are meant to place a sugar cube between the teeth and sip the tea through it. In Afghanistan, tea, served with or without sugar, is sometimes flavored with **cardamom** (•251). In Morocco sweetened mint tea is traditionally served in a special engraved silver pot and poured from high above the table into decorative glasses.

Ayran
Frothy **yogurt** (•244) drink

Ayran, reminiscent of buttermilk but thinner, is a refreshing beverage made by diluting yogurt with water and salting it lightly. It is commonly served with meals, especially during periods of warm weather. Iranians call it abdug, while Afghanis call it dugh.

SPANISH
cuisine

★

Cheers–*Salud* (sah-**lood**)
Bon appétit–*Que aproveche* (kay ah-pro-**veh**-chey)
Thank you–*Gracias* (**grah**-theeas)

BECAUSE SPAIN IS A COUNTRY OF MULTIPLE CUISINES rather than one national style of cooking, most Spanish restaurants in the U.S. offer a selection of typical dishes from all over the country. As quality Spanish restaurants multiply, distinctive, authentically prepared regional fare, sometimes centering exclusively on foods from Catalonia or the Basque country in the north, has begun to appear on menus. Nevertheless, time-tested dishes that have gained American acceptance, such as gazpacho, paella, and seafood in green and garlic sauces, still predominate.

Spanish Regional Cooking

Spain is a country of diverse climates, terrains, and cultures, and in each of the country's 17 regions the produce and style of cooking vary greatly, even though certain ingredients, like olive oil, garlic, sweet peppers, and tomatoes, are used everywhere. Spaniards are avid seafood eaters; from the coastal regions of the Atlantic Ocean and the Mediterranean Sea, as well as in landlocked Madrid, seafood is the star and is featured in many of the country's most characteristic dishes. Along the eastern shore, rice, in a wide variety of preparations including popular paellas, is a diet staple. In the northeast region of Catalonia, casserole dishes that date back to medieval times but are surprisingly modern predominate, combining meat with fruit in sauces flavored with ground nuts. In the interior, pork, lamb, and bean and chick-pea dishes play a major role. And in the south, cold soups, refreshing marinades, and light sauces are the appealing foods appropriate to the warm climate. In all regions *tapas*—appetizers made with fine-quality wholesome ingredients—are not only an important aspect of local cuisines, but an integral part of Spanish lifestyle. Spanish cuisine, which rarely includes butter or cream, is, therefore, the basis for a healthy diet that is generally low in cholesterol.

Principles of Flavor

Spanish cooking relies on hearty Mediterranean flavors, such as olive oil, tomatoes, garlic, onion, and sweet red and green peppers, then adds its own distinctive touches. Cured ham and chorizo sausage, for example, are common cooking ingredients, and what is called a *picada*—typically a blend of garlic, parsley, saffron, and almonds or pine nuts, mashed to a paste in a mortar—adds wonderfully complex flavor to fish, poultry, and meat sauces.

Foreign Influence

The Romans brought olive trees and garlic to Spain, but it was the Arab occupation—from the 8th century until 1492—that left an indelible impression on Spanish cooking and is in part why it is different from other European cuisines. With these Eastern invaders came rice, almonds, saffron, and other seasonings like cumin and coriander.

The Spanish exploration and colonization of the Americas brought a wealth of previously unknown ingredients, such as tomatoes, peppers, potatoes, and chocolate to the Old World, revolutionizing the diet in Spain and eventually in the rest of Europe.

Ordering

Tapas, Spain's appetizer foods, can be ordered as a first course or, if a Spanish restaurant specializes in them, they can replace a traditional meal. When *tapas* are eaten as a prelude to a meal, they should be ordered as soon as you sit down at the table.

Service and Dining

A Spanish menu is subdivided into traditional categories, i.e., appetizers, soups, fish, meat and poultry, and desserts, often with a separate listing for paellas and other rice dishes. In Spain vegetables do not automatically accompany a main dish but are ordered as an appetizer or first course or even as a main course. Spanish restaurants in the U.S. rarely adhere to this tradition. Spanish egg dishes, also included on a lunch or dinner menu in Spain, are more likely to appear on a brunch menu in a U.S. restaurant.

Condiments

Some Spanish rice and fish dishes are served with a small bowl of garlic mayonnaise (*alioli* in Spanish). Other fish dishes may come with a Romesco sauce of mashed garlic, almonds, and dried or fresh red bell peppers on the side. Diners are expected to spoon a small amount of the sauce onto the side of their plates.

Rice and Bread

Rolls or sliced bread are placed on every table in Spanish restaurants in the U.S. Spaniards will break off a bite-size piece and butter it (or leave it plain). Bread is useful for pushing small pieces of food (like peas or rice) onto the fork and for soaking up sauces. In deference to American customs, a small dish of potatoes or "saffron" rice (sometimes colored with food coloring rather than saffron) is also offered with every main course in most restaurants.

Signature Dishes

Gazpachos; Paellas; Tortilla Española (potato omelet); *Shellfish* or *Chicken al ajillo* (in garlic sauce); *Zarzuela* (seafood stew); fish *en salsa verde* or *a la vasca* (in a parsley, garlic, and white wine sauce); *Mariscada* (shellfish, in green, garlic, or white sauce); *Caldo Gallego* (beef, bean, and vegetable soup); *Empanada Gallega* (meat or fish savory pie); *Txangurro* (seasoned crabmeat served in a seashell); *Bacalao a la Vizcaína* (salt cod in onion and red pepper sauce)

Common Misconceptions

Spanish cooking is hot and spicy. Far from it. Except for an occasional touch of dried red chili pepper in some *tapas*, there are no herbs or spices that will startle an American palate.

Spanish cooking is the same as the cuisines of Cuba, South America, and Mexico. Despite their efforts to educate the American public, Spanish restaurants in the U.S. have had great difficulty correcting the common confusion between the cooking of Spain and that of Cuba, South America, and Mexico. In fact, there is little connection. The cooking of Spain is not at all spicy or hot; it is a European cuisine, closely related to French and Italian, but with its own unique qualities. Tacos, tamales, enchiladas, and the like do not belong on a Spanish menu.

Spanish MENU

APERITIVOS, TAPAS (APPETIZERS)

Tapas, or appetizer foods, represent the most convivial part of a Spanish meal; traditionally they are placed at the center of the table and shared, each diner taking directly from the serving dish with a fork, toothpick, or his or her fingers. Dunking bread in the sauces is encouraged.

TAPAS BARS

Tapas bars, which may be part of a Spanish restaurant or separate eating establishments, are becoming increasingly popular in the U.S. because of their casual atmosphere and the opportunity they provide to taste small portions of dozens of different dishes. In Spain they are a way of life, enormously popular before lunch and before dinner as places to meet friends and socialize. *Tapas* are typically displayed on the counter of the bar (there is sometimes a printed menu as well), while other *tapas*—usually those needing some last-minute preparation—may be announced on chalkboards. Because of the tantalizing array of foods offered, Americans often prefer to have *tapas* instead of lunch or dinner. Portion sizes vary according to the restaurant and the kind of food. Choose a well-assorted selection—something grilled, a refreshing shellfish or vegetable marinade, a fried dish, and something with a sauce. Typical drink accompaniments are beer or wine.

Tapas bars have their own peculiar etiquette. It is not necessary to wait for a space at the bar—clients may stand two or three deep (that's part of the fun). There may be some bar stools (usually not the case in Spain) and often there are small tables for those who are not comfortable eating while standing up.

Gambas al Ajillo
Shrimp sizzled in garlic and oil sauce with a touch of dried chili pepper

Gambas a la Plancha
Shrimp grilled in their shells and sometimes sprinkled with garlic and lemon juice

Almejas a la Marinera
Clams in white wine, garlic, onion, and parsley sauce

Tortilla Española
Spanish potato omelet made with sautéed sliced potatoes and onions soaked in beaten egg, then cooked in a skillet into a "cake"

Tortilla Española *(also called* Tortilla de patata*) is not related to the Mexican tortilla except in its round shape. A ubiquitous dish in Spain, it is served in wedges or small cubes and can be eaten as a* tapa *or as a light meal.*

Salpicón de Mariscos
Mixed shellfish in vinaigrette that may include onion, green pepper, chopped pickle, and tomato

Marisco *is the Spanish word for shellfish. Any dish made with shellfish is called a* mariscada.

BABY EELS: A SPANISH DELICACY

Angulas, or baby eels, the thickness of spaghetti strands, are a delicacy of Spanish cuisine, most commonly served in an oil and garlic sauce and eaten with small wooden forks. They are astonishingly expensive but so good that some restaurants continue to offer them to appreciative clients (they may not always be listed on the menu). To sample *angulas* at a reasonable cost, order one portion and share it as a *tapa*.

Mejillones a la Vinagreta
Mussels in an olive oil, vinegar, onion, parsley, and pimiento marinade

Calamares Fritos or a la Romana
Crunchy, deep-fried squid rings; sometimes served with *alioli* (garlic mayonnaise)

Frito *and* a la Romana *are two similar ways of frying:* Fritos *squid are crisper, with a flour or bread crumb coating;* a la Romana *squid are dipped in flour first, then coated with egg just before frying.*

Jamón Serrano

Thinly sliced Spanish cured ham; served on its own or on top of sliced country bread that has been rubbed with garlic and tomato and drizzled with olive oil

Jamón serrano *is not, at present, imported to the U.S., but Spanish restaurants have domestic sources for a similar style of ham.*

Empanada Gallega

A savory pie filled with pork or fish that has been sautéed with an abundance of onions and peppers

Chorizo Frito

Sautéed slices of **chorizo**

Txangurro

Crabmeat seasoned with onion, garlic, parsley, white wine, and brandy; served in a crab or scallop shell

Txangurro *comes from the Basque Country, a lush green region on the rugged northern coast of Spain that has long been celebrated for its fine restaurants and outstanding chefs. Basque restaurants are at the forefront of creative cooking in Spain, but their traditional seafood dishes are still overwhelming favorites. Among them is this stuffed crab—made in Spain with the spider crab found off the Basque coast and in the U.S. with Alaskan king crab.*

SOPAS (SOUPS)

Sopa de Alubias Negras

Thick black bean soup simmered with onion, garlic, green bell peppers, cumin, and sherry

Sopa de Pescados y Mariscos

Fish and shellfish soup, in the style of the chef, but generally seasoned with **saffron** (•265), bay leaf, onion, tomato, and sometimes a hint of anise

Caldo Gallego

Hearty Galician soup of beef, beans, potatoes, and chopped collard greens (or other similar vegetable)

Caldo Gallego *comes from Galicia in the northwest corner of Spain and has become known the world over by way of Galician emigrants. This soup can be a one-dish meal if enough of its principal ingredients are included in a serving, although it is generally offered as a first course.*

INGREDIENT NOTES

• **Chorizo** is a tasty mild sausage seasoned with garlic and paprika. It is eaten at room temperature, sautéed, and in Spanish stews and paellas.

Gazpacho Andaluz
Cold purée of tomato, cucumbers, green peppers, bread, and olive oil

Cooling Gazpacho Andaluz *hails from Andalucía on Spain's southern shore and is the ideal refreshment for this hot and arid land. Andalucía is also known for its outstanding seafood in simple preparations—crisply fried, in marinades, or in light sauces, seasoned with saffron, cilantro, and cumin.*

Gazpacho is generally accompanied by bowls of finely chopped vegetables, such as tomato, sweet green pepper, and cucumber, that are brought to the table by the waiter, who asks which and how much of each garnish to sprinkle on each serving of soup (if the garnish is not offered, you can request it). Besides the well-known red gazpacho, there is a white gazpacho, made with ground almonds and garnished with peeled grapes.

PESCADO Y MARISCOS (FISH and SHELLFISH)

Mariscada en Salsa Verde
Shellfish in a green sauce of parsley, white wine, olive oil, and garlic

Zarzuela de Mariscos
Shellfish stew in a tomato, onion, and white wine broth

Salmón a la Parrilla con Romesco
Grilled salmon; served with Romesco sauce of dried red bell peppers, ground almonds, garlic, and olive oil on the side

A la parrilla is the Spanish term for grilled.

Bacalao a la Vizcaína
Salt cod in an onion and pimiento sauce, often with tomato added

Dishes labeled a la vizcaína *come from the Basque province of Vizcaya, and this salt cod preparation is one of the province's signature dishes. Even before the discovery of America, Basque fishermen sailed to Newfoundland to fish cod, which was salted in order to preserve it for the long journey home. Today, despite the same-day fresh seafood available in northern Spain, salt cod is still a highlight of the cuisine, and when soaked in cold water for a sufficient amount of time, it is not at all salty.*

Merluza a la Vasca
Hake or fresh cod in a garlic, parsley, and white wine sauce, garnished with clams, peas, and white asparagus

A la vasca *means "from the Basque Country," and although a wide range of dishes are referred to in this way, most often it is applied to this specific preparation.*

Calamares en su Tinta
Sliced or stuffed squid in a sauce of **squid ink**, onion, tomato, and wine; served with white rice

Langosta a la Parrilla
Broiled lobster

For whatever reason, inexpensive broiled lobster has become a hallmark of many Spanish menus in the U.S., although in Spain lobster is a specialty item that is not especially emphasized and, in any case, is never broiled— it is simply grilled or boiled.

CARNES (MEATS)

Cochinillo Asado
Roast suckling pig with crackling skin

Suckling pig, the smaller the better, is typically roasted in a wood-burning oven. It is rarely offered in individual portions; rather, it should be requested by special order ahead of time for a group of six to eight people.

Ternera or Solomillo al Vino Tinto
Veal or beef tenderloin in Spanish red wine sauce

Ternera a la Extremeña
Veal cooked in a sauce of onion, sweet peppers, and **chorizo** (•262)

Pollo Villeroy
Chicken breast coated with a thick white sauce, then breaded and fried

Pollo al Ajillo
Chicken sautéed with olive oil and garlic

INGREDIENT NOTES

• **Squid ink** is a dark liquid that comes from a sac in a squid's body.

Chuletas de Cordero
Grilled baby lamb chops, sometimes seasoned with garlic or served with garlic mayonnaise on the side

Pollo or Cerdo a la Riojana
Braised chicken or pork with onions, tomatoes, and sweet red bell peppers

ARROCES (RICE DISHES) Spanish rice preparations, usually prepared for a minimum of two people, represent a major part of traditional cooking on the eastern coast of Spain. In good restaurants these colorfully and artfully arranged symphonies of taste and texture are made to order with short-grain rice and are served in wide, shallow paella pans. In lesser quality establishments they are merely dreary precooked entrées prepared with poor-quality rice.

Paella a la Valenciana
Rice cooked with chicken, pork, **chorizo** (•262), shrimp, clams, mussels, lobster (if so indicated), and peas in a chicken and **saffron** stock

Although Paella a la Valenciana *generally describes paella that is made with both fish and meat, paella is not one dish with set ingredients but a dish as varied as the chefs who create it.*

Paella a la Marinera
Rice cooked with a variety of fish and shellfish in fish stock

Arroz con Pollo
A rice dish of chicken, onion, **saffron**, garlic, and sweet bell peppers

• **Saffron** comes from the stigmas of the purple saffron crocus. It imparts a pale yellow color to foods and lends a distinctive flavor. It is used sparingly because of its assertive taste and extremely high cost.

If the rice in a paella (or the "saffron" rice that often accompanies main courses) is bright orange, it has not been made with saffron, which lends a pale yellow color, but with a commercially produced powdered mixture of food coloring, turmeric, and other seasonings.

Arroz Negro or Paella Negra

Rice cooked in fish stock with squid ink, squid, shrimp, fish, garlic, and peppers; often served with a separate bowl of *alioli* (garlic mayonnaise)

Recently this unusual rice dish, which is very popular in Spain, especially along the coast of Valencia, has begun to appear on the menus of finer Spanish restaurants. The rice is indeed black, colored and flavored with squid ink, a dark liquid that comes from a sac in the squid's body.

POSTRES (DESSERTS) Spaniards often eat sweets with afternoon tea, as a snack on the run, or to conclude a Sunday midday meal. Although fruit is traditional after a meal at home, sweet desserts often end lunch and dinner in a restaurant. Nevertheless, desserts are not an important part of a Spanish meal and tend to be simple and custard-based, like the famous *flan al caramelo*, and flavored with cinnamon and lemon peel. Cakes made with almonds or pine nuts are popular as well.

Flan al Caramelo
Baked individual custards with caramelized sugar

Brazo de Gitano
Custard-filled cake roll with pine nuts

Tarta de Santiago or de Almendra
A simple, moist cake of ground almonds, sugar, and eggs (no flour), dusted with confectioner's sugar

Peras al Vino
Pears poached in red or white wine sweetened with sugar and spiced with cinnamon sticks and lemon peel

Tarta de Piñones
Pine nut cake, often with a custard filling

Crema Catalana
Soft custard with a crackly sugar glaze

Wine

Dining in a Spanish restaurant gives you a wonderful opportunity to sample the country's exceptional wines, which are often poorly represented elsewhere. When choosing one, look for labels that say Reserva or Gran Reserva *because these terms indicate wines of exceptional vintages that have been aged for long periods of time.*

Spaniards generally prefer red wine (vino tinto) *to white wine* (vino blanco) *with dinner, even when the main course is fish. They do not consider sangría, which commonly appears on menus in the U.S., an appropriate accompaniment to a fine meal and will rarely order it in a restaurant, reserving it for more casual meals in the backyard or at the beach.*

Sherry

Spaniards enjoy dry sherry, called fino, *that is chilled (but never diluted with ice cubes) as an apéritif. Sweet sherry, such as* oloroso *or cream, or Spanish brandy may conclude a meal.*

Since sherry is a blended wine made according to extremely high standards, any brand—as long as it is made in Spain—will be very good.

Espresso

Though listed as espresso on menus in the U.S., espresso-style coffee is simply café *in Spain. It comes in three versions: café con leche (lightened with heated milk); café cortado (with a dash of hot milk); or café solo (black).*

THAI
cuisine

★

Cheers–*Yindee* (*yin* **dee**)
Bon appétit–*Cha Roen ar han* (cha roen ar han)
Thank you–*Kop Koon* (kop koon)

THAI COOKING IS A MELDING OF FLAVORS, TEXTURES, and colors. Thai cooks work hard to blend the four main flavors of salt, sour, spice, and sweet harmoniously. Thais also make liberal use of fresh herbs, especially basil, mint, and cilantro, as well as garlic and coconut products. Texturally, the ingredients in a single dish may range from smooth and satiny to crunchy, as in a smooth noodle dish garnished with peanuts or a spicy beef salad topped with crisp bean sprouts. An attempt is also made to vary the colors. For example, a beef salad will be served over green lettuce and will include red tomatoes and a garnish of fresh herbs. Though Thai food is often thought of as fiery hot, in fact the degree of spiciness ranges widely. As more traditional Thai ingredients become available, good Thai restaurants are becoming more widespread.

Principles of Flavor

Salt, sour, spice, and sweet are the contrasting flavors that make Thai cuisine distinctive. Following are some of the most common ingredients used to achieve them:

Salt: dried anchovy and shrimp, fish sauce, and shrimp paste

Sour: lime juice, vinegar, and tamarind water

Spice: peppercorns and dried and fresh chilies

Sweet: white sugar, palm sugar, and fruit

Foreign Influence

Among the major influences on Thai cuisine were the cooking of China and India. The Chinese influence is evident in the large number of stir-fries and noodle dishes. The Indian influence is most evident in the curries. Another significant contribution came from the Portuguese, who introduced chilies in the mid-16th century; prior to that black pepper was the main source of spiciness in Thai food.

Ordering

A good rule of thumb is to order one dish per diner plus one extra dish for the table. Consult with everyone in your party so that all of you do not order the same types of foods, for instance, all spicy curry dishes. A group of four might order one kind of soup, a spicy chicken dish, a non-spicy stir-fried vegetable dish, a medium-hot curry dish, and a seafood or beef salad.

Most Thai menus offer meat, poultry, fish, and vegetables, in any of the basic sauces or styles: Massaman, green *(kaeng kew wan)*, and red curries *(kaeng phea)*; sautéed *(pad)*; with ginger *(pad king)*; with basil and chili *(kaprow)*; with oyster sauce *(nam man hoi)*; with garlic *(kratiem)*; or with chilies *(prik* or *prik Thai)*. Therefore, it is possible to order

without looking at the menu, simply specifying the main ingredient and the sauce or style. When ordering straight from a menu, beware that many dish names vary widely from restaurant to restaurant because there is no definitive English transliteration for the Thai language.

   If possible, before going to a Thai restaurant call or stop by to find out if each order is made fresh or if the restaurant makes certain foods in bulk in advance. While sometimes speedy service is desirable—when you're ravenous or only have a short time to eat—in most cases, the extra wait for a freshly prepared meal is worth it. If you are starving when you walk in the door of a Thai restaurant, immediately order something that can be prepared quickly, such as fried rice or a small bowl of mild soup, then study the menu to decide what else you would like to order.

Service and Dining

In Thailand food is not served in a particular order but is eaten family-style as it comes out of the kitchen. The only time that a Thai meal might be served in courses is at a religious or wedding banquet. Thai cooks try to serve an assortment of dishes with varying textures and flavors so diners can alternate from one to another—for example, from a spicy dish to a refreshing soup or salad to a more subtle noodle dish. Rice is served throughout the meal.

Condiments

Many Thai dishes are served with dipping sauces, such as chili, peanut, and plum sauces. It is customary for each diner to dip his or her food into the bowl of sauce rather than transferring the sauce to the individual plate. Bowls of ground condiments, such as ground peanuts or chilies, plus fish sauce, chili-vinegar sauce, sugar, and lime, are served with noodle dishes and are meant to be sprinkled over the noodles.

Garnishes

When eating at a Thai restaurant you may find
some ingredients on your plate or in your
bowl that are not meant to be eaten. For
example, whole chilies, large slices of
galanga, lime leaves, or tube-like stalks of
lemongrass may be added to a soup or curry
for flavor, or whole uncooked basil leaves may
serve as a garnish. Nevertheless, if you are curious
about the individual flavor of any of these ingredients, go
ahead and take a nibble, except for the chilies: even a nibble
may prove to be too hot to handle.

Rice

Rice is served with just about every meal (except noodle
dishes) in Thailand, but this is not always the rule in Thai
restaurants elsewhere. Thais tend to spoon a small quantity
onto their plates along with some of the particular food
they want to eat, then repeat the process with the next food
item. More informal and inexpensive restaurants may serve
the food over rice. If you are quite hungry and want to
avoid ordering an additional main course, simply order an
extra bowl of rice.

Utensils

In Thailand most dishes are eaten with a soup spoon and
a fork, and these are the utensils you are most likely to
find on a table in a Thai restaurant in the U.S. The fork,
held in one hand, is used to mix the rice with the
meat, sauce, or other food on the plate, and to
transfer food onto the spoon, which, held
simultaneously in the other hand, carries the
food to the mouth. The only time Thais use
chopsticks is with noodle dishes. Knives are not
usually present on a Thai table because most
meat, fish, and vegetables are cut into bite-size pieces during preparation in the kitchen.

Signature Dishes

M*ee Krob* (sweet, crisp-fried noodles); *Satay* (skewers of grilled beef or chicken); *Tom Yum Goong* (spicy shrimp soup); *Pad Thai* (sautéed noodles with shrimp, egg, and vegetables); *Gai Pad Kaprow* (chicken with basil and chilies); *Kaeng Kew Wan* (meat, poultry, or fish in green curry sauce) or *Kaeng Phed* (meat, poultry, or fish in red curry sauce)

THAI CURRIES

Thai curries are made predominantly with coconut milk, fresh herbs, fresh or dried red or green chilies, shallots, and sometimes garlic, in addition to dry spices (Indian curries are flavored mainly with dried spices). All of the herbs and spices are blended together (either with a mortar and pestle or the more modern food processor) to create a paste that can be either incorporated into a dish immediately or stored for later use.

Three of the most popular curries served in Thai restaurants in the U.S. are Massaman, green curry, and red curry. Massaman, the mildest of the three (and the closest to an Indian curry; its name may be a corruption of "Muslim"), is made with dried red chilies, potatoes, and spices, such as cinnamon, cloves, cardamom, mace, and nutmeg, that make it subtly sweet. Green curry, actually pale yellow in color, is made with fresh green chilies and is very spicy. Red curry, made with dried red chilies, falls in between Massaman and green curry in terms of spiciness. A fourth curry found on some menus is the thick, dark, and spicy Panang curry, made with ground peanuts.

The MSG Question

In the past, MSG was sometimes used in Thai cooking, especially in strong-flavored soups and other dishes with large amounts of liquid. It is used much less often today. Always call a restaurant in advance or ask the waiter if you are concerned about MSG in your food.

Common Misconception

All Thai food is spicy. Although some Thai food is very hot, this is not true of every dish. Furthermore, most Thai restaurateurs will gladly tone down the spiciness of a particular dish at a customer's request—easily done because much of the hot spice is added at the end of the preparation process. Among the dishes that tend to be the least spicy are the Massaman curries and foods made with ginger and oyster sauces.

Thai MENU

KUP KAEM (APPETIZERS)

Appetizers are listed on most Thai menus in the U.S. even though an appetizer course is almost never served in Thailand. Always ask the waiter about the size of the appetizer (as well as soup and salad) portions; sometimes they are as large as main courses.

Chicken or Beef Satay

Marinated chicken or beef grilled on small skewers; served with spicy **peanut sauce** and refreshing cucumber salad

Satays (or satés) *are eaten as street food throughout Asia, with each region putting its own flavor stamp on them.*

TO EAT A SATAY: Hold the skewer in your hand, dip the meat in the sauce, then eat the meat off the skewer; it is not necessary to remove the meat from the skewer and cut it up.

Gari Pup

Curry puff made with chopped chicken or beef, carrot, potato, red onion, Massaman curry paste, and chilies; served with cucumber salad dressed with vinegar, chilies, and **cilantro**

Tod Mun Pla

Deep-fried fish patties made with minced kingfish, minced shrimp, red curry paste, and chopped vegetables; served with cucumber salad

Goong Tod

Crispy deep-fried shrimp; served with cucumber in vinegar

Phla Goong

Blanched, quickly cooled shrimp with onion, ground chilies, and lime; often called Dancing Shrimp

Salad Pak

Green salad with bean sprouts, red onion, lettuce, tomato, cucumber, bean curd (tofu), sliced cooked egg, and **Thai peanut dressing**

INGREDIENT NOTES

• **Peanut sauce**, which usually counts peanuts, curry paste, coconut milk, and garlic among its ingredients, is brown in color and creamy in texture.

• **Cilantro**, also known as fresh coriander and Chinese parsley, is widely used in Thai cooking. None of the herb is wasted; the leaves, roots, stalks, and seeds all offer their own distinctive flavor.

• **Thai peanut dressing** will vary from restaurant to restaurant but often includes coconut milk, which makes the dressing creamy, among its ingredients.

Mee Krob

Sweet, crisp-fried rice noodles with **pickled garlic**, bean curd, shrimp, chilies, and **tamarind** sauce

This crispy nest of lightly fried rice noodles combined with a variety of other ingredients, including a sweet-and-sour sauce, is a popular Thai specialty. Served at room temperature, it is a pleasant contrast to a spicy dish and/or a smooth curry. Good mee krob should not be overwhelmingly sweet.

Tofu Tod

Deep-fried bean curd; served with sweet-sour-spicy dipping sauce made with such ingredients as honey, vinegar, herbs, and chili flecks, topped with ground peanuts and a **mint** leaf

YUMS (HOT-AND-SOUR SALADS)

Yums are composed salads made with cooked meat, fish, or shellfish tossed with a thin, spicy dressing usually based on fish sauce (a pungently flavored sauce made from fermented fish) and lime juice. Possible garnishes for *yums* include crushed roasted peanuts, crispy fried onion or garlic, powdered dried shrimp, and herbs, such as mint, basil, and cilantro.

Yum Hoi Shell

Scallops with mushrooms, carrot, red onion, **lime juice**, **roasted curry paste**, and **cilantro**; served over lettuce

Yum Goong

Shrimp with mushrooms, carrot, red onion, **roasted curry paste**, **lime juice**, and **cilantro**; served over lettuce

---

• **Pickled garlic** is used to balance out the sweetness of *mee krob*. It is also used in salty dishes. Garlic is pickled in a mixture of white vinegar, salt, and sugar.

• **Tamarind** is the fruit of a tree in the Leguminosae family. The pods of this fruit contain a sour-sweet pulp that is used in cooking. Lime juice or white vinegar are sometimes used as a substitute for tamarind.

• **Mint** and **lime juice** provide refreshing counterpoints to the hot chilies in many Thai dishes.

• **Roasted curry paste** is a hot chili sauce. This traditional condiment for rice, vegetables, and salads often counts dried red chilies, roasted garlic, onion, shrimp paste, and tamarind among its ingredients.

277

Laab
Pan-fried ground beef, pork, or chicken with ground chilies, onion, mint, and lemon or lime juice; served at room temperature with lettuce, cucumber, and tomato

Yum Pla Muok
Spicy squid with sliced shallot, **pickled garlic** (●277), chilies, **lemongrass**, lime juice, and fresh mint; served over lettuce

Yum Nuer
Beef slices with garlic, cucumber, tomato, chilies, red onion, and lime juice; served over lettuce

S O U P S   Thai soups can be broken down into three categories: *tom yum*, characterized by the simultaneously fresh and hot flavor of the broth; mildly flavored *kaeng jued*, consommés made with meat and vegetables; and *kao tom*, rice soups of Chinese origin that can be light and clear or heavy and porridge-like. Of these three kinds, the highly seasoned *tom yum* are most often featured on menus in the U.S. The milder *kaeng jued* provide a welcome relief when eaten in combination with fiery chili preparations.

Tom Yum Goong
Spicy shrimp soup with **straw mushrooms**, **lemongrass**, **kaffir lime leaves**, shallot, chilies, cilantro, and lime juice

TO EAT TOM YUM GOONG, spoon the shrimp, often presented with their tails on, out of the broth and into your mouth, then remove the tail with your fingers.

INGREDIENT NOTES

• **Lemongrass** is a lemon-scented grass native to Southeast Asia. It has a scallion-like shape and a fibrous woody texture. It is often thinly sliced or bruised to use as a flavoring in soups and sauces. It is also pounded and combined with other herbs and spices to make curry pastes. Thais use lemongrass as a healing herb and believe it to be a powerful cure for colds.

• **Straw mushrooms** are small and globe-shaped, with a musty, earthy flavor.

Tom Ka Gai

Spicy chicken soup with **galanga**, **lemongrass**, **kaffir lime leaves**, cilantro, chilies, coconut milk, and lime juice

Kao Tom Goong

Rice soup with scallions, cilantro, and choice of seafood or chicken

A porridge-like version of this soup (similar to Chinese congee) is often eaten for breakfast or late at night in Thailand. It is less flavorful than many other Thai dishes but is often doctored up with such condiments as scallion, cucumber, lime, sliced green chilies in vinegar, and preserved fish.

KOB (FROG'S LEGS)

Frog's legs are very popular in Thailand, where they are often served on special occasions. Though many Thai restaurants deep-fry frog's legs, they are more commonly pan-fried in Thailand.

Kob Kratiem

Fried frog's legs in garlic sauce, with chilies, cilantro, and tomato

Kob Kaprow

Frog's legs fried in a chili sauce with **basil** (•281)

• **Galanga**, a light yellow root with pink stems, belongs to the same family as ginger and has a similar hot, peppery taste. At one time Europeans considered galanga an aphrodisiac.

• **Kaffir limes** have dark, bumpy skin and a sharp flavor. Both the leaves and the colored part of the skin (zest) are used in cooking, but it is the leaves, which are added to foods while they are cooking so they can slowly release their flavor, that are most important. In earlier times, Thais believed that the fragrance of the leaves kept the evil spirits away.

KWAY IOW (NOODLE DISHES)

In Thailand noodle dishes are sometimes eaten for breakfast and are particularly popular at lunchtime, when they are often enjoyed at restaurants that specialize in them. They are traditionally accompanied by an assortment of condiments—fish sauce, chili-vinegar sauce, ground peanuts, sugar, lime, and crushed dried red chilies—though some restaurants in the U.S. do not offer this assortment to non-Thai clientele. Ask for the condiments, if desired, then add them in small increments until the mix of flavors suits your palate.

Bami Nam
Egg noodle soup with cilantro, scallions, and choice of chicken or mixed seafood

Lard Na
Flat rice noodles with **Chinese broccoli** and choice of shrimp, scallops, chicken, or squid

Bami Lard Na
Fried egg noodles with mixed vegetables, seafood, or chicken

Pad Thai
Sautéed rice noodles with shrimp, **dried bean cake**, **bean sprouts**, eggs, ground peanuts, and chilies

Bami Pad Kee Mow
Fried egg noodles with fresh **basil**, chilies, garlic, and choice of chicken, pork, or beef

Pad Kee Mow
Flat rice noodles with fresh basil, chilies, garlic, and choice of chicken, pork, or beef

Kway Tiow Nam (or Bami) Ped
Noodle soup with flat rice or egg noodles in broth with roasted duck, scallions, and cilantro

INGREDIENT NOTES

• **Chinese broccoli** (more appropriately called Chinese kale) has fewer florets and is leafier and longer than the green broccoli commonly sold in the U.S. It also has a more pungent, bitter flavor that many people deem far superior. Before ordering this dish, check with the waiter to make sure that it is indeed made with Chinese broccoli (kale). Some restaurants use the more common green broccoli because it is less expensive.

• **Dried bean cake** is bean curd (tofu) that has been dried, a process that renders the bean curd firm but porous. Before it is used for cooking, it is rehydrated. Like fresh bean curd, it takes on the flavors of the ingredients with which it is combined.

GAI (CHICKEN)

Gai Pad Kaprow

Sautéed sliced chicken breast with fresh **basil** and chilies

The word kaprow *means "holy basil" in the Thai language. Its inclusion in a dish name, however, is a surefire indication that the dish, when made authentically, is spicy.*

Gai Massaman

Chicken in subtly sweet curry sauce of **coconut milk**, Massaman curry paste, potatoes, onions, and peanuts

The addition of potatoes as well as the sweet-spicy flavors in Massaman curry paste (for example, cinnamon, cloves, cardamom, mace, and nutmeg) attest to the Indian origins of this dish.

Kaeng Kew Wan Gai

Chicken in green curry sauce with eggplant, **kaffir lime leaves** (•279), **coconut milk**, and **basil**

Kaeng Gai

Chicken in red curry sauce with green peas, **coconut milk**, chilies, **kaffir lime leaves** (•279), and **basil**

Gai Yang

Grilled sliced chicken breast marinated in garlic, white pepper, and herbs

Gai Pad King

Sautéed sliced chicken breast with ginger, scallions, **Chinese mushrooms**, and chilies

Gai Pad Pak Nam Man Hoi

Sautéed chicken breast and mixed vegetables with **oyster sauce** and scallions

• **Bean sprouts** are a crunchy, cooling counterpoint to the spiciness of the noodles in dishes like *pad Thai*.

• Thai cooks use several different kinds of **basil**, including Italian or Greek and balsam (also known as purple or holy basil). Sometimes it is cooked and sometimes it is added raw to a finished dish.

• **Coconut milk**, which is used instead of dairy cream in Thai cooking, is made by combining the meat of a coconut with boiling water and straining the mixture to obtain as much liquid as possible. It adds a silky creaminess to curries—as well as a fair dose of fat.

• **Chinese mushrooms**, also known as black mushrooms, are often dried, which intensifies their flavor considerably.

• **Oyster sauce**, made by reducing oysters, water, and salt to a thick rich concentrate, is an ancient seasoning. It is brown in color and has a rich, savory flavor that neither tastes nor smells fishy. Thai dishes made with oyster sauce tend to be among the mildest.

NUER (BEEF)

Kaeng Kew Wan Nuer
Sliced beef in a green curry sauce with eggplant, coconut milk, chilies, **kaffir lime leaves** (•279), and basil

Kaeng Phed Nuer
Sliced beef in red curry sauce with green peas, coconut milk, chilies, **kaffir lime leaves** (•279), and basil

Nuer Yang
Sliced beef marinated with herbs, garlic, chilies, green peppers, and cilantro, then grilled

Nuer Pad King
Sliced beef sautéed with ginger, **Chinese mushrooms** (•281), scallions, and chilies

Nuer Ka Na
Sliced beef sautéed with mixed vegetables, **oyster sauce** (•281), and scallions

Nuer Massaman
Sliced beef in subtly sweet Massaman curry sauce of coconut milk, peanuts, potatoes, and onions

Nuer Kaprow
Sliced beef sautéed with **basil** (•281) and chilies

MOO (PORK)

Moo Yang
Grilled sliced pork with herbs, green peppercorns, and lime juice

Kaeng Kew Wan Moo
Sliced pork in a green curry sauce with **bamboo shoots**, chilies, coconut milk, and basil

Kaeng Phed Moo
Sliced pork in a red curry sauce with green peas, chilies, coconut milk, and basil

Moo Pad King
Sautéed sliced pork with ginger, **Chinese mushrooms** (•281), scallions, and chilies

Moo Pad Pak Nam Man Hoi
Sautéed sliced pork with mixed vegetables and **oyster sauce** (•281)

Moo Kratiem Prik Thai
Sliced pork sautéed with chilies, garlic, white pepper, and cilantro

INGREDIENT NOTES

• **Bamboo shoots** are the conical, fibrous inner shoots of young bamboo plants. Most restaurants in the U.S. use canned bamboo shoots.

AHAN TALAY (FISH and SHELLFISH)

Seafood dishes derive mostly from the south of Thailand, which is sandwiched between two bodies of water, the Andaman Sea and the Gulf of Thailand.

Pla Kew Wan
Pan-fried salmon (or other fish) fillet in green curry sauce with basil, chilies, and coconut milk

Although salmon is not consumed very often in Thailand because it is scarce (and, therefore, very expensive), it is well liked.

Pla Pad King
Pan-fried fish (such as flounder) with ginger, chilies, scallions, and cilantro

Pla Mouk Kratiem Prik Thai
Pan-fried squid with chilies, garlic, white pepper, and cilantro

Goong Kratiem Prik Thai
Pan-fried shrimp with chilies, garlic, white pepper, and cilantro

Hoi Shell Kaeng Kew Wan
Scallops in green curry sauce with coconut milk, basil, **kaffir lime leaves** (•279), and chilies

Hoi Shell Kratiem Prik Thai
Pan-fried scallops with chilies, garlic, mushrooms, scallions, red pepper, and cilantro

Goong Choo Chee
Shrimp cooked in red curry sauce with coconut milk, basil, **kaffir lime leaves** (•279)

Choo chee curries are thick and rich. They are made with a red curry paste, often minus the cumin, coriander, and peppercorns, and with less coconut milk than other curries. Choo chee tofu is another common dish made with this sauce.

Pla Muok Kaeng Kew Wan
Fried squid in green curry sauce with coconut milk, **bamboo shoots**, chilies, **kaffir lime leaves** (•279), and basil

Pla Jearn
Whole fish sautéed with ginger, chilies, mushrooms, and scallions; sometimes topped with ground pork

Pla Lad Prik
Whole red snapper stir-fried with **roasted curry paste** (•277), red curry paste, chilies, garlic, and **tamarind** (•277)

Pla Nueng
Steamed whole fish topped with ground pork, mushrooms, and ginger

Goong Pad Preaw Wan
Sweet-and-sour shrimp (or other seafood) cooked with cucumber, tomatoes, pineapple, onions, and scallions

KAO (RICE)
Thailand is one of the world's top rice-growing nations and is affectionately known as "the rice bowl of Asia." *Kao* is the word for both "rice" and "food" in the Thai language.

Kao Pad Pak
Fried rice with mixed vegetables

Kao Pad
Fried rice with choice of shrimp, chicken, or pork

Steamed White Rice
Better Thai restaurants in the U.S. offer jasmine rice, a long-grained white rice that has a subtle, somewhat nutty flavor.

Kao Pad Goong
Fried rice with mixed seafood (usually shrimp) and chilies

Thai fried rice, which is less oily than Chinese fried rice, is usually made with leftover rice. Commonly flavored with fish sauce and lime, it may also include onion, egg, garlic, and sliced tomato. In Thailand, it is often served with a fried egg on top and slices of cucumber and scallion as well as lime on the side. Some American restaurants will serve it this way upon request. When ordering fried rice, be sure to check the size of the portions. Many restaurants serve it as an entrée rather than a side dish.

KONG WAN (DESSERTS)

Thai desserts other than custard are not commonly found on menus in U.S. restaurants despite their popularity in Thailand. This is because they can be complicated to make and because they are not often appreciated by American diners who prefer ice cream over small cakes made with mung beans, yams, sticky rice, and agar (a gelatin-like ingredient).

Sang Ka Ya
Steamed pumpkin custard made with coconut milk

Khao Niew Mamuang
Sticky rice flavored with coconut cream, sugar, and salt, and paired with mango slices

KONG DUEM (BEVERAGES)

In the past Thai people tended not to drink anything with their meals (soup was considered the beverage). Today many men choose to consume alcohol, either whiskey or beer (especially when they are eating very spicy food), while women usually stick to non-alcoholic choices like ice water, fruit juice, soda, and iced tea.

Thai Iced Tea and Thai Iced Coffee
Tea or coffee made with sweetened milk and ice; may be flavored with cinnamon, star anise, vanilla, and other sweet spices

Thai iced tea and iced coffee are very refreshing but because of their sweetness are sometimes more pleasing as a dessert or a refreshing snack on a hot day rather than as the beverage served with the main part of a meal.

Hot Coffee and Tea
Thais are not big consumers of hot beverages because of the climate in their country (which can be described as hot or hotter). Nevertheless, hot tea is much more popular than hot coffee and is sometimes served at the end of a meal.

Beer
The best-known Thai beer is Singha. It is a strong, pale lager; very hoppy, aromatic, and flavorful.

VIETNAMESE
cuisine

★

Cheers–*Chuc mung* (chook mung)
Bon appétit–*Moi* [NAME OF PERSON BEING ADDRESSED] *An*
(moy [NAME OF PERSON BEING ADDRESSED] ang)
Thank you–*Cam on* (cam uhn)

VIETNAMESE COOKS TAKE PRIDE IN THE LIGHT, healthful qualities of their food as well as its beautiful presentation. Many dishes are simmered, steamed, or grilled, and when a Vietnamese cook does stir-fry, it is with a minimal amount of oil. Each dish features not only clean, clear flavors but also contrasting textures and colors. One of the healthiest and most representational aspects of a traditional Vietnamese meal is a table salad, an array of vegetables, herbs, and meat or seafood that is rolled in lettuce and/or rice papers by each diner. Some Vietnamese restaurants also offer an assortment of French classics, such as *chateaubriand* and *coq au vin;* this is a reflection of the 95 years during which France occupied Vietnam.

Principles of Flavor

Though Vietnamese cooks rely on many flavor sources, none is more prevalent than *nuoc mam*, a fish sauce made from fermented anchovies. Replacing salt in the Western kitchen and soy sauce in the Chinese, *nuoc mam*, like an anonymous benefactor, enhances other flavors while keeping its own presence hidden. Fresh herbs, such as cilantro, mint, basil, and garlic chives, are used in such abundance that they provide nutrients as well as good taste. Additional flavor comes from chilies, lemongrass, garlic, ginger, shallots, and lime juice.

Foreign Influence

Vietnamese cooking reflects many strong foreign influences but, at the same time, retains a strong, individual character. From the Chinese, who ruled Vietnam for nearly 1,000 years, the Vietnamese adopted stir-frying in a wok, deep-frying, chopsticks, and such cooking staples as tofu and noodles. The Chinese also introduced Buddhism, which spurred on the development of a Vietnamese vegetarian cuisine. Mongolians invaded Vietnam in the 13th century and introduced many beef dishes. By way of India, Vietnam acquired curries.

From 16th-century European explorers the Vietnamese acquired such foodstuffs as watercress, corn, tomatoes, potatoes, and peanuts. And from the French, who ruled Vietnam from 1859 until 1954, the Vietnamese adopted a passion for coffee as well as a taste for such foods as French bread, pâté, butter, cream, and asparagus.

Ordering

A typical Vietnamese family meal consists of a non-noodle soup, rice, vegetables or salad, and meat and/or fish. Noodle soups are very popular for breakfast and for one-dish meals at other times during the day. All of the components of a family meal are brought to the table at the same time and eaten in whatever order each diner prefers.

To create an authentic Vietnamese meal in a restaurant, order as a group and share each dish around the table. Be sure to order an assortment of dishes that represent different flavors, textures, and cooking styles.

Service and Dining

In some Vietnamese restaurants a bowl of shrimp chips is brought to the table automatically when diners sit down for a meal (in Vietnam they are enjoyed as a snack with drinks or used as a scoop with salads). These light, airy chips are made by combining finely ground shrimp with egg whites and tapioca. This mixture is dropped into hot oil, causing the chips to puff up and double or triple in size. Most restaurants buy mass-manufactured dried chips, then fry them before serving. Unfortunately, high-quality shrimp chips, which boast a strong, fresh shrimp flavor and melt in the mouth, are very expensive and rarely encountered in restaurants. Some restaurants serve shrimp chips tinted pastel colors; these are among the poorest quality of all.

Waiters usually offer instruction to the uninitiated on how to wrap food in rice papers. Some restaurants bring the rice papers to the table predampened, which actually makes the wrapping process much more difficult than it need be because the longer the rice papers sit after they are dampened, the stickier and more difficult they become to handle. You will have a much easier time if you dip the rice papers in a bowl of water as you are ready to use them. For specific instructions, see page 295.

Condiments

Nuoc cham, a blend of fish sauce *(nuoc mam)*, small red chilies, vinegar, lime juice, finely shredded carrot, and sugar, is Vietnam's principal table condiment, the equivalent of salt and pepper in the U.S. It is served to each diner in a small, individual saucer into which other foods are dipped.

Noodle soups are served with an assortment of condiments, such as chili sauce, hoisin sauce, and fish sauce, all of which are meant to be added at the diner's discretion, either directly into the soup or into a condiment saucer into which solids from the soup can be dipped.

Garnishes

Vietnamese cooks take great pride in the presentation of their food. On your plate you may find such edible garnishes as cilantro, scallions, garlic chives, and crisp fried shallots (served over noodles, soups, and salads); thin pieces of lemongrass, not meant for eating; or the very small, very hot red or green bird chilies (also known as Thai chilies), to be eaten at the diner's discretion. In certain soups you may find pieces of dried orange peel, cinnamon stick, and star anise, all of which contribute to the flavor of the broth while it is cooking but are not meant to be eaten.

Rice

In most Vietnamese restaurants, long-grain white rice, an integral component in the Vietnamese diet, is served with all entrées except those accompanied by noodles. Some of the better establishments offer fragrant jasmine rice, a Vietnamese favorite.

Utensils

Each place setting for a traditional Vietnamese meal includes a rice bowl, a set of chopsticks, a saucer for dipping sauce, and a soup spoon.

To eat in traditional Vietnamese fashion, place a portion of rice in your rice bowl, then take, with your chopsticks, a biteful of another food, such as a piece of meat or a vegetable, eat it with some of your rice, then take a biteful of the next food you desire. The Vietnamese even ladle their soup into the rice bowl, either pouring the soup on top of the rice or, if they don't want to eat the two together, only taking soup when the rice bowl is empty. It is considered impolite to pick up a serving platter in order to serve oneself (instead reach with your chopsticks) or to take more than a bite-size portion at one time.

Signature Dishes

C *ha Gio* (spring roll: pork and often seafood, cellophane noodles, and vegetables wrapped in rice paper and deep-fried); *Goi Cuon* (fresh spring roll: shrimp, pork, vegetables, rice vermicelli, and herbs wrapped in rice paper and served at room temperature); *Pho* (beef-noodle soup); *Canh Chua Ca* (hot-and-sour fish soup); *Chao Tom* (shrimp paste grilled on sugarcane); *Bo Nhung Dam* (beef fondue)

The MSG Question

MSG is used by many Vietnamese chefs.

Common Misconceptions

Vietnamese and Chinese food are the same. Although Vietnam was ruled by China for about one thousand years, ending in the 10th century, the cuisines of these two countries remain distinct. Whereas soy sauce is a key ingredient in Chinese cooking, it is used in much smaller quantities in Vietnamese cooking. While the Chinese appreciate lamb, the Vietnamese rarely make use of it. While the Vietnamese use oil very sparingly, the Chinese use it, at least in comparison, rather lavishly.

Many ethnic Chinese have emigrated from Vietnam to the United States and opened Vietnamese restaurants, sometimes offering Chinese dishes on their menus, a source of some confusion to the public.

Vietnamese food is spicy. Unlike some other Southeast Asian cuisines, Vietnamese food is not fiery hot. In general, Vietnamese cooks leave it up to individual diners to spice up their foods with condiments rather than incorporating spicy seasonings into a dish during the cooking process.

Vietnamese MENU

MON AN CHOI (APPETIZERS) The
Vietnamese are quite fond of the appetizer course, which
often includes pickles enjoyed with beer or whiskey.
Appetizers in restaurants in the U.S. tend to be small portions of dishes on the main course section of the menu.

Banh Mi Chien Tom (Shrimp Toast)
Shrimp plus such ingredients
as garlic, shallots, and ginger
processed to form a paste, then
spread on small slices of French
bread and deep-fried

Nem Nuong
Pork meatballs grilled on a
skewer; served with lettuce,
herbs, pickled carrot and cucumber, and rice paper for wrapping

Banh Cuon
Steamed rolled crepe filled with
ground pork, black mushrooms,
and onion; sometimes served
with boiled Vietnamese sausage
on top

Banh cuon *is popular
Vietnamese breakfast fare.*

Cha Gio Chay (Vegetable Rolls)
Rice paper wrapped around
such ingredients as **cellophane
noodles**, lettuce, mint, **garlic
chives**, and cilantro, then
deep-fried

Cha Gio (Vietnamese Spring Rolls)
Rice paper wrapped around such
ingredients as pork, crabmeat,
shrimp, **cellophane noodles**, and
onions, then deep-fried

*In Vietnamese restaurants in
the U.S.* cha gio *are sometimes
listed as imperial rolls.*

FRIED VIETNAMESE
ROLLS, such as *cha gio*, are
traditionally served with lettuce leaves, cilantro, mint,
and pickled carrot and
cucumber. To eat, spread
out the lettuce leaf, then use
your chopsticks to place the
spring roll plus the other
ingredients on the lettuce;
roll everything up in the lettuce, dip in *nuoc cham*, if
desired, and eat with your
fingers, taking small bites.
Do not try to cut *cha gio* or
other Vietnamese
rolls because
they will most
likely fall apart.

INGREDIENT NOTES

• **Cellophane noodles**, also
known as bean thread, mung
bean, clear, transparent, or glass
noodles, are made from the
starch of mung beans. They are
translucent in color, light and
slippery in texture, and bland in
flavor.

RICE PAPERS: Like tortillas in Mexico, rice papers are the all-purpose food wrappers of Vietnam. They are made by combining finely ground rice, water, salt, and sometimes tapioca (cassava) flour, then rolling out the mixture into paper-thin rounds and drying the rounds on bamboo mats in the sun. When dry, the rounds look glassy and brittle, the cross-hatch pattern from the bamboo showing through. When wet, they are translucent and pleasantly chewy.

To use rice papers for wrapping, first submerge the dry round in a bowl of warm water until malleable and relatively soft. Then remove the rice paper from the water and let sit for a minute or so to soften a bit more.

To fill and roll rice papers, use your chopsticks to transfer the desired fillings onto the center of the paper in a fairly neat straight line, spreading each ingredient so that with every bite you will taste every flavor, then roll and fold into a neat package.

Goi Cuon

Rice paper wrapped around shrimp, pork, lettuce, mint, **garlic chives**, and rice vermicelli; served at room temperature with **peanut** or **hoisin sauce**

In Vietnamese restaurants in the U.S., goi cuon *are listed under several different names, such as garden roll, summer roll, or soft spring roll.*

Bi Cuon

Rice paper wrapped around shredded roast pork and lettuce

• **Garlic chives** (also known as Chinese chives) look like long blades of grass and boast a strong garlic flavor.

• **Peanut sauce** commonly counts among its ingredients roasted peanuts, fresh red chilies, garlic, mint, lemon juice, fish sauce, and coconut milk.

• **Hoisin sauce**, made with soybeans, garlic, chili peppers, vinegar, and sugar, is thick and reddish brown in appearance and sweet and spicy in taste. The quality, taste, and thickness vary greatly from brand to brand. Your opinion of this condiment may therefore vary from restaurant to restaurant.

GOI: VIETNAMESE SALADS

Vietnamese salads are traditionally composed of numerous ingredients of contrasting color, taste, and texture, including meats such as shrimp, chicken, or pork; fruits; vegetables; egg; herbs; and nuts. Each component is carefully cooked, tenderized (raw vegetables are often tenderized by marination in a mixture of vinegar, salt, and sugar), and/or decoratively sliced to create a salad that is satisfying to both the eye and the palate. Dressings, often made with such ingredients as fish sauce, rice vinegar, lime juice, chilies, garlic, and minimal oil, are used sparingly and are sometimes presented as a dipping sauce on the side rather than drizzled over the top. In Vietnam as well as Vietnamese restaurants elsewhere, salads may be served as appetizers or as part of a main meal.

NOODLE SOUPS Noodle soups are eaten for breakfast, and sometimes lunch and dinner, throughout Vietnam. Because they require many ingredients, these meals-in-a-bowl are, for the most part, eaten outside the home. They are traditionally served in large bowls with an assortment of goodies on the side, such as bean sprouts, mint, basil, lime, and sliced chilies, as well as such table condiments as chili sauce, fish sauce, hoisin sauce, and sugar.

Mien Ga
Chicken and **cellophane noodle** (•294) soup

Hu Tieu
Seafood, pork, and rice noodle soup

Hu tieu *is the southern Vietnamese version of* pho *(see page 297). There are many different varieties of this soup, which is sometimes served without broth.*

Pho Bo (Hanoi Beef Soup)
Sliced beef and rice noodles in broth; served with bean sprouts, basil, cilantro, lime, and sliced chilies on the side

In Hanoi this soup is not traditionally served with bean sprouts, but in other parts of Vietnam and in the U.S. they are a common addition.

NOODLE SOUPS are traditionally eaten with both chopsticks and a short porcelain soup spoon. To do so, hold the chopsticks in your strong hand and use them to eat the noodles, meat, and other solids, to transfer bean sprouts and other foods served on the side to the soup bowl, and to dip the meat into the condiment saucer (alternatively, the condiments can be poured directly into the soup bowl, especially if the condiments are in bottles in the center of the table and you have not been given a condiment saucer). Hold the soup spoon in your other hand and use it for the broth. The Vietnamese do not consider

it impolite to slurp hot broth or noodles; in fact, it is considered a necessary measure in order to cool off the food as you are putting it into your mouth.

Pho Ga

Chicken and rice noodles in broth; served with bean sprouts, basil, cilantro, lime, and sliced chilies on the side

PHO

Pho bo from the north of Vietnam is the most popular of all phos, and is commonly called just "pho." Noodles and raw meat are placed in a bowl, then covered with boiling stock. Vietnamese cooks pride themselves on their special stocks, and secret ingredients include marrow, cinnamon, coriander seed, star anise, dried orange or tangerine peel, and "burnt" onion, ginger, and shallot (made by grilling the onion, ginger, or shallot until the

skin is black, then discarding the skin, and adding the inside flesh to the stock).

In a restaurant that specializes in pho, diners choose the cut of beef they want in their soup. Beef options include:

Tai: medium-rare eye-of-round steak
Nam: well-done flank steak
Gau: well-done fatty brisket
Chin: well-done brisket
Sach: tripe
Gan: beef tendons
Bo vien: meatballs

CANH (NON-NOODLE SOUPS)

In Vietnam *canh* are a common accompaniment to a meal. In restaurants in the U.S. non-noodle soups are commonly offered as appetizers. *Canh* are sometimes listed on menus as *sup*, a corruption of the French word *soupe*.

Canh Chua Ca
Fish in a sour and slightly sweet-and-spicy broth made with such ingredients as tomatoes, bean sprouts, celery, **tamarind**, pineapple, chilies, and herbs

This popular southern Vietnamese soup, sometimes called Vietnamese bouillabaisse, is often made with shrimp instead of fish.

Canh Kien
Vegetables, such as squash and sweet potatoes, in a coconut milk-based broth

Canh Bap Ga
Chicken and corn soup

Canh Mang Cua
Asparagus and crabmeat soup

After the French effort to grow asparagus in Vietnam failed, canned white asparagus were imported, and it is hypothesized that it was a French cook who created this soup. In restaurants in the U.S. it is often made with green asparagus, either fresh or canned.

Hoanh Thanh or Won Ton Soup
Delicate dumplings in broth

BUN (NOODLE DISHES)
In Vietnam these meal-in-a-bowl noodle dishes are very popular at lunchtime. Rice vermicelli is combined with shredded lettuce, carrots, cucumber, bean sprouts, and fresh herbs, such as mint and cilantro, then topped with meat or seafood that has been grilled, stir-fried, stewed, or poached. Everything is seasoned generously with *nuoc cham* (see page 289) and sprinkled with ground, toasted peanuts.

Bun Ga Cari
Rice vermicelli topped with chicken curry

Bun Thit Nuong
Rice vermicelli topped with grilled pork slices

Bun Bo
Rice vermicelli topped with stir-fried beef with **lemongrass** (•300)

Bun Cha Gio
Rice vermicelli topped with fried spring rolls

Bun Nem Nuong
Rice vermicelli topped with barbecued pork balls

Bun Bo Kho
Rice vermicelli topped with spicy beef stew

HEO (PORK)   Pork, commonly cooked to the well-done stage, is the most popular meat among Vietnamese cooks because of its versatility and low price.

Banh Xeo (Happy Pancakes or Crispy Cake)
Vietnamese-style crepe made with rice flour batter and any number of fillings, including a mixture of pork, shrimp, mushrooms, and bean sprouts, or simply bean sprouts

Properly made banh xeo *have a crispy bottom crust and are served with* nuoc cham *(see page 289).*

Banh Hoi Thit Nuong
Grilled pork over steamed rice vermicelli noodle cakes

Heo Kho
Pork simmered in **caramel sauce**

INGREDIENT NOTES

• **Tamarind** is a fruit that grows on a tree native to Asia and northern Africa. The pods of this fruit contain a sour-sweet pulp that is used in cooking.

• **Caramel sauce**, made of caramelized sugar and sometimes such ingredients as fish sauce and shallots, is a common component in simmered dishes, where it brings out the flavor of other foods and lends them its golden color.

BO (BEEF) There is not a lot of land for cattle to graze in Vietnam, so beef prices are high. As with all meat, lean cuts are preferred. Many beef dishes are served with *mam nem*, a dipping sauce made with anchovy paste, pineapple, and fresh chilies.

Bo Bay Mon
Seven courses of beef

Bo bay mon *is a Vietnamese favorite that is offered in the U.S. and Vietnam at restaurants that specialize in this presentation and sometimes at restaurants with broader menus. One by one, beginning with* bo nhung dam *(beef fondue) and ending with* chao thit bo *(thick porridge-like rice soup), different beef preparations are brought to the table, each one meant to enhance the next.*

Bo Xao Xa Ot
Sliced beef sautéed with **lemongrass**, peanuts, and chilies

Bo Nhung Dam (Beef Fondue)
Beef cooked at the table in a seasoned vinegar or coconut broth; served with rice paper, mint, cilantro, lettuce, and pickled carrot and cucumber

Fondues like this one are often served on special occasions in Vietnam. The beef plus the herbs and vegetables are meant to be wrapped in the rice paper (see page 295). The beef in bo nhung dam *is sometimes replaced with pork, chicken, shrimp, or squid.*

Bo Nuong La Nho
Ground beef marinated with spices, wrapped in grape leaves, and grilled on skewers; served with rice vermicelli and **peanut sauce** (•295)

Grapes leaves are the Western stand-in for la-lot leaves (also known as pepper leaves because they are in the same family as the vine that yields black peppercorns). La-lot leaves are large, round, and crinkled in appearance, and very delicate in flavor.

The word nuong *in a Vietnamese dish name indicates that the food is grilled.*

INGREDIENT NOTES

• **Lemongrass** is a woody grass valued for the lemony flavor and aroma it releases in cooking.

GA (POULTRY) Poultry is appreciated for its versatility in Vietnam but is served mainly on special occasions because of its high price.

Ga Nuong Chanh

Chicken marinated in spices and lime juice and grilled on skewers; served with rice papers and/or lettuce leaves, herbs, and pickled vegetables for wrapping

Ga nuong chanh *is sometimes served, without the rice papers and accompaniments, as an appetizer.*

Ga Xa Ot

Pan-fried chicken with **lemongrass** and chilies

Com Tay Cam

Rice and chicken and vegetables, including **tree ear mushrooms** and **bamboo shoots**, cooked slowly in a clay pot

Vit Quay

Oven-roasted duck

Ca-Ri Ga

Chicken curry

Vietnamese curries, which are a specialty of the south, are often made with frog's legs and goat in addition to chicken. They are milder than Indian and Thai curries and are, most often, made with prepackaged curry powder rather than fresh spice blends. Like Thai curries, they often include coconut milk and lemongrass among their ingredients. A special Vietnamese touch is the use of sweet rather than white potatoes.

• **Tree ear mushrooms** are small dried black fungi (about $1/2$ inch across) valued for their chewy and crunchy texture and ability to absorb other flavors. They grow out of tree trunks, giving the visual impression of floppy ears, thus their name.

• **Bamboo shoots** are the young, sprouting stems of the bamboo plant.

HAI SAN (FISH and SHELLFISH)

Vietnam is blessed with 1,400 miles of coastline, so it is not surprising that seafood provides a significant amount of the protein in the Vietnamese diet.

Chao Tom

Barbecued shrimp paste on sugarcane; served with lettuce leaves, scallions, mint leaves, rice paper for wrapping (see page 295), and *nuoc cham* or **peanut sauce** (•295) for dipping

Ca Kho To

Chunks of fish in a salty **caramel sauce** (•299)

Ca kho to *is traditionally served with* canh chua ca *(sour fish soup)*.

Ca Hap

Whole steamed fish

Tom Nuong Vi

Grilled shrimp in the shell; served with vegetables and rice papers for wrapping (see page 295)

TO EAT CHAO TOM, remove the shrimp paste (a mixture of shrimp plus such ingredients as sugar, pork fat, and salt and pepper) from the sugarcane. Place a piece of the shrimp paste along with whatever accompaniments you desire on a moistened rice paper, then roll to close, dip in the sauce, and bite. Even if the roll is big, do not try to cut it with a knife because it will break apart; instead hold the roll in your hand and take small bites. If desired, suck or chew on the sugarcane.

Cua Rang Muoi (Salt and Pepper Crab)

Crab pieces in the shell seasoned with salt, pepper, and possibly garlic and tomato paste, then fried in minimal oil

Cua rang muoi *is meant to be eaten with the hands. Traditionally, to clean up when finished eating, diners squeeze lime juice on their fingers, then rinse them with warm tea. This dish may also be made with shrimp.*

VIETNAMESE VEGETARIAN DISHES

Vegetarian dishes form an important category of foods in the Vietnamese diet as many Vietnamese are Buddhists. However, unlike the Buddhist monks who follow a very strict regime, most Vietnamese Buddhists follow a vegetarian diet only during spiritually significant days of the month rather than all the time. Among the Vietnamese vegetarian dishes most likely to be encountered on a menu in the U.S. are *rao xao* (mixed vegetables with tofu), *mi don xao chay* (mixed vegetables with tofu and crispy egg noodles), *mi mem xao chay* (mixed vegetables with tofu and soft egg noodles), and *cari rau cai* (vegetable curry). The principle liquid flavoring in Vietnamese vegetarian foods is soy sauce.

COM (RICE)   At lunchtime in Vietnam combination rice dishes, called *com dia*, are very popular. Diners can generally pick a type of rice (either long-grain or broken) and a stir-fry, stew, or grilled item listed on the menu as a topping. Standard accompaniments are pickled and fresh vegetables.

Com Chien
Fried rice prepared with shrimp, pork, chicken, beef, crabmeat, or a combination of meats

Vietnamese fried rice is very similar to Chinese fried rice, though it is flavored with fish sauce instead of soy sauce.

Chao Thit Bo
Thick porridge-like rice soup topped with beef

Like the Chinese congee, *Vietnamese chao is a common breakfast food but is also enjoyed at other meals or as a snack.*

Com Tam
Broken rice, usually topped with pork

Com tam, broken rice kernels reminiscent of couscous, are usually cooked with coconut milk.

Com Xuong Nuong
Grilled pork chops over rice

Com Ga Nuong
Grilled chicken over rice

Com Cari
Curried stew over rice

BANH MI: VIETNAMESE SUBMARINE SANDWICHES

Trained by the French colonists, Vietnamese *charcutiers* developed their own repertoire of pâtés, hams, and sausages, which they serve on French bread. Condiments include mayonnaise, marinated vegetables, such as shredded Chinese radish and carrot, fresh cucumber, cilantro, and fresh chili peppers. These sandwiches are a popular lunch on the run.

DO TRANG MIENG (DESSERTS)

The Vietnamese favor fresh fruit (such as papaya, pineapple, and banana) after a meal and reserve sweets for snacks or special occasions.

Lichees

Lichees (or litchis) have spiny red or brown skin and jelly-like grayish white flesh with a distinctive, delicate sweet flavor. While they make frequent appearances on menus in the U.S., they are not a common choice in Vietnam. Most lichees in the U.S come from a can (in which case they are preskinned).

Che
Coconut-flavored pudding

Che is sold on the streets of Vietnam and in some U.S restaurants in different flavors and colors. A very popular choice is che ba mau, *a three-color extravaganza made with ground mung beans (which are yellow) and red and green agar (a gelatin made from seaweed).*

Banh Flan
Caramel custard

Chuoi Chien
Batter-fried bananas

THUC UONG (BEVERAGES)

The Vietnamese drink a variety of beverages with their meals, including hot tea (without sugar or milk), beer, sweet soybean milk, iced French coffee, orange juice, and sugarcane juice. Wine is popular among those who can afford it.

Da Chanh
Freshly squeezed lemonade

Chanh Muoi
Salty lemonade made with whole lemons preserved in salted water

Fruit Shakes
Available in such flavors as **jackfruit**, papaya, or coconut

Café Sua Da
Iced espresso with sweetened condensed milk

Americans have been known to become addicted to this refreshing iced coffee concoction reminiscent of a milk shake.

Café Sua
Espresso with sweetened condensed milk

To make Vietnamese-style espresso, freshly ground, dark-roasted coffee beans are placed in a special single-serving filter. Boiling water is added and left to drip into a glass into which a hefty portion of sweetened condensed milk has already been poured. The coffee is brought to the table while still dripping.

Jasmine Tea

Jasmine tea is a Chinese green (unfermented) tea that is scented with dried jasmine flowers.

INGREDIENT NOTES

• **Jackfruit** is a very large tropical fruit with thick, yellowish-green, spiny skin and mildly sweet, pale yellow flesh that is remininscent of pineapple, though less sweet and juicy.

AMERICAN REGIONAL
cuisines

★

THE OTHER CHAPTERS IN THIS BOOK DEAL with cuisines of foreign countries, but American menus can, in their own way, be just as "exotic" as the menus at Thai or Indian restaurants. While the words will be written in English, some of the them—such as "weck," "fiddleheads," or "rivvels"—may be totally unfamiliar.

This chapter introduces regional specialties, explains some regional cooking styles, defines unique menu terms, and calls attention to local treats to look for when traveling—or when a New York-style deli or a Cajun bar opens in your neighborhood. (Tex-Mex and Cal-Mex cooking, important subsets of the American regional category, are handled in the Mexican chapter, starting on page 209.)

NEW YORK DAIRY and DELI

These are Jewish cuisines and, at one time, restaurants serving these foods would have followed the Jewish dietary laws, which prohibit the serving of meat and dairy dishes at the same meal and forbid the consumption of pork. Today, the rules are often relaxed (or tossed out), but in Jewish neighborhoods you'll still find kosher deli restaurants that serve no milk, butter—or cheesecake—and kosher dairy restaurants that serve dairy, vegetarian, and fish dishes only. These restaurants are likely to be closed during the Jewish sabbath—from sundown Friday until after dark on Saturday—and on major Jewish holidays.

NEW YORK DAIRY

You get the best of dairy cuisine at breakfast or brunch—an unparalleled assortment of breadstuffs, spreads, and toppings. Slather your bagel, bialy, or onion roll with cream cheese or farmer cheese, then pile on smoked fish, onion, tomato, and cucumber.

Bagels

These dense, ring-shaped rolls come in plain, pumpernickel, and egg versions; topped with onion, garlic, sesame seeds, or poppy seeds; or swirled with cinnamon and raisins (sample more exotic varieties, such as blueberry, at your own risk)

You'll know you have a "real New York bagel," which is boiled and hand-shaped before it is baked (imposters are only baked), because it will be quite firm and will have a rather tough, glossy crust and no little bumps on the bottom.

Bialys

Chewy disk-shaped roll with a puffed edge and a flat center that is sprinkled with browned onions

Matzoh Brei

"French toast" made with matzoh (unleavened, cracker-like bread); served with sour cream, applesauce, or cinnamon sugar

Farmer Cheese

Dry pot cheese, pressed into large loaves, available plain or with scallions or chives, chopped vegetables, pineapple, or blueberries mixed in; spread it on bagels, bialys, or pumpernickel bread

Farmer cheese is sometimes served warm, which brings out its flavor and makes it more spreadable.

Cream Cheese

A good dairy restaurant will provide flavorful, non-gummy, homemade cream cheese delicious enough to eat with a spoon; however, ask for a "schmear" if you want just a thin coating of cream cheese rather than a thick layer

Borscht

The Jewish version is a meatless beet soup; served cold with sour cream and chopped, hard-boiled egg

Gefilte Fish

Small, loaf-shaped "dumplings" made of finely chopped whitefish (usually carp or pike) poached in broth; served with head-clearing horseradish

Latkes

Thick, crispy pancakes made from grated raw potato, onion, and eggs; fried in oil and served with sour cream or applesauce

Latkes *are traditionally served on the Jewish holiday called Hanukkah.*

Blintzes

Cottage cheese-filled crepes (blueberries, cherries, or other fillings may be mixed with the cheese) browned in butter; served with sour cream

Smoked and Pickled Fish

Lox (cured salmon) is the classic with bagels and cream cheese, but you can also choose cold-smoked Nova Scotia-style salmon, which is less salty than lox; rich, fatty sablefish; smoked sturgeon; whole smoked white-fish; or herring prepared in a variety of ways—smoked, pickled, in cream or wine sauce; herring or whitefish salad are other options

NEW YORK DELI New York-style delis are famous for their overstuffed sandwiches—a half-pound or a pound of meat is not uncommon. Order your sandwich on rye or a hard roll, with spicy mustard (a request for mayonnaise—or for white bread—may raise eyebrows), Russian dressing (a mixture of mayonnaise, pimiento, and ketchup or chili sauce), sauerkraut, or coleslaw. It will be accompanied with half-sour pickles, garlic dills, pickled tomatoes, and pickled peppers. Each deli has its special combination sandwiches, often named after celebrities. For example, the Stage Deli in New York City fills two rolls with corned beef, pastrami, coleslaw, and Russian dressing and calls its creation a "Dolly Parton."

NEW YORK DELI SANDWICH FILLINGS

In addition to the usual turkey and roast beef, some favorite sandwich fillings include:

Pastrami: dry-cured spiced beef
Corned beef: salt-brined brisket
Tongue: smoked or pickled, thinly sliced
Salami: a dense, garlicky all-beef version
Brisket: pot roast made from a deliciously fatty cut
Chopped liver: made with sautéed onions, chopped hard-boiled eggs, and lots of chicken fat; also served as an appetizer

Kishke

Bread "sausage" made by stuffing a highly seasoned bread crumb or flour mixture into a natural beef casing; sliced and served hot

Chicken in a Pot

A cut-up chicken cooked in broth with vegetables and noodles

One order of chicken in a pot is often large enough to serve two. Ask the waiter when ordering.

Knishes

Thin dough stuffed with potato, cabbage, **buckwheat**, or chopped liver, then baked

In New York dairy restaurants, knishes are filled with cheese.

INGREDIENT NOTES

• **Buckwheat** is a nutty-tasting, brown rice-like kernel that is ground into granules called groats. When the groats are roasted, they are called kasha.

Kasha Varnishkes

Roasted **buckwheat** groats cooked with bow-tie noodles; served with gravy

Chicken Soup

Limpid and golden, with matzoh balls (matzoh-meal dumplings), fine noodles, rice, or kreplach—meat-filled, noodle-dough wrapped "won tons"

Hamantaschen

Three-cornered pastries made with cookie dough or yeast dough, filled with poppy seeds, prune butter, or apricot butter

Hamantaschen *are traditionally eaten on the festive Jewish holiday called Purim, which takes place in the spring.*

Rugelach

Cookie-size rolled pastries filled with nuts, dried fruit, jam, or a chocolate filling

PENNSYLVANIA DUTCH
The serving of "seven sweets and seven sours" characterizes a traditional Pennsylvania Dutch meal. In addition to meat and vegetables, you'll be offered seven or more side dishes or condiments, which may include pickles made from cucumbers, watermelon rind, beets, onions, mushrooms, or beans; pickled eggs tinted with beet juice; sauerkraut; pepper-and-cabbage relish; mustard-flavored piccalilli made with chopped vegetables; homemade ketchup; apple butter, jellies, preserves, and fruit fritters; pudding (often tapioca and custard); and cake and cookies. Everything goes on the table at once, and you mix and match as you please: Some people eat a little cake and/or pudding before beginning the meal (while their appetites are sharpest), while others enjoy these sweets between "courses." Pie is the usual dessert.

Chicken Potpie
Not really a pie (and nothing like the frozen dinner), this is a chicken and potato stew made with thick squares of noodle dough

Schnitz und Knepp(e)
Pieces of smoked ham cooked in broth with dried apples and brown sugar, then topped with biscuit-like dumplings

Corn Soup with Rivvels
Rich chicken broth with diced chicken, corn freshly cut from the cob, and *rivvels*, rice-like noodles made by rubbing together flour and eggs

Filling
A "comfort-food" mixture of mashed potatoes, coarse soft bread crumbs, milk, eggs, onion, and butter, baked in a casserole

Shoofly Pie
A molasses-and-crumb-filled pie that may be "wet" or "dry" (or somewhere in-between); for a "wet" shoofly, the crumbs top a moist molasses filling; in "dry" shooflies, the molasses and crumbs are mixed for a cake-like filling, and the slices are firm enough to dip in coffee

The name shoofly may come from the need to shoo flies away from this sugary dessert.

SOUTHERN The South is the territory of what Calvin Trillin, writer and aficionado of American regional cuisines, respectfully calls "serious eaters." Much Southern food is hearty country fare, and this includes soul food, dishes specifically identified with the South's African-American community. However, culinary boundaries between the races blur when it comes to standbys such as fried chicken or catfish, greens and pot likker, rice and beans, and sweet potato pie. Many rustic Southern dishes are centered on or flavored with choice or humble parts of the pig—barbecued ribs, salt pork cooked with greens or beans, sliced ham with red-eye gravy—and throughout the coastal region, shellfish is celebrated in hundreds of ways. Cajun and Creole food, important subsets of the Southern cooking tradition, are addressed separately (see pages 315–320).

Grits or Hominy Grits
Dried, hulled corn kernels ground into coarse particles, cooked up into a bland, creamy cereal; commonly served with butter or gravy as a side dish

Grits can also be flavored with cheese, enriched with eggs, or cooked into a soufflé.

Spoon Bread
Not really a bread but a rich cornmeal "soufflé," made with milk, eggs, and butter; delicate and custardy, it is served and eaten with a spoon

Red-Eye Gravy
Ham gravy made by adding water or, frequently, coffee to the pan in which ham has been fried

Hoppin' John
Black-eyed peas and rice, flavored with salt pork, onions, garlic, and chilies or hot sauce

Hoppin' John, introduced to the South by slaves, is traditionally eaten there on New Year's Day.

Chicken-Fried Steak
Thin, round steaks or cubed steaks, dipped in egg, dredged in flour, and fried; usually served with **cream gravy**

INGREDIENT NOTES

• **Cream gravy** is a milk-and-flour gravy made with the pan drippings from fried chicken or chicken-fried steak.

Maryland or Baltimore Crab Cakes

Lightly spiced, broiled, deep-fried, or pan-fried patties of crabmeat, egg, mayonnaise, and bread crumbs; served with tartar sauce and coleslaw

She-Crab Soup

A specialty of Charleston and coastal South Carolina, this is a bisque made with blue sea crabs, seasoned with Worcestershire sauce, red pepper, and sherry; the roe from female crabs gives it an orange color and a unique, tangy taste

Maryland Steamed Crabs

Blue crabs steamed and served with liberal coating of spices, such as a mixture of celery salt, allspice, red and black pepper, dry mustard, and clove; served whole on a table covered with butcher paper along with a roll or stack of paper towels and bowls of additional seasoning and vinegar

A crab feast is a messy but memorable meal commonly featured at large, informal waterfront restaurants. Order your crabs by the dozen and by size—the bigger they are, the meatier they are and the higher the price. Pitchers of beer, shared among everyone at the table, are the standard accompaniment.

DIPPING MARYLAND STEAMED CRABS in the bowl of extra seasoning spices with which they are served is, for many people, gilding the lily but, if you desire, go right ahead; alternatively, if you find the seasonings with which the crabs are already coated too intense, either dip the crabs in the vinegar to wash them off or simply ask that the seasonings be washed off prior to serving.

When ready to dismantle the steamed crabs, begin by twisting off the meaty claws; set them aside and save them for last. Pull off the six legs and suck out the meat and juice. Pry off the triangular "apron" from the bottom of the shell; if you have a female crab, you'll find orange roe, a delicious bonus. Pull off the top shell and remove the spongy gray lungs and the intestines from the body. Break the body in half, then twist off each of the back fins and eat the meat. Pick out and eat the meat from the body shell. Using your mallet and knife as a hammer and chisel, crack open each claw: If you do this properly, you can remove the meat in one piece.

Chicken Perloo (or Perlow, Pilaf, Pilau—or one of many other spellings)

A South Carolina one-dish meal of rice baked in broth with tomatoes (sometimes), onion, celery, and shrimp or strips of chicken; subject to many geographical and personal variations

Burgoo

A slow-cooked Kentucky stew made with several types of meat, such as chicken, beef, and pork, as well as squirrel or other game; it also contains potatoes, peppers, carrots, onions, okra, or other vegetables, and is seasoned with hot pepper

Brunswick Stew

A hearty stew made with chicken plus onion, potatoes, and corn

Brunswick Stew was created in Brunswick County, Virginia, in the early 19th century using squirrel meat.

Frogmore Stew

Hot sausage, shrimp, and chunks of corn on the cob, cooked in a highly spiced broth (or beer)

Although Frogmore Stew originated in the Sea Islands off the Carolinas, it is now served elsewhere in the South.

Iced Tea

The Southern beverage of choice, served in huge tumblers; unless you specify otherwise, it will be sweetened—usually heavily—before it is served to you

---

SOUL FOOD While the following dishes belong to the pantheon of soul food, most are eaten by all Southerners, not just blacks. The term "soul food" probably arose in the early 1960s, when African-Americans rediscovering their heritage took a renewed interest in the traditional foods of their Southern forebears.

Oven-Barbecued Spareribs

Different from the open-pit version (see page 322) but delicious, these spareribs are first baked without sauce, then baked further with a tomato-vinegar-brown sugar sauce

Chitterlings

The lining of a pig's intestines, painstakingly cleaned, then stewed and eaten with cider vinegar, hot sauce, and chopped raw onion; or the chitterlings may be battered and fried after stewing

Pot Likker

The well-flavored broth remaining after cooking greens with ham or pork; it may be eaten as a soup, with corn bread, or used as a base for other soups

Fried Catfish

Fillets or the whole skinned fish dipped in cornmeal, fried in a skillet, and often served with coleslaw and hush puppies (see right)

Black-Eyed Peas or Cowpeas

Black-eyed peas (cream-colored dried peas that bear a single black spot) cooked with ham hocks or slab bacon slices; served with corn bread

Hush Puppies

A cornmeal batter (seasoned with chopped onions, scallions, and/or garlic) deep-fried by the spoonful

Greens

Collard, turnip, or mustard greens, sliced and cooked with some form of smoked pork; the greens may be flavored with chilies in cooking or served with hot sauce

Sweet Potato Pie

Mashed sweet potatoes, sweetened and blended with eggs, milk, and spices, such as cinnamon, cloves, and nutmeg, and baked in a crust

Sweet potato pie tastes similar to pumpkin pie.

CAJUN and CREOLE   These two time-honored Louisiana cuisines have many ingredients in common, but certain distinctive differences in their cooking styles. To oversimplify somewhat, Cajun is country cooking; originally the make-do food of poor folks, it has gone far beyond subsistence cooking, but still includes local game, freshwater fish, and robust seasonings. Creole, on the other hand, is a more sophisticated, cosmopolitan cuisine, exhibiting Italian, Spanish, and African as well as French influences; more expensive, delicate foods such as veal, oysters, and artichokes figure in Creole menus. Seafood is preeminent in all Louisiana kitchens, but ham, sausage, and chicken are also important; bell peppers, onions, celery, scallions, tomatoes, chilies, and hot sauce are basic to both cuisines. Using a variation on a standard French technique, both Cajun and Creole cooks begin their sauces and stews with a roux, a slow-cooked blend of flour and fat that gives body and deep flavor to the dish. Cajun cooks use oil, while Creole roux are based on butter.

BOILED CRAWFISH:
For an "immersion course" in eating boiled crawfish, order three to four pounds to start (as you gain speed in shelling the critters, you can work your way up to more). Twist apart each crawdad's tail and "head" (it's actually the body) and crack the top section of tail shell. Gently squeeze the tip of the tail and the meat should pop out in one piece. If the black vein adheres to the tail meat, pull it off and discard. If desired, use your thumb to scoop out the yellow fat or "butter" from the head and savor it as it is considered a delicacy. If the claws are sizable (and you're patient enough), crack them between your teeth and suck out the meat and juices.

Boiled Crawfish

Cooked in a highly spiced broth, these are served in the shell and ordered by the pound; often served with boiled potatoes

The crawfish (also called crayfish, crawdad, or mudbug) is a small, freshwater, lobster-like crustacean and a staple of both Cajun and Creole cuisine. It appears in many guises, and there is quite a bit of overlap between the Cajun and Creole methods for cooking it.

Cajun Popcorn or Fried Crawdaddies

Shelled, batter-coated, deep-fried crawfish tails; served as a bar snack or appetizer with a piquant tomato-based sauce

Crawfish Étouffée

For this "smothered" crawfish, the tails are shelled, then stirred into a thick, peppery, tomato-based sauce and served with rice

In addition to crawfish, an étouffée *can also be made with fish or other shellfish, such as shrimp.*

Crawfish Bisque

A creamy soup with stuffed crawfish heads

Crawfish heads may be stuffed with such ingredients as chopped crawfish meat, bread crumbs, onion, parsley, and scallions.

AFTER YOU'VE finished the soup and scooped the stuffing out of the crawfish heads, if desired, pick up the shells with your hands and suck out any remaining stuffing.

Crawfish Balls

Chopped crawfish meat combined with white sauce and herbs and spices, formed into balls, crumbed, and deep-fried; served with drinks or as an appetizer

Crawfish Pie

Cooked crawfish combined with onions, scallions, garlic, herbs, and spices, baked into a double-crust pie

Blackened Redfish

Redfish rubbed with a hot, robust spice-herb blend (paprika, red, white, and black peppers, garlic and onion powder, oregano, and thyme, among other seasonings) and cooked in a smoking-hot iron pan

Soon after this dish was created by nationally known Cajun chef Paul Prudhomme, other cooks felt compelled to offer Blackened Everything Else— fish, seafood, meat, poultry— much of which, it must be said, does not take to the treatment.

Seafood Rémoulade

Cooked chilled shellfish—often crabmeat or shrimp—topped with a piquant mayonnaise flavored with ground red pepper and sharp Creole mustard

Shrimp Creole or Shrimp Sauce Piquante

Whole shelled shrimp cooked in a thick, sharp tomato sauce/gravy; served with rice

Redfish Courtbouillon

Redfish cooked in a dense, roux-thickened tomato sauce flavored with chilies; served with rice—a very common meal in Bayou country

Jambalaya

Rice cooked with onions, garlic, celery, tomatoes (sometimes), and seafood, chicken, ham, and/or sausage

Perhaps more than any other Cajun or Creole dish, jambalaya bears the signature of the cook, who brings to it his or her own family heritage, personal instincts, and keen eye for what's best in the market. Jambalaya resembles a Spanish paella.

Boudin

Links of pork sausage (**boudin blanc** or **boudin rouge**) cooked in liquid and then broiled or grilled

INGREDIENT NOTES

• **Boudin blanc** is a white sausage made from pork shoulder and liver, rice or bread, onions, garlic, herbs, and hot pepper; **boudin rouge** is a similar sausage colored red by the inclusion of blood.

BREAKFAST IN NEW ORLEANS

A simple New Orleans breakfast might consist of a cup of dark, somewhat bitter Creole coffee (blended with roasted, ground chicory root) made with equal amounts of coffee and milk (*café au lait*) accompanied by a *beignet*, a pillow of fried dough dusted with powdered sugar, or *pain perdu*—French toast. A more bountiful sit-down breakfast or brunch starts with milk punch (a light version of eggnog made with plenty of bourbon or brandy) or a creamy cocktail made with anise-scented liqueur, followed by poached eggs Sardou (served on artichoke bottoms atop creamed spinach with hollandaise sauce) or eggs *hussarde* (served on rusks—rounds of crisp, dry toast—with tomato, ham or Canadian bacon, and a mushroom-wine sauce). Another option is *grillades* and grits, thinly sliced veal braised in a Creole tomato and pepper sauce, served with buttered grits. You can even have a classic dessert like bananas Foster, invented at Brennan's restaurant in the French Quarter in the 1950s—bananas sautéed with brown sugar in butter, flamed with rum and banana liqueur, and served over vanilla ice cream.

Turtle Soup
A thick, smooth, Creole soup made with chunks of turtle meat and flavored with sherry and lemon

Andouille
A sharply spiced smoked pork sausage, often sliced and added to gumbo, jambalaya, and other dishes for seasoning

Muffuletta
A gargantuan round loaf of sesame seed-topped bread split and filled with Italian cold cuts and cheeses and olive salad (a mixture of chopped vegetables and olives with parsley)

Tasso
Cajun-spiced, intensely smoked ham, minced and chopped and used as a seasoning

Dirty Rice
White rice cooked with chopped vegetables and hot peppers, chopped chicken giblets and liver, and gravy (and sometimes chopped pork), all of which turns the rice a "dirty" brown

Red Beans and Rice
Red kidney beans cooked with a ham bone, onion, garlic, bell pepper, herbs, and hot sauce; served over fluffy white rice
This is a traditional New Year's Day dish.

Gumbo

A hearty roux-based stew that, like jambalaya, is subject to hundreds of variations. It can be made with chicken, duck, turkey, sausage, shrimp, crab, oysters, or other meats and seafoods; the liquid is thickened either with cut-up okra, which releases a thickening substance as it cooks, or with *filé* powder (aka gumbo *filé*), made from pounded sassafras leaves. The dish is seasoned with onions, chilies, garlic, and hot sauce. Gumbo *z'herbes* (a contraction of gumbo *aux herbes*), a traditional variation of gumbo that is served during Lent, was originally meatless and made with seven kinds of greens (such as cabbage, spinach, collard and turnip greens, scallions, or even carrot tops) for good luck; the modern version may also contain meat. Gumbo is served in a soup plate, spooned over a portion of rice.

OYSTER PO'BOYS: Some people have been spotted eating oyster po'boys (an admittedly large and messy affair) by taking off the top piece of bread, dishing out the oysters, and cutting the bread to eat with them. Whether or not that is acceptable is subject to great dispute. A similar but larger sandwich is an oyster loaf, made with a whole loaf of white bread—definitely knife-and-fork material.

Oyster Po'Boy

A split loaf of hot French bread that is slightly hollowed out, buttered, and lightly toasted, then spread with mayonnaise and filled with breaded fried oysters, lettuce, and tomato

Po'boy is also the local term for hero sandwiches (see page 330) made with the full range of fillings, such as roast beef or ham. (Order roast beef with "debris" and you'll get the crusty extra little bits of meat along with a hefty dose of gravy.) Food scholars speculate that the po'boy (Southern lingo for "poor boy") may have gotten its name because it is something of a bargain—a large loaf of bread with plenty of filling at a reasonable price. They go on to hypothesize that in New Orleans, an oyster po'boy—something of a luxury for all its humble appearances—might have been brought home by late-roving husbands to their waiting wives, earning the sandwich another name: "la médiatrice," or peacemaker.

Stuffed Artichoke
For this Creole first course, the artichoke is filled between the leaves with a mixture of chopped shrimp, bread crumbs, garlic, and Parmesan or Romano cheese; the top leaves are eaten with the stuffing and the lower leaves and artichoke bottom are dipped in an accompanying vinaigrette

Oysters Rockefeller
Oysters on the half shell topped with a garlicky, spicy spinach sauce; baked (and served) on a bed of rock salt

Oysters Rockefeller was invented at Antoine's Restaurant in New Orleans in 1899. The dish was dubbed Rockefeller because it is so rich.

FLORIDA
With a long history of Latin influences—Spanish, Cuban, and South American—Florida has developed a unique cuisine based on the region's native fruits and vegetables, seafood, and game.

Hearts of Palm
Locals call it swamp cabbage, but this vegetable delicacy is pricey and epicurean; the cores, or hearts, are chopped from young palmetto trees and painstakingly unwrapped from layers of fiber. They can be eaten raw or cooked (and, in fact, most often come from a can), and are usually featured in salads dressed with a vinaigrette

Spanish Bean Soup
A chick-pea soup made with potatoes, bacon, beef, and chorizo (spicy pork sausage) in a **saffron**-tinted broth

Cuban Black Bean Soup
A thick bean stew made with browned salt pork, seasoned with vinegar and topped with chopped onion; sometimes served over white rice

Gaspachee
Based on Spanish gazpacho, this Floridian salad is made with hardtack (dry biscuits) that are soaked in water and then layered with sliced tomatoes, onion, cucumbers, and mayonnaise

INGREDIENT NOTES

• **Saffron**, the stigmas of the purple saffron crocus, gives food a distinctive flavor and a pale

yellow color. It is the world's most expensive spice and is, therefore, often replaced by less expensive substitutes, such as turmeric or food coloring.

Conch Chowder

Chopped **conch** cooked with salt pork, tomatoes, bay leaves, and rice or potatoes; thickened with evaporated milk

Conch Fritters

Ground **conch**, onions, and peppers, mixed with eggs and flour and deep-fried by the spoonful

Pompano and Red Snapper

These fine Floridian fish, often stuffed with shrimp or seasoned with orange juice and orange zest, are cooked *en papillote* (in a parchment paper envelope).

Stone Crabs

Only the huge claws of this creature are eaten; they are cracked before serving so you can tease out the juicy meat with a pick and dip it in lime or lemon juice, melted butter, garlic butter, or mustard sauce

Spiny Lobster (Rock Lobster)

A small-clawed, large-tailed crustacean native to Florida waters; the tails are grilled with butter and lemon (the claws are not eaten)

Green Turtle (Cooter)

The tough meat is pounded, then the steaks are braised, or floured or battered and pan-fried

Bolichi

A beef roast that's partially hollowed out, then restuffed with the ground beef mixed with ham, sausage, bacon, and olives; served sliced with vegetables and gravy

Cuban Sandwich

A 5- to 8-inch loaf of thin-crusted bread (similar to French bread but flatter) stuffed with sausage, ham, barbecued pork, cheese, and pickles; served with pickles

When ordering a Cuban sandwich you may be asked if you would like it pressed (heated and flattened in a steam press reminiscent of a waffle iron) or plain.

Key Lime Pie

A mixture of juice from small, round yellow limes native to the Florida Keys, sweetened condensed milk, and eggs in a crumb or pastry crust, often topped with meringue

In addition to being used for pie, Key lime juice flavors custard, soufflés, cheesecakes, ice cream, and cocktails, and is also blended with butter, mustard, or oil to make seafood sauces and salad dressings. Often bottled rather than fresh Key lime juice is used.

• The beautiful scrolled **conch** shells with pearly pink interiors that many tourists take home from Florida as souvenirs also provide sweet, rather tough meat that, for cooking, is pounded and sometimes marinated in lime juice to tenderize.

BARBECUE

Barbecue (or Bar-B-Q or Barbeque or BBQ) is subject to striking regional and personal variations. The word refers not to grilling or backyard barbecue—steaks or burgers quickly charred over a hot fire—but to a large cut of meat (sometimes a whole pig) cooked over a slow, smokey fire for 12 hours or longer, basted with water or a thin vinegar sauce to keep it juicy and never doused with a thicker sauce until shortly before (or after) the meat is done; additional sauce may be slathered on after the meat is sliced, "pulled" into shreds, or chopped. Barbecue joints are never fancy—often unadorned cinder-block structures with minimal identification—and service and etiquette are casual, to say the least. Your meal may come on a paper plate—or a sheet of butcher paper—with standard side dishes and condiments, depending on where you're eating: pit beans (baked beans cooked with barbecue sauce), slaw, potato salad, pickle, onion, and even Brunswick stew (see page 314) are barbecue go-withs. You can ask for "inside" or "white" meat, which is moist and tender, or crisp brown "outside" meat, also called "burnt ends" or "brownies,"

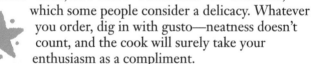

which some people consider a delicacy. Whatever you order, dig in with gusto—neatness doesn't count, and the cook will surely take your enthusiasm as a compliment.

REGIONAL BARBECUE VARIATIONS

Alabama

Pork ribs or shoulder are cooked over hickory and basted only with water in order to keep the meat juicy. When the meat is ready, it is sauced with a tomato-based mixture and served on what Southerners call "light bread," otherwise known as plain old white bread.

Arkansas

In the western part of the state (which borders on Texas), beef ribs or brisket are as popular as pork. Elsewhere, pork shoulder is the favorite, chopped and served with pit beans (baked beans made with barbecue sauce) and slaw. You can also order a barbecue salad, but be warned that it's no light lunch—tepid barbecue is served over a salad of iceberg lettuce, tomato, and onions, and topped with barbecue sauce or bottled salad dressing.

Georgia

Georgians favor pulled (into shreds) and/or chopped pork shoulder, with a mild or hot tomato-based sauce and a bowl of Brunswick stew (see page 314) on the side; you can also get a "sandwich" of a few ribs, bread, and sauce.

Kansas City

Many people consider Kansas City the capital of barbecue in the U.S.; the local style is pork or brisket mopped with a tomato-vinegar sauce, cooked over hickory for 12 hours or more, then chopped or sliced and piled on white bread. Side options include French fries and coleslaw.

Kentucky

In the western part of the state, burgoo—close kin to Brunswick stew (see page 314) but made with mutton—is served alongside barbecued sliced mutton (a quarter sheep is cooked at a time) or pulled pork shoulder with tomato-vinegar-pepper sauce; sandwiches made with the meat are topped with dill pickle and onion.

North Carolina

In the eastern part of the state, the whole hog is barbecued and basted with a distinctive peppery vinegar sauce; after cooking, it's chopped, mixed with hot sauce, and served with coleslaw on top or hush puppies (see page 315) or corn bread and potato salad alongside. Western North Carolinians prefer chopped pork shoulder with a tomato-vinegar sauce, served on a bun, with hush puppies, slaw, and baked beans.

South Carolina

Here, many barbecue experts go "whole hog," literally cooking the whole pig, then chopping or slicing the meat. The sauce may be tomato- or vinegar-based, or it may be a sweet, spicy mustard sauce peculiar to this state. The favorite side dish is liver hash, or pork hash, a sort of dense pork "giblet" gravy served over rice.

Tennessee

Pulled pork shoulder or ribs are served on corn bread batter cakes or a toasted bun, with coleslaw and pit beans (baked beans cooked with barbecue sauce). The Memphis specialty is pulled or chopped pork shoulder on a bun, with tomato-based sauce and slaw on top, onion rings and baked beans on the side. In western Tennessee, you'll find barbecue salad (see Arkansas; page 322).

Texas

Beef is king here; the brisket is rubbed with dry spices first, basted with a vinegar-based sauce (or just its own drippings) while cooking, and served with a tomato-vinegar sauce or bottled hot pepper sauce. The meat is served on soft rolls or white bread—or with saltines. Pinto beans, coleslaw, pickles, onions, and whole chilies come with the barbecue.

NOT-TO-BE-MISSED REGIONAL SPECIALTIES

Some of the regional dishes that follow have found their way onto menus in far-off states, while others seem unlikely to be eaten beyond their place of birth. When you find yourself in an area that's new to you, make a tasting tour: Pass up the chain restaurants (reliable though they may be) and sample the local specialties.

Fiddleheads (Maine, Vermont, and the Northwest)

Served steamed or boiled as a vegetable side dish

Fiddleheads, which are picked in early spring, are the tightly furled tops of ostrich ferns. They boast a woodsy asparagus-like flavor.

Clam Chowder (New England)

Salt pork and onion flavor a milk- or cream-enriched soup filled with diced potatoes and clams (see page 326 for New York version)

Indian Pudding (New England)

Cornmeal, molasses, milk, eggs, butter, and sweet spices, such as ginger or cinnamon, baked into a dense pudding; served with vanilla ice cream

L O B S T E R : You needn't worry about style too much in an informal "lobster pound," but you can watch other diners crack and smash away to get a feel for how to eat a lobster.

Start by twisting off the claws and cracking the very hard shell with a nutcracker, mallet, or rock. Then separate the tail from the body by bending it backwards. Break off the tail flippers (even they contain some nice meat) and push the tail meat out with a fork. It should come out in one piece, but if it resists, break down the underside a bit and try again. Remove and discard the black vein that runs the entire length of the tail meat; a waxy red mass in the tail (and body) is "coral" or roe, which some people find very tasty.

Open the body by cracking it apart sideways and remove the meat in the four pockets where the small walking legs are attached. The legs should be broken off one at a time; suck on the ends to remove the meat. The green soft stuff is tomalley (the liver and pancreas), which is considered a delicacy by some and eaten as a dip with potato chips. Because these organs filter out contaminants such as dioxin, tomalley consumption should be limited, especially by pregnant or nursing women and women of child-bearing age. Lobster meat is not similarly affected and is considered wholesome.

Shore Dinner (Maine)

Whole lobster (sold by weight), corn on the cob, and steamers (clams), and/or mussels boiled together in saltwater (food for each order is put in a net bag that is placed in an enormous kettle of boiling saltwater); served with melted butter for dipping

The Shore Dinner is generally served at large, informal, family-run restaurants called lobster pounds or pools along the Maine coast; often the lobster served at these restaurants comes from the family's own fleet of lobster boats. Tables are usually equipped with nutcrackers, mallets, or just rocks for cracking lobster shells. The most popular weights for the lobsters are between $1^1/_4$ and $1^1/_2$ pounds, but smaller ("chicken") lobsters and larger ones are usually available. Lobsters in the midst of molting, called new-shell lobsters or shedders, have soft shells and less but sweeter meat than hard-shell lobsters; shedders are also filled with more water, so watch out for small floods when you crack them open.

Wild Blueberry Pie (Maine)

Homemade pie filled with tiny, hand-picked wild berries (fresh only in August)

Pies vary greatly among Maine's restaurants, roadside stands, and church bake sales. Therefore, according to the top pie-eating experts, when visiting Maine it is imperative to order blueberry pie at each and every meal (including breakfast, of course) in order to find the vendor whose pie boasts the lightest crust and just the right amount of sweetness.

Clam Cakes (Maine)

Chopped clams and onions stirred into a milk-flour-egg batter and griddle-fried like pancakes

Clam Cakes (Rhode Island)

Chopped clams mixed into a batter, formed into spoon-size fritters, and deep-fried; a common accompaniment to clam chowder

Johnnycakes or Journeycakes (Rhode Island)

A cornmeal batter griddle-cooked to make pancakes

In eastern Rhode Island, johnnycakes are thin and lacy, while in the western part of the state they're thick and substantial.

Stuffies (Rhode Island)

Stuffed shells of quahogs (KWO-hogs)—large clams—filled with chopped clam and cracker crumbs, and baked

Manhattan Clam Chowder (New York City)

Tomato-clam broth with chopped clams, onions, carrots, celery, and potatoes

Egg Cream (New York City)

A fizz-topped fountain drink made with milk, chocolate syrup (Fox's U-Bet Chocolate Flavored Syrup to be authentic), and seltzer from a syphon (no egg, no cream)

EGG CREAM: Though the origin of the name of this eggless, creamless beverage is subject to debate, the way to drink it isn't: quickly, before its ingredients subside into thin, watery layers.

Beef on Weck (Buffalo, NY)

Thinly sliced roast beef on a salt-and-caraway-seed-topped *weck* (a German word for roll); served with gravy (or the roll may instead be dipped in gravy before the beef is added)

Horseradish is the required condiment with beef on weck.

Buffalo Wings
(Buffalo, NY)

Just ask for "wings" and you'll get a basket of deep-fried chicken wings tossed with melted butter and hot sauce, served with celery sticks and blue cheese dressing for dipping. Order the wings mild, medium, or hot; if you're a real fire-eater, dunk the wings in additional hot sauce (and cool the fire with the local Genesee beer).

Spiedies
(Binghamton, NY)

Skewered chunks of lamb, beef, or pork marinated in a garlic-herb vinaigrette, then grilled

Cheesesteak (Philadelphia)

Order "cheese with" and you'll get the full treatment—strips of thin, griddle-cooked steak and sautéed onions, topped with Cheez-Whiz (or provolone or white American in some of the more sophisticated places), on a crisp Italian roll; the sandwich is yours to top with such condiments as ketchup, hot sauce, mustard, barbecue sauce, hot or sweet peppers, sautéed onions, or mushrooms

Pepperpot Soup
(Philadelphia)

A hearty soup made with tripe and veal bones, seasoned with both black and red pepper

This dish was supposedly created by a Philadelphia cook during George Washington's winter campaign of 1777–78.

Philadelphia Scrapple
(Pennsylvania and
Delaware)

A thick cornmeal mush blended with cooked ground pork scraps, sometimes flavored with sage, summer savory, marjoram, or clove, to form a sort of starchy country sausage that is sliced and fried for breakfast; may be served with ketchup or maple-flavored syrup

Scrapple is also considered a Pennsylvania Dutch food, but is particularly popular in Philadelphia. A similar dish, called goetta, is popular in Cincinatti, Ohio.

Hot Brown Sandwich
(Louisville, KY)

A knife-and-fork sandwich made open-face on white toast with turkey or chicken, bacon or ham, tomato, and a thick cheese sauce; the sandwich is broiled with a sprinkling of Parmesan

Cincinnati Chili (Cincinnati)

A thin ground-beef chili with cinnamon, cloves, and other sweet spices—but not much "heat"—as well as garlic and oregano; the chili is served over spaghetti, plain, or with various toppings, each of which has a traditional name: "Three-way" is buried under a cloud of thinly shredded Cheddar; "Four-way" has Cheddar and chopped raw onions; "Five-way" boasts Cheddar, onions, and kidney beans. Oyster crackers are a common accompaniment. The chili is also served over small hotdogs called "Coney Islands," or "Coneys."

Chicago Pizza (Chicago)

The original deep-dish pizza with a thick crust filled with mozzarella cheese, sausage, tomatoes, and extras, such as spinach, onions, and olives, until the pie is about two inches high. There's also a double-crusted "stuffed" version, and either type is knife-and-fork fare, not finger food.

Toasted Ravioli (St. Louis)

Breaded and deep-fried meat-filled ravioli; served with meat sauce, tomato sauce, or butter sauce—plus a shower of Parmesan

Fish Boil (Door County, WI)

A fish boil is a summer weekend event at family-oriented resorts on this Lake Michigan peninsula and the surrounding "lake country." All diners are invited to watch (from a safe distance) as the "Master Boiler" tends to the cooking. Red potatoes, onions, and whitefish steaks are added at precise intervals to a special steel basket in an immense iron pot of boiling water set over a huge wood fire. A hefty dose of kerosene is poured on the fire, causing the flames to lick the treetops and the water to boil over, thus dousing the fire. The basket is carted off by a crew of workers who carry it slung from a pole to the dining room, where tables are set with such accompaniments as coleslaw and melted butter.

Cornish Pasties (Upper Peninsula of Michigan)

Diced or ground beef and vegetables in hefty-crusted turnovers; the related Finnish pasty has ground beef and pork and a more delicate crust

Brat (or Double Brat) on a Semmel (Sheboygan, WI)

Bratwurst—spicy pork sausage—served two to a large *semmel* (a German word for roll) with onions, pickles, and mustard

Fried Brain Sandwich (St. Louis)

Batter-fried calf brains served on rye bread with pickles and onions; one regional specialty whose fame seems unlikely to spread nationwide

Loosemeats Sandwich (Sioux City, Iowa)

Like an "unpattied" hamburger or sauceless sloppy Joe, this is ground beef skillet-cooked with onions, garlic, and spices; served on a hamburger bun

Runzas (Nebraska)

Soft-dough turnovers (topped with caraway seeds) filled with ground meat, cabbage, and onions

Originally a generic term spelled runsa, "Runza" is now the trademark of a Nebraska drive-in chain.

French Dip Sandwich (California and the West)

Thinly sliced roast beef on a crusty roll with mustard: The roll is either dipped in natural beef gravy before the beef goes on, or the gravy is served with the sandwich so diners can dip for themselves

Cioppino (San Francisco)

A seafood stew made with shellfish and/or finfish; served with garlic toasts

Fry Bread (Southwestern Native Americans)

Baking powder or yeast dough formed into 8- to 9-inch flat rounds and deep-fried; served drizzled with honey butter, dusted with powdered sugar, or with a savory topping, such as chili and cheese, as individual "pizzas"

Rocky Mountain Oysters (the West)

Don't say you haven't been warned: These are calf testicles, sliced, marinated, floured, and deep-fried

Hangtown Fry (northern California)

An omelet made with crumbed, deep-fried oyster nuggets; served with bacon

Dungeness Crabs (Pacific Northwest Coast)

These one- to three-pound sweet crabs yield a higher ratio of meat to shell than most other crabs and are traditionally boiled and served cracked for you, with fresh mayonnaise for dipping

Alder Planked Wild Chinook Salmon (Pacific Northwest Coast)

Salmon baked (or roasted opposite an open fire, Native American style) on a plank of alder, a local sweet wood, for an aromatic, smokey flavor and distinctive texture

Wild Mountain Blackberry Cobbler (Pacific Northwest)

Deep-dish pie with a tender, flaky, sweet crust filled with tiny, intensely flavored berries hand-picked from secret patches scattered among the Cascade Mountains; served warm and topped with vanilla ice cream

ALL YOU WANTED WAS A SANDWICH AND YOU ENDED UP WITH A SUBMARINE

Some of the most basic menu items are sometimes called by quite different and totally unrelated names in different parts of the U.S. For the most part it's hard to determine why or even exactly where the names originated, but trust us, this is the lingo that you can expect to hear. General area of use is included to the extent possible:

Big Sandwiches on French or Italian Bread: Hero (New York); Hero Sandwich; Hero Boy; Italian Hero Sandwich; Bomber (Upper New York State); Hoagie (Philadelphia and mid-New Jersey); Grinder or Italian Grinder (New England); Italian Sandwich (New England); Submarine (New York-New England); Po'Boy (Deep South); Wedge

Pizza: Tomato Pie (Mid-Atlantic); Apizza (parts of New England); 'za

Hot Dog: Frankfurter; frank; weiner; dog; Coney or Coney Island (parts of Midwest); red hot

Milk Shake: Frappe (New England); Cabinet (Rhode Island); Frosted

Soft Drink: Soda (Mid-Atlantic); Pop (Midwest); SodaPop; Tonic (New England)

Ice-Cream Soda Made with Root Beer and Vanilla Ice Cream: Black Cow; Black-and-White

Black Coffee: Regular (all U.S. except New York City, New England)

Coffee with Milk: Regular (New York City, New England)

INDEX To find individual dishes, look up their names in the menu section of the appropriate chapter. Use this index to look up key ingredients, culinary terms, and other special information, and to see where sections begin.

A FRIENDLY PIECE OF ADVICE

DRINKING is a wonderful part of dining out, and for certain cuisines it is considered an essential part of the meal, but please keep in mind that even a little alcohol can impair your driving skills. Don't drive if you've had any alcohol to drink—use a designated driver or take a cab. If you are the driver, choose from among the non-alcoholic alternatives offered in every restaurant.

PERSONAL FAVORITES